D0286172

GOD I AM

From Tragic To Magic

By
Peter O. Erbe

TRIAD

For information address:
TRIAD Publishers Pty. Ltd.
P.O. Box 731
Cairns, Qld. 4870
Australia
Fax: +61 07 4093 0374
E-mail address: triad@austarnet.com.au
Web site: http://www.triadpublishers.com

Book Title:
GOD I AM - From Tragic To Magic
Author:
Peter O. Erbe
Cover photo: Horsehead Nebula.

National Library Of Australia: ISBN: 0 646 05255 1
Printed in the United States of America

*If you are truly happy,
if your life is an expression of joy
filled with deep purpose,
if you lack no thing – in short, if you are at One
with the Spirit that causes you to be –
then you have no need for this material,
for you walk with God.*

*Then, perhaps, you may pass this book on to a
friend, or someone who is in need of
of the gift of your blessing.*

Ask not: Who or What is God?
Ask: Who or What is He not?

Contents

Author's Foreword

There is a silent aching in the human soul for hope and joy – a void that longs to be filled. Hope is expectancy for something to come. To go beyond hope, to arrive at what we hope for – to lift the soul from the dense clouds of turmoil, sorrow and stagnation to heights of clarity into Light and love – is our purpose here. This message tears the veil of make-believe and reveals our time – against all appearances – as the most exciting to be in. It inspires the soul to soar again – to release itself into freedom, the on-going adventure of Spirit where all things are made new.

****

Observing humanity as a whole, the need for answers to some fundamental questions becomes more apparent than ever before. With man in stress, economies in distress, and the list of woes endless as time itself, an onlooker from on high would certainly not perceive mankind as serene and filled with a quiet sense of purpose.

It is most astonishing, to say the least, that lack of noble purpose is the common trait in the lives of even the most learned intellects of our time. To challenge anyone into questioning his reality, which is cemented in the belief system of fear and lack, is generally met with resentment. It is this belief which constitutes man's Holy Shrine. To empty this shrine of its contents is almost perceived as an act of blasphemy.

What we identify with constitutes our reality, and lack of true identity is reflected in the individual's insecurities, regardless of the many attempts made to cover these by seeking safety in numbers. It is not union, when one disunited individual joins with another disunited individual. Such union compels itself to a mere reaffirmation of each other's disunity.

The tenacity of such 'union' is always in direct proportion to the ignorance of its individual members. Croaking individuals do not make a choir by joining.

Institutions, associations of any kind, educational systems, these are but bodies representing collective insecurities – resulting in a society where the crippled lead the infirm. The hunger of the human Spirit for knowledge shall never be satisfied with the food scholastic efforts provide. Hypocrisy and double standards, however blatantly displayed, have become the norm, the accepted way of life. As long as humanity remains in its slumber of SELF denial, how can it even hope to tap its grand and promising potential.

Despite the impact spiritual giants have made – I think of Gautama, Yeshua Ben Joseph and hundreds of seers and prophets and a maze of superb literature to show humanity, that there is a state transcending social consciousness, attainable by all, promising the end of grief – man has stirred little in his sleep.

Although we have been given all the ingredients we could possibly need to create a virtually paradisical world – a magnificent planet and unlimited human potential – we turned it into a wasteland of spiritual ignorance, completely out of touch with the Spirit that causes all things to be – the Creator, our very Source. Behind the flimsy veneer of progress we hide the emptiness of a world dedicated to material values and in the process of it destroy not only ourselves but the Earth as well. As a society we have run ourself into the ground. Although our Mother, the Earth, erects flaming warning signs in whichever direction we turn, we still attempt to repair the effects of our attitude instead of healing the attitude itself, which means healing ourself. A healed Self is a whole SELF and the actions springing forth from such a SELF must of need be wholesome as well. As a spiritual Being man has become sterile, resulting in a society with vision in exile and any faith barred.

Without vision there is no direction, hence we continue to run in circles, try to patch up this hole, then that, re-use outdated, archaic solutions to our problems, such as war, and still insist, not only in the field of medicine, on treating symptoms as the cause. We substitute entertainment for joy, and insist on filling the void in our soul with material things. We stubbornly refuse to deviate from ways which lead progressively away from where they ought to lead us. We look persistently from what we should look at. Churches with their dogmas do not have the answers, neither do governments. In fact both would have much to answer for if put to the bench.

So what is there to do? Instead of accepting responsibility for our lives, we continually commission institutions and official bodies to find the answers. An easy way out but presenting no answers. Responsibility is in essence the ability to respond – to our true needs, and not to wait until someone else responds. For the result of that mental stand we are facing only too clearly today. Now, what we think we need and what we truly need are two very different things. The infant thinks its needs are candies – its mother knows its needs are nourishment and love.

If we asked anybody for the meaning, the purpose of life, even the most self-assured person, we would find the answer, in all likelihood, to be either silence, or an embarrassed muttering of sentences unfinished. The meaning is either not known or very blurred. Where there is a life without meaning, we can safely call it meaningless. Where life has lost its meaning, its sense, it becomes non-sense. To face oneself and admit to the non-sense of one's life, seems at first glance fairly nonsensical. Yet it is the first step toward the recapturing of that meaning, the lost sense.

To sound the clarion with the intent to shake the sleep from man is easy, to be sure. To coax him into opening his eyes, I deem a mighty task.

Ultimately, there is but one question to be asked: Who am I? The answer is: I AM – the rest is commentary. Yet, at this stage in man's awakening in consciousness this answer is, in all probability, of little meaning. Ancient wisdom tells us: Man, know Thyself and Thou shalt be master of the Universe. I speak of Self-Knowledge, the golden key to all doors. I speak of a consciousness the Mystics tried to acquaint humanity with throughout the ages, a consciousness that is the heritage of all and yet transcends worldly experience; a state of Being that puts an end to the perception of the temporal world as it appears to be and knows naught but joy. All man has to do is desire it. To desire it he has to be aware of its existence and potential in the first place.

Fortunately we are not without help in this undertaking. Our ignorance of an unfolding universe does not prevent the universe from doing so. As part of this universe we unfold with it. However, the grasses and the trees bend with the wind but the majority of humanity does not even know from whence it blows. We resist and try to swim upstream, with the result that swimming becomes labour and drudgery, instead of letting the swim be what it was meant to be: a natural flow, allowing the current to carry us gently back to the ocean.

The mark of our time is a universal conversion of energy – a shift from fear to love. In essence it is a redefinition of identity. Contrary to all appearances it is springtime in the Universe. The seeds of human consciousness have slept through the barrenness of a long winter, many preparing to burst asunder to sprout the mighty Tree of Life. Here and there seeds are bursting already and with every passing day more souls promise their awakening by stirring in their sleep.

Evolutionary pressure has built up to a point where its effects are increasingly apparent in all walks of life. A keen observer could not deny the presence of a force, pushing us progressively toward an expansion of awareness. As a result there is now prevalent a general disgruntlement, to the extent of disillusionment with what is generally perceived as reality. This may not be openly admitted – but nonetheless – the feeling is there. The banal learnings and values of society do not quench the thirst of the soul for Light and Truth any longer. For this reason many flee the established scene in search of a way out. Lacking direction, many know not where to turn. They vaguely run in circles, mistaking lateral direction for a vertical one and thus finish up in dead-end streets. And how depicting this word is: Dead end.

In the search for opiates to veil our inner emptiness we find causes to fight for or plainly deepen our apathy by way of escape. War and bloodshed can be found at any time at some place in the world. Man will never be in lack of a cause to fight for or against, unless he opens his eyes and awakens from his nightmare.

There is no atheism except the denial of one's true identity. When Spirit is denied, man travels fast into oblivion on the highway of deprivation. As it is, he definitely has lost his way. A road map would come in handy here – and there are many, to be certain.

To live and not to know one's Self is to live without identity, is to live in darkness. And we have to concede the fact that humanity lives in darkness. That most are not even aware of the quest as yet, is in its place, is alright. These are still on schedule, for their time shall come too.

Yet there are those of us who have probably felt for quite some time a stirring, an uneasiness, or plainly had their 'gut full' of man's old ways. These feel a hunger for answers to a fundamental quest, theirs is a keen awareness of their lack of fulfillment.

Their hearts may be heavy, their minds confused. But there is definitely a way out, to be sure. To show this way is our purpose here. Our questions should be: Who am I? What am I here for? What is the meaning of it all?

Asking these questions means to step in the right direction for the first time since aeons of wandering in the dark. And very well have we asked then, for the sum total of all our experiences is only designed to bring us to the point where we ask these very questions. And where questions are asked with an earnest heart, the answers never fail to come; they are as certain as the sunrise in the morning.

Those who dare to question their reality, I invite to join me in the grand adventure of Self-discovery, the flight of the soul. There is nothing to lose, only to gain! To redefine Self identity and to release fear as a result of it, is the answer to all man's woes. This is our purpose here. To realign our Being with the Divine Intent. This material is not airy-fairy philosophy – its purpose is to develop a practical tool which can be utilized in every situation and walk of life, to actually change our state of existence, that is survival, to the state of Being – to a life lived in exuberance, completely free of fear, or lack, or apprehension, walking in harmony with a healed Earth. There is no single path that leads to the realization of the Oneness of all life. Each soul has to walk its own path. However, all roads lead to the same homeland. In truth there is no road to travel, for what we call a path is but the awakening of a soul from its deep slumber. But remaining with the paradigm of a journey we may recognize major, common land-marks to help us find the way. This is our concern.

So, if you permit, we shall embark together on a journey; no lack of road maps here. We shall travel slowly, for there is much to be seen and to be explained. But, when our destination is in sight, you may find it was the grandest journey you have ever undertaken, because on this journey we are homeward bound.

Our travel luggage? An open, unprejudiced mind and a keen awareness. No more – just that!

So let us begin.

Introduction

Before man discovered the law of aerodynamics, to fly was an impossibility. Yet the law itself existed since time immemorial. So the discovery of the law alone made flying possible, nothing else. The universe is governed by such precise laws. Nothing is left to chance, although there is free choice. To most of these laws we must plead complete ignorance.

Mankind as a whole has entered the era of spiritual awakening and pockets within humanity are stirring in their sleep and are beginning to ask themselves some questions. Not all ask, of course, and this is precisely the reason why we are, in essence, witnessing a split in consciousness. Some adhere to the old, no matter the price, others pioneer to new horizons. All this, of course is exactly according to design. The winds of change are upon the Earth. Man's mind is stretching, is growing, and no one spares us the growing pains.

Most of us are somewhat familiar with the term New Age, a concept which signifies many things to many people. However, its real import on a deeper level of understanding is seldom if ever realized, not the least due to the fact that the idea has been perverted in mainly three directions: firstly, the public media is known to frequently screen programs ridiculing a magnanimous universal process of which it has not even the faintest inkling. As such it is plainly displaying what every first year psychology student would recognize as the oldest, most basic fear symptom: attack. For what we do not understand makes us insecure, therefore we invalidate it.

Secondly, the commercial sector senses the hunger for truth in many – therefore a chance to make a quick Dollar, and thus exploits its fellowmen by feeding them half-truths, miracle remedies, plastic pyramids, maps of secret extraterrestrial bases, survival kits for the 'inevitable' day of doom and what not – all in the name of a New Age.

Thirdly we witness the Guru syndrome. Cults, secret 'initiation' schools, metaphysical counsellors, 'spiritual' healers and New Age workshops spring up like mushrooms after a rain – many of them only discrediting the few authentic individuals and groups who are doing genuine work, often in the most selfless manner and away from the limelight.

Thus we are facing two New Age understandings: one is a worldwide multimillion Dollar business creating just another dogma and sidetracking many searching souls into trips. It is the Isness Business – cashing in on thirsty souls – commercializing God.

The other is the quietest, most powerful process in the universe, the most sacred, divine energy transforming human hearts, returning souls to their source of origin – awakening them to Reality. Humanity is preparing for a mass awakening in consciousness. The era of Social Consciousness is coming to an end, is birthing into Super-consciousness. As Above so Below. The very Earth and universe in which we find ourselves is stepping up its vibratory frequency, and we, as part of it, had better move with the flow and not resist, if remaining part of it is what we desire. To gain a more comprehensive understanding of the 'New Age' we should view this process in two stages: the preparation of humanity for a distinct event and the actual event itself. The preparation period is our now time, giving mankind literally a last-minute chance to realign itself with the Divine Intent. The extraordinary population increase in this our time finds its explanation in this fact. Souls are pressing for incarnation to make a last attempt at a correct choice, before this ten-thousand-year cycle of our cultural epoch is coming to an end – before the era of darkness is merging into the era of Light. Spiritual evolution can only take place within the dark epoch. Only here can the choice be made between fear or love. Although it is not the purpose of this material to elaborate on a coming event, but to help us realign ourself for this colossal change, it is nonetheless of utmost interest and very beneficial to be acquainted to some extent with the nature and purpose of the coming changes. The epilogue of this book is affording that particular subject special attention, but a brief look at a certain pattern in nature may help us comprehend the coming transition better. Nature always catapults life without graduation into new dimensions of experience. The transformation from egg to chicken, from caterpillar to butterfly – the babe that leaves the warmth and protection of the womb and enters an entirely new reality, are good examples illustrating the suddenness of any transition. There is always a long growth process preceding a transition, however, the event itself is an instant shift from one reality to another. So it is with the coming transition into the Age of God, which is but one of many terms for one and the same occurrence. The shift from social to super-consciousness will occur in the twinkling of an eye if we avail ourself, or put differently: if we align with its energies – and this is what we are concerned with, the time at hand, the preparation period.

On an individual level, especially when the greater overall picture is not known, this process can make for much confusion, hopelessness, and can create, temporarily, a fatalistic attitude. A sense of futility may creep in, 'one does not feel like going on', for nothing seems to make any sense. That these are only hurdles on the road we walk, symptoms of an expanding consciousness, rather to be viewed as a reorientation process, is not seen at the time. To overcome these hurdles, to see the greater picture, we need help.

Now, help comes always in the individually most suitable form for us: a fellow traveller, a book, an experience of some sort. The form it takes does not matter. The help matters. In this sense, the author wishes you to understand this journey we embarked upon – this book. Not that the contents represent anything fundamentally new. No – the wisdom of the ages has literally been around for ages.

But as one person might prefer a song interpreted on the piano in a concert hall, and another person prefers the same song played on a flute at the dawn of a new day high up in the mountains, so we as individuals resonate to different forms of one and the same expression more or less favourably.

Everything that exists vibrates in one frequency or another, and according to our individual frequency, we resonate and respond. So the knowledge imparted here may or may not be new to you, however, the form of expression, the frequency, may just be the one suitable for you, may just trigger within you that magic switch. This communication cuts mercilessly through the maze of frills which has historically veiled the very light it tried to shine. This knowledge is vibrant, live, experienced truth, not covered by layers of history's dust. This point cannot be stressed enough! As the subject matter deals with an interdimensional understanding, the tool – the language – used to convey thought, is kept simple.

Yet, sometimes we need to invent a special tool for a special job. So we may, at times, find words and the style of expression not in accordance with traditional ways.

The purpose of words is to express thought, and not to limit this expression to the use of a fixed matrix. Words are sound, colour and rhythm. The three combined convey meaning. The message this material conveys is aimed predominantly at the soul via the intellect and not the intellect alone. The soul remembers – the intellect does not. Certain passages may not be fully comprehended at first. In our present state of Social Consciousness we tend to analyse, that is to split, dissect – and this we do with the intellect. The understanding comes naturally, for as the mind reads words the heart feels the meaning, which lies between and behind the lines.

Communication does not occur on one level only. If certain parts are virgin ground and the reader finds he has to tread carefully, then this is fine. Some time later he may return to the same sentences and find them perfectly understandable. How is this possible? The mind perceives consciously and subconsciously. In the same manner, as we are not consciously aware of digesting food, we are equally not aware of consciously digesting mental and spiritual nourishment. We nevertheless digest.

This knowledge, as it comes across, may shock some reader in its honesty, bluntness and lack of any veil. That is alright – man, as such, has been lulled into apathy for far too long. A splash of cold water does not hurt, but surely does away with sticky sleep. The intention of this book is to help us realign ourself with our God-SELF, to transcend Clay-man and become God-man once again. The issue here is not another religion or dogma of sorts – on the contrary. If we compared man to a crawling babe, then religions are the scaffolding or crutches, helping the babe to crawl about. By realigning ourselves with the Creator Source we drop the crutches and learn how to walk, upright and sure-footed. Fear is the illusory veil separating us from our Divine Source, the God I Am. In order to release fear we must first realize its true nature and cause. To accomplish this most sacred of tasks we have to acquaint ourself with fundamental cosmic principles and then to expound on these to clarify their application. There is a deliberate restraint from indulgence in nonessential matters. Any attempt to disprove certain concepts or delve into great detail of peripheral subjects, however interesting, is avoided.

There is a definite, purposeful pattern in the layout of this material, which if followed in sequence, develops a magnificent tool in our consciousness: True perception. It is the bridge between sleep and awakening. Once True perception is accomplished, walking across the bridge compares to a joyous dance.

So any temptation to 'stop and smell the roses' is ignored as it would only sidetrack the mind. The aim of these discourses is too precious to warrant a failure to arrive at the destiny of the journey we embarked upon. Once our new insights are adhered to in practice, taken into one's daily life, we make a grand discovery: these principles actually work, and with great amazement we recognize that truth is true. We then realize the actual cause of our drudgery and pain: our ignorance of knowledge denied us its fruits. If I am ignorant of the existence of the cherry tree in my garden, I can hardly hope to harvest cherries. A 'fruitless' situation!

Now, it is one thing to be acquainted with a law, and another to put it into practice. That is, it is not enough to know about the cherry tree. It is not even enough to harvest the cherries. Only when we taste the cherry have we knowledge of the cherry. Meaning, experience of cosmic law gives us the final knowledge of it. But first we must know of the existence of such laws. The attitude in our approach to this knowledge is vitally important. We receive from it what we bring to it. If we are convinced we know it all anyway, that is alright. It only means our cup is full and cannot be filled any further. However, if we can empty our cup of concepts, dogmas, opinions and whatever forms of social conditioning we have exposed ourselves to – all those certainties without competence – or if our cup is full but we realize that whenever we drink from it we suffer indigestion, then we have a genuine chance to change our life from drudgery, mediocrity and hypocrisy to one filled with purpose, fulfillment and joy.

Once an individual has made the essence of truth his own, he will find his previous thought system inconceivable, for he has unveiled the common cause of all fears and therefore fears no more. The illusion of Lack of Supply he simply allows to dissipate. Can you, the reader, even faintly comprehend a state of mind that knows no fear, no apprehension? A heart at peace with God ?

What if we took heart and faced that terrible emptiness inside, which we so fervently try to cover and fill with a thousand meaningless activities? Activities to which we give important names and then actually believe in their importance, validity and justification? What if we faced this inner void courageously and began to fill it for the first time with an oh-so-sweet sense of purpose which gives our soul that peace it so yearns for?

It is up to us. But, as we heard earlier, our most important tools in the acquisition of these truths are a very open mind and a keen awareness. Many will plainly not believe much of what is said – this is alright. Acceptance of the truth is not required here, acquaintance with it is. And this is how it works: the next time we experience a situation where the traditional matrix of our truth does not fit or offers not sufficient help, we then remember the Truth we acquainted ourselves with here. And lo, it fits and helps and clarifies. It is application then which stabilizes our trust in it. So an open mind is definitely a prerequisite. We may be genuinely willing to explore new frontiers, however when it comes to the actual confrontation with new thought and the eradication of the mental and emotional grooves which we have carved into our minds, then great resistance shall be felt by many.

There are certain fundamental principles with which we have to familiarize ourselves, before we can actually embark on our journey of Self-discovery. It is for these, especially, that we need an open mind.

The structure of this book is comparable to a flight of stairs. We best take a step at a time to reach the top. Jumping steps may result in slipping. In other words, it is recommended to read these pages in sequence. And there is more to this: the moment an individual changes the direction of his life from darkness to light, the angels (generally a greatly misunderstood term) are with him. For this means that, for the first time, he turns toward his one and only purpose here on Earth, and that is union with his SELF – and this means union with God.

Chapter 1

Metempsychosis
Or The Law Of Reincarnation

The Lost Knowledge.

At the Ecumenical Council (under Emperor Justinian) in the year 533 A.D., the fathers of the Catholic Church removed the teachings concerning reincarnation from the scriptures. With the teachings intact, the image of hell and brimfire, of a God to be feared, could not have been upheld. Therefore the power of the Church would have lacked its foundation, which is fear. The understanding of the wheel of rebirths would have completely done away with the concept of punishment, with the concept of a judging God. Such concept lacking, who would fear God? Who, then, would be in need of a Church? The first Christians, the Essenes, knew this principle, as had the East for thousands of years. And slowly the remembrance of this lost knowledge is seeping back into the Western mind. For what else could explain and justify life's seeming injustices?

Excellent literature exists concerning the idea of Metempsychosis. So it is not the intention here to delve into great detail, but to state its existence as a principle of evolution, to point out its necessity as a tool for the soul's journey into the realm of matter and out again. In other words: involution and evolution. (The understanding of evolution, however, should not be misinterpreted here in the sense of Darwin's theory of evolution.)

The wildest ideas are held about the principle of reincarnation and some clarification is needed. The biggest stumbling block in the comprehension of this concept, for a mind not acquainted with this thought, is the theory generated by the science of the Western world that consciousness is a by-product of matter. Nothing could be further from the truth; matter is a by-product of mind, or better: consciousness.

The English word 'Reincarnation' means re-entry into flesh. The word 'Metempsychosis' points to a more accurate meaning of the concept: the passage of the soul from one tenement to another, the carnate body being only one of the many robes the soul utilises in its journeys.

Such great thinkers and teachers as Pythagoras, Plato, Virgil and Ovid understood the principle of reincarnation. The Gnostics and Manicheans and other Early Christians held to it. Paracelsus embraced this thought, and the German school of philosophers is full of its teaching. The anthropological systems of Kant and Schelling speak of it. The English thinkers of the Cambridge Platonists expound on it with much fervour, and in more recent times the Theosophical Society and similar schools of thought acquainted the West with this lost knowledge. Edward Carpenter and Walt Whitman were great expounders of this truth. And last, but not least, we are faced with the revolutionary findings of Thorwald Dethlefsen, who succeeded, with non-hypnotical methods in a therapeutical environment in his clinic in Munich, Germany, in genuine regressions with hundreds of patients. His experiments, executed under strict scientific conditions, brought final proof to the theory. Detailed publications of his work and thought are available.

The Reason For Reincarnation.

Why at all reincarnation? What is its reason and purpose? Why can we not just settle for that simple concept of being nothing more after physical death than food for the worms? It may be a boring and unexciting concept, but it is so wonderfully uncomplicated. Besides, it gives us an excuse to 'get it while we can', to 'live it up' without any further thought toward a deeper meaning of life. Unfortunately for the ones thinking along these lines and fortunately for those who do not, life has a little more imagination and has assigned a nobler destiny to its children.

So, before we examine the how of the principle of metempsychosis, the question of the why of it may be more pressing. To do that, we shall look at the very 'beginning' of that which has no beginning, meaning: to comprehend an ever present now, with a mind which is conditioned to perceive this now as a linear flow of time, is not easy, and what is more: to define the indefinable, the primal cause which we call God, is to try to comprehend the incomprehensible. God can be known but not comprehended. Comprehension is perception with the mind. To perceive, I have to be apart from the perceived. This indicates division. Physicality is polarity. God is union, therefore not comprehensible by a polarized, that is divided, mind. Only when polarities are unified is union with God possible. From within the realm of polarities we can only feel into the subject matter in a manner which induces the remembrance of an ancient knowing in our soul.

Learning, as such, is in reality only a remembering. We may believe it or we may not, the fact still remains that each soul has all knowledge within itself. Any learning is merely an unveiling of one's own light. That is all enlightenment is. Having limited our awareness more or less to the physical plane only, it becomes difficult, if not impossible, for us to interpret any information correctly which concerns a holistic picture, a multidimensional understanding. It is inevitable that we tend to measure this information by the standards of our physical reality. To overcome this hurdle, analogies may serve as a scaffolding or bridge to project a knowing into our awareness by means of pictures. We use one of these analogies as we return now to the beginning of the beginning. Despite being only an intellectual approach, it nonetheless points in the right direction.

We imagine the number 1. This 1 could never know itself in its capacity as 1, the indivisible, without its reflection which is the extension of itself, the number 2. The 2 contains the 1, without the 1 it could not be. Only now does 1 comprehend itself as 1 by reflecting itself in the 2. By recognizing itself in its reflection, which is 2, the 1 becomes an understanding of itself, which is 3. The Absolute, or God, is all-encompassing, is All-There-Is. What is all-encompassing can have no opposite. It is the ONE. The ONE needs to reflect its SELF in its SELF to know its SELF. Thus it creates an extension of its crystal SELF, the Christ SELF, to gain cognition of itself in its reflection. What reflects must receive the image first which it is to reflect. Thus the Son of God is born, the Christ-SELF; the Christ, created in the image of 'the Father'. The Christ represents the 2, for now there are two aspects of the One (1). The 1 contains the potential 2 within itself – the 2 contains the

1. Without the 1 it could not be. The understanding which arises from the cognition of the One in the reflection of its extension, the Christ, is one of being of ONE Spirit, of being wholly Spirit, is the Holy Spirit, which becomes the 3. This is the TRIAD of God, which is ONE. We may express the same principle as Power – Love – Justice. Justice being the understanding, which recognizes the Oneness of Power and Love as pure being, therefore innocence.

The Father and Son are ONE. ('I and the Father are one.') The Christ is the Christ-SELF of the God-SELF, the crystal SELF of the ONE God. The Christ-SELF carries God within itself as the number 2 contains within itself the 1. And here, a mind limited to a fallen state of consciousness already creates division and sees Father and Son as two, instead of as two aspects of One, as Creator/Creation, as God unmanifested and as God manifested. The Son aspect of God, the Christ, is the Father expressed, journeying through its Creation for the purpose of experiencing its own potential.

The Son, the First Principle, was told by the Father to go out and create. The Son contemplated the thought or better, formed a mental image, the Universal Mind. To quote Ramacharaka in his work 'Gnani Yoga, the Yoga of Wisdom': 'The Universal Principle of Mind is the Great Ocean of Mind Stuff, from which all the phenomenal Universe is evolved. From this Universal Principle of Mind proceeded the Universal Principle of Force and Energy. And from the latter proceeded the Universal Principle of Matter.' Thus we see matter is a creation or 'by-product' of mind.

The Son of God is one singular Being, the totality of God expressed. It is both male and female, but for ease of expression we remain with the traditional 'He'. He explores his own Creation, therefore also the densest realms, which are those of matter. Matter is not restricted to the physical; the physical is merely that part of matter which vibrates at its slowest frequency. As Spirit is Light, which is the highest frequency, it can only experience matter, the low frequency, on the level of that frequency. Therefore it must enter matter to 'view' it from within. In order to do that a vehicle of matter had to be created – the body – through which Spirit could relate to the realm of form. So a process was initiated, which proceeded over aeons in linear time, the process of Spirit gently and lovingly raising matter's frequency to prepare the realm of form for its coming. This process began with the subtler bodies first, approaching slowly the denser frequencies. Spirit sent forth fragments of its consciousness, tiny particles so to speak, to enter the world of form for the purpose of preparing and quickening it. Spirit animated matter, thus plant life and animals came into being, biology in short. There existed, however, the risk that these particles of the Christ's consciousness would lose themselves in the world of form and would assume an identity of their own. This is precisely what happened – consciousness fell from its origin, lost the connection with its own SELF. This fall occurred long before these atoms, or particles, of consciousness entered the densest part of Creation, the worlds of physical form. We are the particles, imagining ourselves to be separate Beings. It is an imagined identity, as there is in truth only One Being.

The soul is the first and immediate cloth or vehicle the Christ SELF uses on its journey of discovery through its own creation. It is the one 'robe' it will never shed. Without it, it could not 'hold' thought. Thought would simply pass through it, could not be stored (for want of a better word). Spirit took on the cloth of matter to experience the realm of polarities, to develop the body and to learn by contrast. The use of the term 'soul' from here on should be understood in its traditional meaning of Being and not so much in its functional aspect as a 'robe' for the Christ-SELF.

The reunion with its Source does not rob the soul of its individual frequency or flavour. Its individuality is never to be lost, but its state of separation is. In order to enter the world of polarities, it had to enter as polarities itself. Therefore, it had to divide itself into its polarities of male and female energies. The 'soulmate' of any soul is, in effect, its opposite polarity, although in the ultimate analysis everyone is the soulmate of everyone, for all are expressions of the one God, the one I AM.

A soul is always present at the physical conception of its body, but its entry into this body may be delayed up to a period of one year in our linear counting of time from the moment of conception. The instant Spirit, the Christ SELF, enters this world of polarities at the moment of physical birth, the moment it partakes of the reality of the realm of polarities with its first in-breath and out-breath, Spirit forgets its origin and purpose. While in the womb it is still knowing; it may be spoken to in any language, it understands. For example, if the position of its physical form is not conducive to a normal birthing process, a 'caesarian' can be circumvented by assuring the soul of one's love and care for it, by asking it to turn its body in the right position. It hears and understands and complies. After a period of time the body has turned. The implication of the soul's understanding while being in the womb is enormous. Now we may consider the discussion of its abortion in a different light, for the soul hears and feels utterly unwanted, therefore experiences trauma.

Once it enters the world of polarities it perceives its new world in an upside-down fashion. As we shall soon see, when we learn about the altered Ego, our perception of this world is a deliberate denial of Truth, of God. As such, everything is perceived as diametrically opposed to Reality. When the newborn begins to see, it sees all images as upside-down, exactly as the retina of its eye receives these. It is the same process as with a camera lens which projects a reversed picture onto the film plane. The new born requires some time until its brain has learned to convert the picture into an upright position.

Here this individual expression of the Absolute, the individual expression of the Christ-SELF, finds itself in the company of countless 'other' Selves and sees these as 'others'. For now it is fenced off by a body, sees itself as separate. Now the illusion of separation is real. But there is great wisdom in this. The body was created for the purpose of separation. For only from the vista of Illusion may Reality be realized as Reality. From within Reality we do not perceive Reality, for it is us, we are it. So we may, more or less readily, see that we descended all-powerful, yet not knowing (our SELF), and on the ascent return again all-powerful, yet knowing (our SELF). So much in the simplest and briefest of manners for the why of it.

Understanding Reincarnation.

Before we return to the how of this subject, a brief look at the background setting for our incarnations may lighten its seeming seriousness a little. Our particular universe is a rather special pocket within Creation. If we regard Creation as such as God's infinite playground, then our playground has different rules to the rest. In actual fact we only have one rule and a very unique one at that; the rule is: 'Everything goes', meaning it is a free-will universe. In a way it is a place where the thrill-seekers from all the galaxies go to experience the most dangerous adventure of all, for only here is the Son of God given the opportunity to forget himself, that is deny his Source and see how far he can slip before disaster strikes. And this is precisely what all of us have done, which makes us all thrill-seekers of sorts. Using a rather liberal comparison, we can say that the potential danger inherent in the process of incarnation is similar to that of a bungy jumper who forgot to connect with the bungy, for the danger rests in the fact that a soul lost in Darkness has to find its own way back to Light, a process which requires with most souls billions of years in our counting. The journey of Spirit entering into dense matter is the most severe test any soul can undergo. Once through the test, once a Son of God has found his way back into the Light of his Source, his knowledge is priceless. He has entered the deepest mystery of Creation and has learned how not to lose himself. This puts him in the position of a grand, grand teacher and helper. In fact his learning is so great that he may be put in charge of entire planetary evolutions, if this be his choice. So much in brief for the background, now we shall look at the how of reincarnating.

During man's sojourn through a physical lifetime, all his experiences, be they ups or downs, are accompanied by emotions. These emotions are recorded in his soul and represent the only 'luggage', or 'capital', he or she may take into the Beyond. The soul of any man or woman has an actual location in the physical body. It is located in the vicinity of the Solar Plexus. The soul does not record actual events, only the emotional essence of these.

Remember the 'holding of thought'? That is what is meant by it. It is the sum total of all these accumulated emotions that furnish the profile for each individual character. At any one time you are the best you that you have ever been, for your character represents the result of the lessons extracted from all your previous experiences. Character must not be confused with personality. The personality of an individual is a conscious choice for a given lifetime serving as a tool, a scaffolding, affording him the learning of a particular set of lessons he set out to learn in that lifetime. If our learning of a particular lesson in this life concerns artistic expression through the physical body, then we may have chosen to act out the role of a dancer, perhaps ballet. For this purpose we most likely selected a strong, but not heavy body. Certain personality traits would, of necessity, go parallel with this role. Whereas one whose learning concerns a long delayed lesson, for example compassion, may choose a crippled body as his vehicle. This way he shall instruct his soul with the feeling of what it is like to be outcast from the mainstream of life. The next time around, in another life-stream, when encountering the crippled form of another soul, he will know what it is like. He will feel compassion. Compassion reaches out to the heart of the other and recognizes him as a brother. Thus he steps in the direction of unification, away from separation. His personality, while experiencing the cripple stage, will be in accordance with this particular drama he has created for himself. Both personalities, the dancer and the cripple, may be diametrically opposed to each other, but their appearance and conduct are nonetheless equally valid as tools for expression and learning. Once this is understood – truly understood with the heart and not merely the intellect – then judging the criminal, the power-broker, the enslaver, the child molester, the thief and the rest of 'the undesirable elements' is an impossibility. When these are seen as beautiful Gods, as innocent souls playing out certain roles on the stage of their particular lifestream for the purpose of enriching their souls with the emotion, for learning purposes, then we do not judge – we educate.

We might as well pause here for a moment and consider the astrological sign a person is born under, for it serves the same purpose as the personality. In fact, both are intricately interwoven. The time of birth is consciously chosen to supply the soul with the make-up, the characteristics, to make the learning of a particular lesson, or set of lessons, possible. By no means does this state a person's bondage to his or her star sign. The learning may go very well in a specific lifetime, so the Zodiac sign may be outgrown and the 'scaffolding' expanded to benefit from the properties of other suitable signs to aid in the learning of further lessons. This may reveal the fallacy of the opinion held by many that one's star sign has control over one's life. The opposite is true. We chose it in the first place and may re-choose if necessary.

Together with the physical shell, the personality is shed at the time of physical death. At this point we may be justified in questioning the idea of the soul recording only feelings and not actual events. For how is a regression into a past lifetime possible, which apparently reveals every single detailed event, with the regressing person reliving, re-experiencing those events and the whole gamut of emotions which go with it, if events are not recorded?

To answer this in an understandable fashion, we will have to seek the help of another analogy. Only in the realm of polarities does linear time and space occur. Why this is so, we shall see later. In reality, time as such does not exist, but rather an eternal now. Without time, future and past cannot exist.

Now, where does this leave us in regard to past or future lifetimes? We may be tempted to conclude: nowhere. Not quite, for the answer is: everywhere, or better, everywhen. Meaning, lifetimes exist in a parallel, rather than a linear pattern. They exist always, the 'future' and 'past' lifetimes alike. At this point we may experience some mental hiccups. The mind tends to refuse this, for this does not fit its 'programming', which is based on linear thinking, based on the principle of polarities. But we can be at ease here – the following illustration shall clarify the picture: We imagine a public library with thousands and thousands of books. Each contains a story. Therefore each story exists already from beginning to end. We may view each book as representing a lifetime. The books have parallel existence in the library. Yet, to experience the story of a particular book, we have to retrace the story in a linear fashion from beginning to end, although beginning and end are already existent. We may now understand a little better how the clairvoyant sees the 'future'. It is a bit like looking ahead in a book to spy on the hero's fate. The library paradigm will, most likely, shed some light into the minds of those who are somewhat familiar with the term 'Akashic Records.'

We imagine for a moment that we enjoy a good movie in a cinema theatre. Now, the story we are following exists, or is recorded in its entirety, on a reel of film. The entire story is there from the beginning to the end. However, to experience this story we have to wind off the film and look at each frame singularly in sequence, that is, in a linear fashion. Although the whole story exists as such already, to experience it we must retrace each step in a linear manner. Thus, time is born. However, let us not fall into the mental trap of assuming that lives are predestined. To sit back in a fatalistic attitude, and see our fate as being 'all in the stars' anyway, only shows that he who feels this way has written this fatalistic attitude in his book of life in the first place. Now he is retracing it. Thus he shall learn from it how not to be. That was the reason for writing this part into his script.

As we can only receive the radio station we are tuned in to, in the same manner the clairvoyant adjusts to the specific frequency of an already existent 'future' or 'past' lifetime or 'future' event of a present life. The fact that only the clairvoyant can do this, and we cannot, is due to his particular gift to do so. Similar to one person having a talent for music and another having a talent for mathematics. However, not having a talent for music still cannot prevent me from being taught to play the piano.

As we can only watch one TV channel at any one given time, so we only experience one lifetime at a time. It does not mean the other TV channels are nonexistent. These beam their programs into the ether all the same, meaning the other programs, or films, are rolling off in the same Now as our Now.

Returning to the cinema analogy, we recognize that the canvas the film is projected upon stands for our physical world, the world of matter. The story of any given lifetime is projected onto and into matter. Now, while watching the movie in the cinema, be the movie funny or sad, we feel with the actors, we rejoice or weep, fear or become angry, to the extent of an increased heart beat and perspiration on our forehead – in short, we become involved. Mind you, it is not real, it is only a movie, remember? And at the end, when we leave the theatre, no matter if we wept our heart out, we are likely to remark on what a good movie this was. Exactly the same happens after our departure from the cinema Earth. The only difference here is that we are author, scriptwriter, director, actor and audience in one. Once we begin to see our particular lifetime as one in a succession of thousands of such lifetimes, its hold on us through its terrible seriousness and drama begins to loosen. We then dare to smile, if not laugh out loud and the serious and sad 'movie' takes on a more light-hearted hue: We begin to actually enjoy it. We then understand the idea behind the roles we have assigned to our lives and the concept of victimization is therefore seen for what it is: an upside-down perception of life.

If the roles we act out in any given life – be it king or beggar, thief or judge, nun or prostitute, murderer or victim – are conscious choices we made before embarking on the journey of that particular lifetime, then the idea of a victim becomes totally unjustified. The inflictor affords the inflicted an experience, a learning opportunity, the entire event being a co-creation. The cripple at the roadside then is no more seen as unjustly treated by life, but rather that his body is the necessary form this fellow soul requires for the learning of his lesson. Whereas before, our heart may have ached with compassion at the sight of him, the compassion now becomes 'dispassionate' compassion. We still feel wholeheartedly for him, yet know his condition to be for a purpose. The general feeling then is one of compassionate understanding.

If coldness is the echo at his sight, or a feeling of superiority, then we shall be assured we will have to come as a cripple ourselves sometime in the 'future', if we do not learn to see aright. For we can only judge what we do not understand. Having been a cripple means that I have been there, I understand. Having been a beggar means I own the feeling in my soul. The lady of good social standing encountering the prostitute at the corner of the street will understand, if she 'has been there', she will not judge. For she knows.

And so the journey goes, from lifetime to lifetime, advancing in our learning a little at a time. But there comes a time when the soul is saturated with the accumulation of experiences. This accumulation may result in the soul's complete boredom with the perceived, for it has been there, has experienced it all; or the result may be the accumulation of sorrow creating a buildup of enormous pressure seeking to be released. And for the first time in aeons, the heart may cry: 'there must be another way.' Thoughts then tend to redirect from the focus on matters at hand to matters concerning life in general and the meaning of it all. It is then that learning is accomplished in gigantic strides. What previously may have taken a hundred lifetimes to learn, may now be absorbed intelligently in one singular life. The focus then is directed rather toward the inner than the outer. (The kingdom of heaven is within). If this learning culminates in the individual's awakening, then further incarnations are superfluous. The soul has disembarked from the wheel of rebirths.

Before we continue on the general aspect of this subject, we ought to take a closer look at the one major pitfall in this learning cycle in the Self's journey: the power of stabilized perception. We experience, therefore we perceive. We cannot help but believe what we perceive. This is a normal pattern. However, perception stabilizes on grounds of repeated experiences and belief becomes limited to that perception. The pitfall sets in when experience is of a nature that contradicts our belief system. For as much as we must believe what we perceive, we cannot perceive what we do not believe. Thus, belief becomes a filter, which filters out what we believe cannot be. This results in lifetimes, repeated over and over, without any progress made. Again and again we re-experience the pain, the struggle, the hatred, the joylessness, although one single experience would suffice to own the emotion. We move in circles, in other words we become 'stuck in a rut'. An example: if experience taught us over and over to fear, then perception of fear becomes stabilized. As we only perceive what we believe, we gravitate continuously toward experiences which cement the belief in fear. In this way, lifetime after lifetime is lived in anxiety without progression toward the next step, and this is exactly the state of affairs with mankind. For what action in this world is not based on fear of lack of some kind?

The next step would see us open to the accommodation of new experiences which would eventually result in the recognition of the actual cause of fear. Whereas before we focused on the form aspect, which manifested the threat causing us to fear, we now look through and past the form at the form's content and recognize the principle of fear as the meaning of the form and therefore realize its cause. The illusion of separation from our Oneness with life would be recognized as the cause eventually.

Once the cause is established, the effect, fear, becomes superfluous. The above example depicts, of course, the learning of the ultimate lesson for mankind. If we could succeed in perception without stabilization of it, then our learning curve would look like a spiral, rather than a flat circle. To perceive without stabilization of perception, however, it becomes imperative to abandon the judgment of that which is perceived, for it is judgment that stabilizes perception. Yeshua's advise: 'Judge not by appearances' may be understood better in this light. Evaluating, that is judging what we perceive results always in false perception.

The thought then, logically and consequently thought to its end, is this: where judgment is not, accusation is absent. Where accusation is not, guilt is absent. Where guilt is not, forgiveness has no purpose and a state without a need for forgiveness must, of necessity, be a state of pure Being, of innocence, a state of enlightenment.

So, in a brief recapitulation of this stabilization effect, we look at the main 'trap' again: repeated experience causes repeated judgment. This creates habits of perception. Habits of perception may be seen like grooves in the mind. The deeper the groove, the more fixed becomes our belief in what the groove contains. The more repetitions, the deeper the groove and the harder it becomes to jump out of that groove. We seem to trapped in a vicious circle. The obvious question then, arising from this, is how to leave the groove? This material shall give us the key. While we are within the groove, we are attached, are entangled in the groove experience. Here we tend to want to improve conditions, not realizing its nature as an effect, but seeing it as cause. The form always represents the effect, not the cause. Treatment of the effect, being only a symptom, can only displace or shift the symptom. Now remember: The root cause of 'evil' of any kind is the illusion of separation. In our mistaken identity we see ourselves over here and life over there and God is a 'pie in the sky'.

By embarking on this journey into the realm of matter, the Self expelled itself from 'paradise' and forgot its origin, its Source. The truth, however, is: we are travelling in a dream while safely at home. For what else is the illusion of separate existence but a dream. No matter how realistic the dream may be, a dream is a dream.

Imagine you sit by the bedside of your child and witness the effects of the nightmare it is experiencing. The child moans and groans, tosses and turns. It experiences fear in its dream and perspires, so great is the fear. What would you do as a loving parent? Creep into your child's dream and fix the dream? But this is exactly what happens when we pray to God in desperation to change an unbearable condition we suffer. This statement intends to depict the 'fixing of the dream' syndrome, instead of awakening from it. It does not in any way diminish the value of prayer. In fact, prayer is one of the highest known ways and most splendid tools for man to re-establish contact with his own Divine SELF, his Christ-SELF, providing prayer comes from the heart.

Let us return to the bedside of your child: the help you would offer your child would rather be this: you gently stroke its forehead and say: 'Wake up, my child, it is not so!'

From a dream one can only awaken. So the answer to the question of how to leave the groove is to wake up to reality, the very purpose of the soul's sojourn through the world of matter. And the very purpose of these writings: to help us awaken from the grand dream, which the wisdom of the East has known for thousands of years as Maya, the Great Illusion. True perception of this illusion will set us free from the bondage of this dream. It allows the miracle in to heal. A miracle is devoid of degrees. It cares not what we perceive our problem to be, how big or small – it matters not. For where we see many problems, it only knows of one: Separation from Oneness. And to the one problem, it can only bring one answer, provided the miracle is invited and allowed in. For what we call a miracle is nothing else but the truth rushing in if we surrender our defences. The healing then is instant. And be assured with emphasis: these words are based on personal experience.

Between Incarnations.

The state of Being, after physical death, may be termed the respite of the soul. It is a period of rest, recuperation and digestion. The first realm the soul finds itself in is the astral plane. It is not a place, rather a state of consciousness. Death does not free the soul of its misperception of reality, indeed, death is the major part of the illusion; only the degree of its learning in the physical realm achieves this goal. Nevertheless, even if the earthly experience was in general a happy one, the astral plane is experienced as 'heaven'. However, the higher the soul has climbed in recognition of its Oneness with all life, the happier is its astral experience. Here the soul is freed from the gross materiality of its physical shell. This alone releases its perception of heavy limitations. The soul has still a body, yet this body is infinitely less dense than its physical counterpart was. According to its level of consciousness, the soul moves on, after a period of rest, to the etheric or on to the mental realm or chooses to reincarnate for the purpose of further learning. If its past lifestream concerned itself only with the daily details of survival, then no significant learning has been achieved. Thus another incarnation is needed to provide further opportunities for learning. This cycle of rebirths may literally entail millions of incarnations.

Once a human being learns to look beyond his physical needs and opens his heart aspect, learning begins. Then, after its rest period in the astral, it moves to the etheric realm for a period proportionate to its learning stage. The higher the learning the longer the periods between incarnations. Any learning that concerns other than matters of survival shall be digested here.

If the earthly experience accommodated lessons regarding the greater, overall understanding of life's Oneness, then the soul shall move from the etheric to the mental or even to the causal realm. Needless to say that the higher the realm, the greater the experience and thrill of joy and happiness. Once the earthly experience is 'processed', and the essence of the learning assimilated, then the soul is ready for the next incarnation. If the learning culminates in the realization of the Self being One with the universal SELF, God, then further learning on the physical plane becomes superfluous. It is then when an individual leaves the wheel of rebirths. Thus we see, perhaps more clearly, how Earth becomes a schoolhouse for the aspiring soul.

Peripheral Questions.

Before we can safely leave the great principle of metempsychosis, it would be well to digress temporarily to seek answers to some peripheral questions, which sooner or later would rise to our awareness in any case. First the subject of 'change-over' or 'crossover' souls. A soul whose intent it is to experience its Self in its female polarity (we remember it is both male and female), will incarnate as female energy, and naturally gravitates to clothe itself in the realm of matter with a body that is in alignment with its energy, a female body. And so it is with the soul wanting to experience itself as male energy. Should such a 'male' soul, however, become 'bogged' down through repeated experiences of extreme pain and fear, conditions which soldiers may be confronted with on a battlefield for example, then the soul may feel pressurized enough to want to flee the male scene (in physicality), for women do not have to fight wars. This soul then chooses a female body on its next round of re-entry into matter – without having changed its polarity of male energy to female on a soul level – only to find that things are not what they seemed. A soul incarnating as male energy in a female body makes for a misalignment, creates heavy confusion. Perhaps the next time around, in meeting a butch lady, we are not so apt to judge her harshly.

The soul incarnating as female energy, especially when journeying through certain parts of the Orient, may be utterly disillusioned with the conditions it finds. It is not granted a 'soul' in that society, but is regarded as of little value as a female, to the extent that newborn babies of female gender are often literally thrown on dung heaps. This soul desires to escape the female scene in physicality and chooses on its next adventure a male body. So, the next time we encounter a homosexual, let some wisdom guide our thoughts.

Secondly, some light ought to be shed on the mistaken concept of the 'inheritance' of talents. A Mozart, for example, did not inherit his musical genius from his father, he rather chose his parents – mainly – for the background this family offered. Rich in musical tradition it supplied a conducive environment for his own intentions. And so, we might add, did the parents choose their son. It is always a co-creation. The body, however, which springs from such parents, does carry the necessary refinement of the nervous system and thus assists the development of such a soul. Genius or not, the process is the same with any incarnation. As nature knows not of good or bad, a misaligned soul, intending evil deeds in a given lifestream, is aided all the same by the choice for a misaligned body. It is easy to imagine a body with a coarse, not yet refined nervous system to be of far greater support to an act of malice than its highly refined counterpart.

Thirdly, we look at the question of individual or group learning. Is each individual soul requested to learn by going through the entire spectrum of possible experiences, or does humanity learn as a whole? Fortunately, the latter is true. How is it possible for a male soul to comprehend, for example, the quality of mother-hood, if motherhood was never part of that soul's experience?

We shall use a little crutch, another analogy in the analysis of the matter. We have been told that the Absolute, or God, is All-There-Is. Therefore we, the Christ-SELF, dwell within the Absolute, are ONE with the Father, are part of the ONE, as the drop is ONE with the ocean. So the analogy of a drop of water in relation to the ocean is an appropriate one here. The drop sets out on a mighty journey, experiences the lofty heights of skies in the form of clouds, the thundering might of lightning, the staleness of a muddy water-hole, the frisky dance of the salmon in a fresh mountain stream, the impurities of pollution, and more. The string of impressions is virtually endless.

The drop will eventually find its way back to its source, the ocean. Here, its accumulated experiences become the property of the ocean and in return the properties of the all-powerful ocean become its own. Being One with the ocean, it gains the properties of the ocean. For as much as the ocean is the drop, the drop is the ocean.

For as much as God is the I AM of us, the I AM of us is God.

This explains the pressing force at this time in the conscious-ness of man, causing him more than ever before to stir in his sleep.

The learning of the few became the property of the many. First, some thousands of years ago, there were a few daring souls who not only stirred in their sleep, but awakened completely. These were the spiritual trail blazers who imparted their learning to the whole. Thus, the most difficult hurdles for man had been cleared out of his way, enabling him to build on this foundation.

Other souls, adding their properties to the whole, spiralled the learning of the race again, until we have now a situation where procrastination, the insistence on remaining asleep, is becoming increasingly painful. Man is urged to awaken. That this event of a mass awakening is 'just around the corner' is reflected by the enormous population increase on this planet – the influx of souls wanting to be part of this greatest of all events, and simultaneously affording them the final choice for love or fear.

Recalling the major points we familiarized ourselves with in this discourse on the Principle of Metempsychosis, two facts emerge as major recognitions: firstly, we are not the body. We may have one, but apart from its service as a vehicle for the soul to gather experience, it has no value. So let us honour it for what it is and no more. Any worship beyond its purpose as a citadel for Spirit would result in setting up a God beside God.

Spirit, the I AM of us, is eternal, is apart from time or space, is incorruptible, therefore the second recognition should tower above the rest: there is no such thing as Death! For what we call death is but a transition. And how could there be death, the opposite to life, if life, or God, is All-There-Is. For God to be God, God must be absolute, and what is absolute must, of necessity be all-encompassing. And what is all-encompassing cannot, by the sheer logic of it alone, have an opposite.

If God IS, then I AM – always! May the peace which comes with this understanding soothe your soul.

Chapter 2

Satan Or the Altered Ego

Belief in something is worship by degree.

Since time immemorial, we have worshipped a force we call by many names. In essence, this force represents the voice against God. We believe in its existence as an outside force, as if it were a separate entity. The same applies to the belief in God. Both are, in general, seen as individual, separate deities, apart from and outside of us. As if Heaven were somewhere in space and God to be found in some place.

Heaven is not a piece of real estate, neither is 'hell'. Please, let there be no consternation here as a reaction to the fact that Satan is deified in the same breath as God. For is not what we believe Satan to be deified in one form or another by the minute day by day? The moment we give credence, even if ever so minutely, to fear or anything we may define as evil, we have deified and worshipped what the Christian terminology knows as Satan, the opposite of good, of God. You recognize the sad, mad twist?

The fathers of the churches profess to believe in one almighty God, yet simultaneously lay sacrifices down at the altar of one whose very existence would negate God's. So much for sanity and purity of thought.

The sacrifice of Oneness is the price we pay for worshipping two Gods. In truth it is no sacrifice, for Oneness always is, only the awareness of it may be temporarily lost.

Yet millions upon millions lay their faith in madness such as this. In any other walk of life, society would label this, rather readily, as double standard, as hypocrisy. But not here, where recognition of the falsity of conduct would really count and put an end to sorrow of any kind for all eternity. For let us squarely face the fact that recognition of one God and only God and no thing beside God, would leave no room for anti-good or anti-God.

If God is Absolute and therefore All-There-Is, what is it then that we give credence to as a force opposed to God? In all fairness then must we admit it cannot be, and what is not, though we invest belief in it, must then be an illusion, a deceit, a lie. The Absolute

IS, or is NOT. This is the only choice. But if it IS, then only illusion can breathe the breath of life into a being that can have existence outside the Absolute.

There are certain things we definitely cannot do. We cannot make water wet, burn fire or sustain a contradiction. Yet the entire population of this world, five billion souls to name a number, eagerly serves at the feet of two masters, for it believes in Good *and* Bad. Therefore disunity is the result – confusion – and the heart is split. If I believe a brother to be evil, then I have robbed him of his God. His mind may be clouded for a time, deluded – yes, misguided by erroneous thought, perhaps – but evil he is not. If evil IS then God is NOT.

So what is it that we see as the Lord of darkness, Satan, Anti-Christ, Lucifer, Evil, Rebel Ray or Anti-God? A pilot never having seen a cloud before, yet heading straight toward this solid looking wall of rock, would certainly believe his end has come. Yet what appeared as solid and impenetrable revealed itself then as a dissipating cloud. No more – no less, just that. Now we can pierce the cloud of Anti-Christ and see it for what it really is: a creation of the mind, looming in threat, dark and inducing fear.

We only fear what we don't know, as little children fear the dark. Where light is shed, darkness is not, so we dissipate the cloud of Satan, take a good, close look and we shall see that fear then will have lost its fertile ground, is doomed to wither, fades away.

Have we not heard before, from One who knows, we shall not judge by appearances?

In the beginning, Spirit-SELF, the Christ, recognized the need to set aside part of its energy to prepare material abodes – physical bodies – for the greatest of adventures: for Spirit to enter in its fullness into matter. Part of its consciousness entered and developed physical bodies – supervised the management of Spirit's potential material home. Thus Spirit could experience the things of Earth, not hampered by 'householding' tasks. All the involuntary activities like digestion and assimilation of food, excretion, etc., were part of the task of this particular part of the SELF. Simple decisions, for instance, where not to set a foot, if treacherous ground promised a fall, were part of its domain.

In time, however, this part of the ONE SELF began to be preoccupied with things of matter, the greater sight was lost and it expanded its activities beyond the originally intended task. It claimed autonomy, denied the presence of the greater SELF and so in time lost knowledge of the real Ego, its own true SELF. That which is its SELF, which it was, and still is ONE with, it forgot and therefore found itself in an altered state of being.

And so came into being what we now know to be the altered Ego. It had separated itself from the ONE and naturally, as a result of wanting to be a 'God' of its own, it had to appear as the exact opposite of God. As if that which is absolute could have an opposite. Let it be emphasized once more: this separation is an imagined state of mind, it is not real. Much in the way a little girl plays 'house' and assumes the role of a mother. If now the game becomes its sole reality, it certainly forgets its true identity as a daughter and thinks it is the mother.

Attempts are made then to awaken it from its game of pretence. If all attempts should fail, we call the girl lost, insane. This is what the Altered state of mind is really like. Fortunately, in God no soul is ever lost forever, though aeons may pass before the soul decides to stop pretence and awaken from its game.

To be opposed in every way to the ONE SELF, it had to be the opposite of the ONE SELF and as the ONE is omnipresent, omniscient and omnipotent it had to give all this away and project an image of frailty and powerlessness. And this is precisely how human beings, separate Selves, perceive themselves.

At this point we may remind ourselves: 'the root cause of all evil is separation from Oneness'. Encircled by a tiny body, this body was perceived as a fence, yet any fence by its very nature is a defence. Defence defends what it perceives as its reality and leaves no space for greater recognition. The true, the undeluded SELF still lived side by side within this body, but was denied acknowledgment. And much in the same manner as a straight ray of light is bent the moment it enters another medium such as water, so was pure thought and knowledge bent that came from the ONE Source, the true SELF, when it met the part of itself which mutinied, and thought now to be separate – the Altered Self.

The greater SELF not being recognized, all truth emanating from it had to be opposed, was perceived as a threat to the altered Ego's very existence. Now truth became distorted, bent and turned into what it was not. For given credence to the truth, truth would have simply been restored and the altered Ego would have ceased to see itself as separate entity, would have simply recognized itself as what it had always been: an integral part of the ONE Whole.

We have already learned about the Principle of Stabilized Perception. This is exactly what occurred. Through repeated evaluation or judgment of its false perception it believed itself to be a separate entity and any acceptance of truth would have put this belief in jeopardy. To twist, contort and contradict the truth, which springs from the inexhaustible fountain of the crystal SELF, the ONE true SELF, became the sole task of the altered Ego. "Get Thee behind Me, Satan!" Yeshua said. In different words the meaning is the same: "Out of my way, do not distort the truth – for I desire naught but the voice of God!".

That part of the SELF, whose original task it was to manage the body, this part which was all-one with its SELF, was now alone. So the soul became accustomed to listen to two voices, the Spirit's, the true SELF's voice and one opposed to it in every way. This in essence was the Fall, the expelling from a state called paradise.

No one expelled us but ourselves. The altered Ego's identity henceforth became the body. And what would it not do in defence of this tiny speck of dust. Henceforth every activity was dedicated to the worship of this minute fence, this miserable little kingdom where it reigned supreme and was now king.

To serve the body now became a full-time task. To shelter, feed and clothe this frame busied the soul enough to lose sight completely of things that really count. To beautify and decorate, to degrade and elevate, to work by 'the sweat of one's brow' just to survive, to diligently and completely obey the altered Ego's insane claims became thus the meaning of man's life. And at the end, when all is done, the servants of the altered Ego stand in line to receive death as their grand reward. Thus is the altered Ego's victory complete. A funeral hardly bears witness to the glory of ONE life, ONE God.

The powers that were once its own were given now to each and everything 'outside' itself. Devoid of power, powerless, it obviously was subject to the things it gave its power to. The very things it had once created in the first place as the ONE SELF. The ONE SELF, of which it still was wholly part of but whose existence it denied. Now it could say with vehemence: see, God is not – for what I see I have to fear, there is but danger all around. And every meaning the ONE SELF had given its creation was now turned upside down. Where God only created love the altered Ego turned it into fear and hate and where abundance filled the universe it could perceive but lack. Where every creature was unharmed because it was unarmed the altered Ego said, to be unharmed we must be armed. Where every creature was at ease, dis-ease took now its place. Where once was peace, war now reigned, at times disguised as truce. Where life knew only its own eternal crystal SELF, there was now death. Attack now became justified for every other Self was naturally seen as it could only see itself: a body, separate from its One true SELF, fenced off by its tiny shell and fending for its Self. So every other soul henceforth became just some-body.

Insanity can only birth insanity, of course, how else could sanity be contradicted? And so the idea of gain and loss was born and that a soul must fend for itself just to survive. This in itself shows no ONE cares, and therefore God is not.

Where once we knew ourselves as innocent and loved by God we now were wretched sinners, guilty and condemned and destined for some burning pit. Where God sees sin only as error, a mistaken way of seeing things, the altered Ego established sin as truth. Where once was heaven now was hell. Life was diametrically opposed in every sense, right down to a simple little word in the very language, these words are written in: the little word to 'live', when reversed, becomes life reversed.

And sly the altered Ego is, and cunning, to be sure. The soul that listens day by day to what the altered Ego says, records all fear, anxiety and pain. Thus, as we learned, all lessons are eventually returned to the One SELF and this is exactly where the altered Ego would have them be, the final finger pointing against God. Now, it knows only too well the soul could and would never accept only Bad, therefore it leaves some Good. This way the seed of doubt is spread, its own continuance assured.

And this is why and how we find ourselves to this very day paying tribute to two Gods. Torn, split, confused and powerless and frail, just as the altered Ego would want us to be. We easily see now how our lives are lived in complete defiance of the truth. We see some Good but counterbalance it with Bad and feel quite justified in doing so.

All of us are only too familiar with the media delighting in reports of accidents, wars and disasters of all kinds, in short, reports of negative content. That this is special diet for the altered Ego is not seen as such, for when questioned: "Why do you consume such mental food? " we all have heard an answer very similar to this: "But this is real life, this is what life is really like – I have to keep myself informed."

And thus is madness doubly reassured. Of course, life is what we would have it be and so is perception further stabilized, the finger kept erect, faithfully pointing to the skies, accusing God for life to be such misery. Let us desist from blaming God, for God does not punish – nor does He reward. Men punish themselves through their actions – this concept of God as a judge is gravely in need of correction.

As long as we still condemn a brother for the 'wrong' he did, we see not yet that we obey the same insane voice as he. As long as we believe in Good, yet still find some-body out there deserving punishment, we are insane. Where does that leave the social structures we have built, the punishment of crime, nations at war, where vengeance is sanctified and our brothers murdered in the name of God? A God we do not know, whose denial we have perfected to almost a fine art. It leaves them just where they belong: in madness, in the insane world of altered Egos, whose constant cry is, "There is no such One as God."

We heard repeatedly that separation from our Source is of necessity an illusion, is but a dream. To dream we first must fall asleep and this we did, to the extent it can be likened to a coma. In this light we may now better understand why Yeshua once felt urged to say: "Let the Dead bury the Dead". In other words:

"Leave the dreamers to their dream". And fortunately it is just that – a dream. If it were reality – if God were not, then help us... who?

But God is Love and love sees only innocence, sees but a child that erred, that lost its way, is weary of its game. All we need to offer is our willingness to be led home. Christian terminology, once more, acquaints us with the Holy Spirit as the ONE that lights the way. We faintly sense some truth here but we really do not understand.

The Holy Spirit, the Whole-I-Spirit, The ONE SELF, the Christ-SELF we so 'religiously' denied, the ONE that remained whole, becomes the saving force, the Saviour. It alone still sees aright, perceives the Truth we have denied – thus True perception is its gift to us to build the bridge from dream back to Reality.

All that is ever needed is our call for help. Not to fix the dream but to awaken. With its help alone shall we become all-one, shall we be lifted and awakened from the heavy, sticky dream.

Now – many people 'on the path', familiar to a degree with the concept of the altered Ego, fight it all the way, try to get rid of it with all their might to free themselves from its heavy yoke and do not realize that in doing so, they only fall into another trap of that which they so vehemently fight. Their hearts sincere, they truly desire to awaken but know not as yet that fight of any kind is resistance, presents an opposition and for this reason belongs to the domain of opposites, the world of altered Egos. And thus illusion fights illusion.

We cannot meet with the altered Ego on its own battleground, meaning resistance only strengthens it. Whatever we fight, we shall strengthen, for the mere fact of fighting it is witness to our belief in it. And we recall: belief is but worship by degree. To fight what we worship is a contradiction in itself.

Resistance of any kind achieves the opposite of its intent.

To "turn the other cheek" means just that. To practically apply this knowledge, let us remember what the altered Ego really is: a mistaken part of our SELF, to be loved and cherished as our very SELF. To fight part of our Being divides but further, disunites. A mother does not disown her child on grounds of misbehaviour or for the fact that it misunderstood. Not to mention the fact that 'disowning' the altered Ego would be literally impossible – how can we disown ourself?

No, we do not fight or resist it in any way. But we can gently call it home and tell it that it was mistaken in its perception of reality, in short we shine a light into its world of darkness, confusion and despair. Reintegrate it to where it really belongs: the ONE true SELF. Where light IS – darkness is NOT. There is no fight, no struggle to be suffered. Darkness gives way to light – that is all. Our altered state of mind would interpret nonresistance as a wilful, defenceless exposure to attack. But this, again, is truth reversed. Nonresistance is the balance of polarities. Once we learn how to do that, we have arrived at True perception.

Although our soul remembers that life is really happiness and the carefree thrill of pure Being, this memory is drowned by our altered state of mind. And though the cry of the soul is strong enough for us to yearn for our original state of Being, we never-theless – the altered Ego's voice – cannot, somehow, imagine that life is really just that – joy and happiness. If we face this state of mind courageously – we see it for what it really is: a state of total confusion, a dream state of the mind.

So how and where do we walk from the dream world to the real world? First we need a bridge to span the abyss we have created between the two. The bridge is True perception which leads us from false perception, our world of opposites, to the real world. And where is this bridge? Exactly at the point of balance of these opposites!

Here is the bridge which leads from life denied to life re-claimed. Up to this point the objective was to bring the illusory nature of our perception of life to our awareness. Differently expressed: we learned, in part, what false perception is.

Before we move to the Balance of Polarities, which shifts the perspective of an altered state of mind to the development of True perception, it is essential we understand the nature of the global thoughtform.

Chapter 3
The Global Thoughtform

The Hundredth Monkey Syndrome.

As fish swim through the various currents of the ocean, so does man move within an all-pervading thoughtform, the collective thought pattern of humanity.

To surface from this thoughtform and to ride the crest of its waves sets him apart from illusion. Looking at this thoughtform a little closer, an acute awareness of its existence and nature shall help us greatly in the stabilization of True perception.

For those of us not familiar with the idea behind the Hundredth Monkey Syndrome, the tale is quickly told. The setting is a group of islands in the Land of the Rising Sun. In 1950, a group of researchers, studying a certain species of monkey inhabiting these islands, decided to introduce them to sweet potatoes. Keenly inspecting the unfamiliar vegetable, one brilliant monkey disliked the beach sand coating it and took his potato to the sea and washed off the sand. Observing the treatment of this new diet, another monkey followed suit and soon the entire clan had grasped the trick how to consume sweet potatoes without the unpleasantness of having grinding sand between their teeth! Within a very short period fellow researchers on all the other islands observed the same process with their monkeys.

A similar event occurred in England some years ago. A certain small bird discovered how to open the caps of milk bottles left in front of house doors. These could be punctured and so gave access to a delicious treat of cream. In an extremely short time span, apparently between three days and one week, all birds of this species in the whole of England – Scotland included – knew how to open milk bottles and did so.

What had happened in both instances? The underlying principle is resonance. In reality, there is only one Universal Mind, the one SELF. An individual mind is merely that particular individual expression of the Universal Mind or God or SELF.

In the case of animals, we may see the individual animal rather as part of a group mind or group consciousness. We all have seen a flock of birds or school of fish changing direction within a split second as one whole group. With primates, the mind becomes already much more individualized. One monkey's mind pattern or frequency affected his next of kin, those within his family. Once the family knew about the potato washing trick, the emanation of thought frequencies was already enhanced – multiplied by the number of family members. The vibratory body of the monkey species as a whole began to resonate at the same frequency as the monkey family. It did not do this immediately. The resonance needs time to build up, similar to an avalanche which gathers momentum. The number of monkeys needed to make the entire vibratory body of the monkey species resonate to this frequency, is called the critical number. The term 'Hundredth Monkey Syndrome' seems to indicate the figure one hundred to be the critical point. Obviously this figure is of symbolic value only. If the source of a thought emanates this thought intensively enough, then it is plausible that a single mind is sufficient to set a thoughtform into motion. The time interval necessary to develop this energy into a major thoughtform would be very dependent again on the intensity of group-thought emanation. However, knowledge of an actual figure for the comprehension of the principle is negligible in any case.

This principle holds true for human beings all the same. If the number of individuals adhering to a specific thought pattern reaches its critical figure, this thought pattern becomes the property of all. In other words, the frequency of the collective thought of a group becomes strong enough to force the surrounding resonant body of humanity into resonance.

An example: A certain person contemplates 'influenza'. His thought vibrations affect the vibration of his family in like manner. The family carries these vibrations over to friends, the children bring the influenza vibrations into school, and before long the critical number of persons thinking influenza has been reached. Their thought pattern vibrates at the specific frequency which is peculiar to influenza. Being a fear-based frequency, the thought of influenza is one of a low frequency, and thus the most receptive minds to this frequency belong to two groups.

Firstly, the group of affinity, which vibrates already on that frequency or one close to it. This group need not necessarily think 'influenza', but certainly their minds adhere to values such as contagiousness, which is of like frequency. This group can be likened to a tuning fork, which instantly resonates to the sound of its own frequency.

The second group represents those minds which have a low level of frequency emanation. These minds, not emanating definite thought patterns themselves, are very susceptible to outside stimuli, meaning the laxity of a mind determines its involuntary impressionability.

Before long, the frequency of the lax mind reaches the frequency of the stimulant frequency. Thus, this group added to the first, more and more people think influenza. The occurrence of an epidemic then comes as no surprise. As we think – so we are and as such we create our reality. Should the stimulant frequency be emanated in rhythmical waves, then we observe an interesting phenomenon. The amplitude of the thought frequency of this group becomes greater by multiples compared to the amplitude of the stimulant which caused the resonance.

We are perhaps all familiar with the picture of soldiers marching across a bridge. The rhythm of their step causes a vibratory build up which may result in the collapse of the bridge. The amplitude of the soldier's step frequency remained the same, yet caused the amplitude of the resonant frequency to increase to the point of collapse of the bridge. In this manner, the amplitude of the resonant thought frequency may build up to a critical point which can express, for example, as mass hysteria. This depicts an extreme case, of course.

Presumably, everyone has experienced, at one time or another, an inexplicable feeling of listlessness or a feeling of elation for no apparent reason. Let us be very specific here. In most cases we can trace the cause of such feelings. What we speak of here is that 'general feeling' in the air, which seems to superimpose itself, at times, onto our present state of mind. This is when a thoughtform can be recognized. For that is exactly what it is; a thoughtform. In most cases this syndrome is not recognized.

A good example are thoughtforms triggered by national or international affairs. Although these are results of thoughtforms already, they may act as causes all the same. A war, somewhere in the world, may affect stock markets and oil prices. The media is swift in reporting these events, mostly in inflated form, and within a short period of time a feeling of gloom and lack pervades the ether. This thoughtform affects, in time, the more resistant minds and they in turn, reinforce the already prevailing thoughtform and a worldwide depression is the result. Everyone restrains financial spending and the spiral descends further. As we shall learn, this illustrates an extreme case of love withheld.

By now, we may already suspect thoughtforms within thoughtforms within thoughtforms. And so it is. That this collective thoughtform has an all powerful influence on our daily thought and the activities which spring from this thought, should not surprise. Yet, its influence is nullified if we are consciously aware of its presence and realize it for what it is.

Having come this far in our understanding of our altered state of mind, we may recognize without difficulty the nature of the Global Thoughtform: This Global Thoughtform, also known as morphogenic resonance, is nothing less than the collective, impersonal altered Ego of humanity – the sum total of every individual's altered state of mind; a mind caught up in the denial of reality. And probing further, we observe a 'ping-pong' effect, which is stabilization of perception: the individual mind nourishes the group resonance of his family which in turn feeds the particular resonance native to the area in which that family resides. The group thoughtform of this area projects on to the resonance of that nation and this one adds to the Global Thoughtform and the Global Thoughtform projects back in reverse order. Now we seem to be perfectly trapped and we wonder why our world does not improve!

Social Consciousness.

Another term for this thoughtform is social consciousness. This thoughtform, in which we move, has a similar effect on our consciousness as rails have on the wheels of a train. It keeps us 'in line' with popular attitudes. Such a consciousness is really a state of hypnosis, a state of mind under the spell of the altered Ego. Here reality, the state of Being, is reversed to the state of 'Having'. Our need for love and to love is substituted with the need for material things and conditions. The severity of this spell is witnessed in the so-called spiritual awakening of many a man where the want for things is only exchanged for the want of spiritual powers and status. It still remains a state of mind under the spell of want, that is such a mind continues in its desire to 'have', yet honestly believes it has initiated a genuine change in identity.

It is not that the one who aims sincerely at an expansion of awareness from a materialistic view to a spiritual understanding of life has surrendered all want. On the contrary, in a sense he is as selfish as his brother who is still steeped in social consciousness, but with a difference: his want is for the whole of life and not fragments of it. He is through with settling for crumbs, for material values only. He claims greater riches, hence asks for everything, the very Source itself. To claim his heritage he realizes he has to lose himself to find himself, that is he has to surrender his Self-image together with the values with which this image has entangled itself.

Our general understanding of the word spiritual merely reflects our upside-down perception of life. Because this word associates with the realms of the unseen, its meaning to us carries a vagueness of sorts and connotes in many minds to religion. Spirit in any context relates to the essence of things and as such means reality; to spiritually unfold is to awaken to reality.

In social consciousness life is reduced to survival, a fear based state of existence. Society's religion is the hunt for supply; the Dollar has become the almighty God of the merry and the wretched alike – this is where security is seen. If not for lack of virtue alone, one should assume that the sheer monotony and boredom of a life spent in the pursuit of the Dollar should generate sufficient impetus to seek new ways – but rarely so. The soul should become very alarmed when life is reduced to mere arithmetic. Our heart is where our attention is and this is where our treasure is. Is it really so intolerable to breach the vows of the Ego and reinvest trust in the very Power which sustains our every breath? The ocean separates not from the water – the wind does not divorce the air, neither is the branch forgetful of the tree – only man is in ignorance of his Being which is God.

Our investment in fear is staggering: the energy spent in keeping fear alive and well drains our very life blood. As it is, that is denying our Source in an altered state of mind, we only receive a trickle of the normally abundant flow of life-force. The little we have available to us of this vital energy is generally dissipated through fear and guilt.

If we compared man's life-force in his natural state to a fully pumped balloon, then an altered state of mind would be analogous to the same balloon being almost deflated, due to punctures in its surface. Each one of fear's offspring, such as hate, jealousy, envy, greed, lack, pride, attack, defence, blame, guilt and the rest of all the colours on the palette of fear represents a puncture. The balloon is grounded – has lost its bounce and the ability to float.

To help us regain the bounce we shall look at a very interesting aspect: the human brain, the chakras and the DNA, for they represent the link between the physical and the non-physical. We may have all heard about the seven chakras, the energy 'gates' in our etheric body. These chakras have their counterpart in the physical body as the endocrine glands. There exist five further chakras external to the physical body, but they are not our immediate concern here. The chakras, or energy centres, wield the life-force in the body and distribute information, that is, thought, to the DNA in the chromosomes of our cells. In the majority of the race, at present, only approximately ten to thirty per cent of the brain's full capacity is utilized and only two chakras are open or active: the chakra at the base of the spine and the navel chakra, which relate to procreation and survival. The activation of the dormant chakras is dependent on the stimulus of higher thought frequencies. This leads us to the human brain, which is a receiver of thought only, it cannot create thought, contrary to common belief. It can broadcast thought, but it is unable to create it. The brain processes the thought it receives in a similar fashion as a computer processes the data it is fed. The thought we receive comes from the universal storehouse of thought, from the All-That-Is. As thought is frequency, we only receive the frequency our state of consciousness allows in, meaning it filters out what is not of its own frequency. This filtering process is governed by the law of Resonance and Affinity. Thought enters through the pituitary gland, at the crown of the head, 'funnelled' in via the external chakras. Depending on the soul's awareness we accept or ignore certain thought frequencies. As the greater part of humanity dwells in social consciousness, we only receive enough thought and energy to keep the physical vehicle functioning plus a little extra for the most basic actions. Thought is light, or better, information. The information or light carrier in our physical body is the double helix of the DNA in our chromosomes. As each chakra corresponds to one helix, the activation of all twelve chakras will see a fully restored DNA with twelve helices. As it is, it resembles an electric circuit with a few loose connections. It is split. The split in our consciousness, the denial of our Source, is reflected in the physical body by the DNA. How this was originally and actually once instrumented is another and very long story. However, the story's bottom line reads: Denial of our Source. Our concern here is the repair of this circuit, for only when all light filaments are reconnected can higher information attach itself to this carrier. It is a receiver of information very much like a radio or TV antenna, consisting of segments. If the segments are disconnected, only limited information can be received and stored.

So, the sequence is this: thought enters, but only low-level frequencies are allowed in. A low-level consciousness filters out the higher frequencies, as they do not correspond to its own frequency. Therefore, higher frequencies lacking, the higher chakras – the more or less dormant energy points – are not being aroused into action, only the two lower chakras are fully stimu-lated. As the chakras, the energy 'gates', determine which infor-mation reaches the DNA, only the lowest frequency reaches the DNA.

Our analysis reveals then two shortcomings: the restriction of higher thought frequencies and a split DNA. On the surface this may indicate a vicious circle, but in truth it is not so at all. The emotion of fear acts like a cork or plug in a pipeline. It is solely fear which restricts the incoming thought to the lowest frequencies. In proportion to the release of our fear-based attitude we allow higher frequencies in. This activates the dormant chakras, which in turn channel information to the DNA.

We may be tempted now to believe that this is the end of the line, as higher thought cannot attach itself to a split DNA, the broken circuit. But not so at all. As the body is a direct mirror of our consciousness, a split consciousness beginning to unify with its Source begins to heal the DNA, in different words, it too becomes whole. In proportion to its healing an increased inflow of information is enabled. Most have heard reference made to the light-body. The process of rebuilding the DNA is building the light-body. When the rest of the chakras – heart, throat, third eye and crown chakra – are open, the DNA carries enough information to change the actual atomic structure of our cells. A person in that state would, for example, be immune to diseases and hard radiation. There would be sufficient information present that he could control the atoms which constitute his molecular structure, meaning he would have the ability to grow a lost limb, or reassemble his body elsewhere – another term for this is teleportation. We would become true masters of our destiny. Throughout the ages there have been pockets within humanity who kept the flame of truth alive; the holy men of the East, for instance, and the Shamans of native America. Many of both of these groups were able to change their actual molecular structure and assume a different physical form or travel any distance through teleportation. If some reader finds that the above-mentioned human potential belongs in the realm of fantasy or that of wild speculation, then (and take no offence) this is only an indication of the degree to which consciousness has been limited.

Now, what prevents the activation of the dormant chakras is the 'plug', which is fear. This results in a repetitious energy flow between the two lowest chakras in males, sexuality and survival. Females are somewhat better off, as their third chakra, the solar plexus, feeling, remained intact. Their DNA could not be tampered with to the same extent as that of males, as woman creates life and needs her feeling centre active to support that life.

So we run in circles – we have become stuck. We do this since the last 12 grand cycles (approx. 300,000 years). It is like listening to the same old tune over and over again. As the release of a fear-based consciousness terminates this vicious cycle, the compelling question is then: what determines the release of fear? In a nutshell the answer is desire. But desire for an expansion in consciousness cannot be generated if this expansion is not perceived as a possible reality. The next logical question imposing itself is: Why do we not hold greater realities possible? Simply because of stabilized perception, which sustains the extremely low frequency of fear. All that is needed is a push, to move the 'needle out of the groove'. This in itself is not too difficult, once an individual recognizes the true state of affairs. However, this recognition is complicated through an additional factor, which reinforces our stagnation: fellow humans who have fallen prey to the Ego's promise of happiness through power. They are deliberating a process which keeps humanity ignorant, meaning humanity is continuously encouraged to believe in the reality of fear. You see, if we would let go of fear we could not be controlled. We would naturally evolve to a recognition of fear as an illusion, hence we would become unmanageable for the power-hungry, who derive an immense stimulus from the feeling of being 'in control'. They feed on fear as much as a sane soul finds sustenance in joy. They need us, and they need us badly. We would be utterly useless to them if we would be masters of our own destiny, if we could do without Dollars, passports and petroleum. We could not be ruled. What a frightening thought for these, mainly male, individuals.

If this paints a picture of humans being helpless little victims, then nothing could be further from the truth. Never, ever buy the victim-ticket. It is our choice to accept suggestions of fear or laugh them away as mere shadows on the wall. There is an ongoing process of purposely designed subliminal and not-so-subliminal suggestions inducing anxiety in all its forms by way of the media and a few dozen other means, very cleverly orchestrated to keep society under fear's spell. Those humans implementing these methods are not their inventors. They again are being used by the greater forces of Darkness, because they can be used, as hunger for power arrests growth of character and this makes for an absence of moral refinement.

Even these greater forces are puppets all the same, puppets of the universal altered Ego. In the early days of the recent human history, the maintenance of fear-frequencies was instrumented partly through the help of a western Church. The actual tool, in this case, was a belief system called the doctrine of depravity, a dogma which states that man is innately sinful and corrupt. This induced guilt on a gigantic level. It is just one of literally thousands of examples. As the house of darkness is a house of cards, rapidly collapsing, the occupants of that house revert to more drastic means in recent times by purposely introducing certain diseases, designed to make individuals fear each other on the most intimate level. You see, it would be disastrous for the powers in charge if you actually knew that there is nothing to fear, that there is not one single disease that can affect you, by simply rising beyond the extremely low frequency of fear. Whatever it is that we give our energy to we empower. If we love we empower love – if we fear we empower fear and what we empower we attract. If you knew who you really are then you would know as a fact that you are provided for, that you are perfectly taken care of, by the Spirit that causes you to be. If you knew this as clearly as you know that water is wet, then you could not possibly be controlled. If you knew with unshakeable certitude that there are no two beings in all the universes – that there is only One expressing as many – then nothing, absolutely no thing, could affect you adversely, because All-There-Is, is I AM. Who could you fear? To fear, you would have to fear yourself.

This is precisely what we are doing, and to maintain this illusion we must be surrounded by a constant emission of the frequency of fear, the Global Thoughtform. This keeps us divided and in survival mode, hence keeps us in a dormant, controllable state. It makes us obedient slaves. For you see, if fear is released, we cannot be manipulated. If all this sounds rather utopian, then let me tell you that the story is much, much, bigger, and reads for the greater part like a cosmic soap opera. It could fill volumes and is certainly highly interesting, but it still would move in the realm of effects. For think not that the forces of darkness are the cause – they reinforce darkness, but they are not the cause. The cause is our loyalty to an altered state of mind.

So, however interesting above-mentioned story might be, it does not even come near the impact of the story we tell here: the story of how to heal a fallen consciousness by expanding into a consciousness of light. The reason for mentioning global manipulations designed to keep humanity in anxiety is not to induce suspicion against fellowmen. If this is what you feel then you have misunderstood. The reason is that those readers unfamiliar with the facts mentioned above begin to recognize the unreality of certain 'facts', and to help them pierce the veil of make-believe and see life in a light-hearted way.

In looking once more at the restoration of the split DNA, two most interesting facts come to light: For one, it is folly to attempt an activation of the dormant chakras by means of pure techniques. The best technique will fail or even cause damage, if the 'plug' is not removed, and once fear is absent, techniques are obsolete in any case. Secondly, one who is in the process of healing his or her own DNA begins to emit a different electromagnetic frequency, which effects the healing of his fellow humans, in contrast to the previous emission of a frequency which only reinforced the damaged, broken circuitry of the DNA through the low frequency of survival consciousness. Such an individual becomes a light beacon, modulates the frequencies around him, hence his task – in technical terms – is frequency modulation.

So to return to our thought of activating the remaining five chakras, to become masters of our destiny once more, masters in the truest sense, we have to know how to release the thought patterns of survival, that is social consciousness. Without the release of fear, progress is impossible. A state of mind devoid of fear is unconditional love, is a soul conscious of its Oneness with the Creator. It is a superior consciousness, therefore superconsciousness. It is an individual unaffected by any worldly adversities. In order to remember Oneness, survival thinking has to be surrendered and to enable us to do this, much dross has to be removed first. This process cannot be implemented if the layers and layers of stifling thought-patterns are not recognized for what they are. Only when we clearly realize the fallacy of hitherto-accepted values can we replace them. We do not have to consciously accept mass-consciousness, the Global Thoughtform, to be affected by it. A newborn knows nothing of social consciousness but exposes itself to its effects all the same – it may still 'catch' pneumonia. By the simple act of entering third density it becomes part and parcel of the consequences of separation. Granted – it comes here for the very reason to experience these consequences, that is limitation, however, it also comes here to learn how to become whole again. So we look at social consciousness in order to reveal the gross perversion of life's values.

Social consciousness is the illness of separation. Here the ideals of noble virtues are inverted, hence substituted with idols. A mind in separation from Oneness perceives only fragments of it, because only a fragment of its SELF is present, the rest is denied. A human being in the state of separation from his Source identifies with an image of itself but not with his God-SELF. This results in a contraction of awareness of such magnitude that the following illustration comparing this state of limitation with reality is perfectly justified:

If we imagined ourselves living in a cellar without any windows, only lit with a tiny oil lamp, and considered the house, of which the cellar is but a tiny part, to be situated in the most magnificent, flourishing garden, bathed in golden sunlight, then this picture portrays, only faintly, our true state of affairs. But not enough: each time a loving soul visits the cellar to call us back into the garden, or a fellow inhabitant of this dark hole discovers the garden and encourages us to leave this dungeon as he did, we either slay him or consider him to be 'crackers'. This dungeon, this darkness of consciousness, constitutes our reality. Here we know fear and death to be real, here we have to fend for a living and anyone who says otherwise must be off the deep end of his mind.

Since the year dot we have been told about the garden, but who of us took the messengers of light seriously enough to make the 'effort' and actually step out into the garden?

We took the message, crucified the messenger and called ourselves piously Christians. Having slain the messenger we now glorified him and started the greatest personality cult in the history of mankind and called it Christianity. We filed the message away and now worship the messenger instead, even send 'missionaries' out into the four corners of the cellar and continue playing 'hard done by', remaining in the cellar. Now, who is really 'crackers'?

If you, the reader, have wondered why Yeshua is referred
material by one of his other names and not by the name Je
this is why: There is a stigma attached to this name, which reeks
of personality worship, the very thing Yeshua rejected at the very
outset of his mission. He is my brother as much as you are my
brother and sister. His greater knowledge puts him in charge of
things, entitling him to honour and respect, but he is still my
brother and he never wanted to be seen as anything else but a
brother. As much as he is the Son of God so are you and so am
I.

What does it take to bring a soul to light, to its natural state of
Being, void of sorrow and lack, to pure joy? I shall tell you what
it takes – in the majority of cases anyway: It takes pain and pain
and more pain, until a soul is so tired of its game of SELF denial,
so exhausted from its endless cycle of rebirths that it becomes
humble and looks within instead of without. It is then when it cries
out: There must be another way. If there be a God, so help me,
please!

Again, in most cases, after help is delivered, we proceed with
the game and forget God. For it is not really God we desire – what
we really want is to have our dream repaired.

It need not take pain to return to light, every lesson can be
learned in joy, without the need for pain. We have heard it so often:
'Whatever comes, comes for a reason'; so we hang in there and
suffer it out, because it is 'for a reason'. What this statement really
implies is that there is a mysterious force outside of us that sends
painful experiences our way for an equally mysterious 'reason'.

Yet the statement that things come for a reason, is correct –
our interpretation of that statement is not. The reason why these
experiences come to us is the fact that we can only experience our
own thought patterns – that is the reason; and that I say, is the
Evangelium, the glad message, for it is proof of the fact that we
are truly masters of our own destiny; that there is no force 'out
there' governing our lives but we ourself.

Yet we cling, for clinging is what we are familiar with, never
mind the pain. See, the pain does not really bother us (although we
forever lament its presence), what really bothers us is sailing
unfamiliar waters. Pain is familiar; in a twisted way we feel

comfortable with it, because it constitutes our reality – in contrast to joy. Joy is not familiar. There is a remedy for that and it has nothing to do with intellect, concepts or methodologies. The remedy is to be a daredevil, to have an attitude of 'all or nothing' – not born of desperation, but of a will for adventure and excitation, in the high spirit of youth – the young eagle, so to speak, who does it for the 'heck' of it, for anything less to him would be living death.

All that is ever required is the sincere desire to awaken from the human drama. To do just that, we have to recognize this drama for what it really is. But as it is we are so caught up in the game of survival that we fear we have to give everything up to come to light. There is only one 'possession' we have to surrender and that is the sum total of all our anxieties. In other words: it is misery which we have to give away. As long as we cling to it, that is believe in its reality, there is absolutely no way out. Clinging we shall remain paupers in Spirit.

To give up misery, we first have to recognize its lack of value. Once we realize that our daily, 'normal' mode of operation is an actually altered state of consciousness, attitudes and beliefs which serve us no longer, then we can establish its worthlessness. Only then are we able to heal and transcend it. To heal something the existence of which we have no cognizance of is an impossibility. This is the sole reason this material puts heavy emphasis on the recognition of the altered Ego first, before any step can be taken to heal it.

The mark of social consciousness is limitation, which is perception of fragments of life and not life itself. A fragmented perception of reality makes for a fragmented reality, which then, of course, is no more reality. To experience the physical realm the soul, admittedly, has to fine-focus on the physical, and the finer we focus, the more we un-focus from the grander picture; but when the physical is seen as the only reality, then the physical is worshipped and not the Spirit that causes it to be. This is materialism, which always hinges around the body. We heard before: the particles of consciousness of the One Christ-SELF who entered matter to prepare it for the coming of its SELF, became preoccupied with matter and identified with it and not with its

Source. They became lost in matter. There is hardly an activity that does not aim at worshipping the Golden Calf, the body, directly or indirectly. Life in a fallen state of consciousness pivots entirely around health, shelter, food, entertainment, beautification and education, the latter only being a tool to help the body survive. Power and financial achievements are dedications to the body all the same, for the first can only dominate bodies, not thought, the second increases 'security'. This is how the Ego executes its denial of Spirit, through the continuous offering of sacrifices at its altar – the body. Ponder this thought, its implication is horrendous. Be not deceived – this is not dishonouring the body, this is not criticism or judgment, but to be understood as plain, sober, constructive self-reflection.

We feed the body thrice a day, we keep it fit, treat it against a dozen and one illnesses, vaccinate it against the ones waiting in a queue, keep it warm, keep it dry, scrub it, wash it, keep it well groomed, paint it, supply it with 'ergonomic' furniture and soft cushions to keep it comfortable. We build the body, we punish it, imprison it. We fatten it when too thin, we starve it when too fat, we create mammoth industries to clothe it – a different fashion per annum – and if this does not attract sufficient attention we design garments with the aim to hide in order to reveal. Legions labour tirelessly their entire life to ensure the ongoing supply of millions of powders and creams to keep the wrinkles at bay – but the body shrivels anyway. Multitudes are kept in their jobs busily creating thousands upon thousands of sprays, deodorants and per-fumes to veil the body's fumes. We mollycoddle it nonstop, only to put it in the end into a wooden box to let it rot. And it is here that the Ego's great mischief reveals itself. First it establishes the body as its reality, to be tirelessly tended for, then it discards it to legitimize its claim that life is misery. If this does not unveil the Ego as psychotic then what does?

For you see, all this care for the body is not born of love but of hate. It imprisons us, eludes us, never does as it is told – on the contrary – it shrinks into decrepitude before our eyes. Only for a short spell does the Ego dangle the carrot of youth before our eyes, saying: 'See, how it could be?', only to take it away to deliver 'proof' of its untruth.

If love would be the motivation for our worship, then we would not try to improve it. We only attempt to improve what proves to be unsatisfactory.

When all is done, we feel something is missing: the elation and exhilaration of simply living. To substitute this most vital but lacking component we add stimulus by way of drugs, alcohol, 'thrill' games or plainly resign to it as a 'fact' of life and remain cheerless. The more appropriate description is dispirited, for how much attention did Spirit receive during all this?

There is more to come. All this care for the physical vehicle must not come easy (says the Ego). For if it would, life would be a dance and this it cannot allow, because its very purpose is to oppose reality. The fulfillment of its demented claims must now be accompanied by either (mostly both) pain or drudgery, and where one is absent the other waits in lure. The implementation of paying the price for our loss of identity, substituted with the body, is by way of money. This becomes now a lifelong dedication. Everything has to have its price. It is astonishing that the Ego did not discover the very air we breathe as a saleable commodity, though in some parts of the globe it put a price tag on water already. Even before the body's arrival the bills are being presented, as well as after its departure. What is more than perplexing is our acceptance of such lunacy. Without further thought we accept such a 'life' as life.

Spirit has no price – it is price-less, hence asks no price. A person in union with his Creator, the God I AM, need not focus on any worldly concerns, but executes his secular duties as a matter of fact, and is perfectly taken care of. It is the denial of our true identity which is the cause of all shortcomings.

Guided by the altered Ego the excessive attention to the physical results in a grave imbalance. If a cyclist shifted his body weight constantly to the left, then this would be his direction. His balance would be lopsided – he would move in circles, exactly as humanity does. To enable us to regain balance, our weight, that is our attention, must, of need, be shifted to the middle. The remaining question then concerns our destiny, for as much as we can ride straight into heaven we can ride straight into hell – meaning joy or torment. Guided by Spirit the body cannot be lacking for it becomes a natural extension of one's Being. It becomes part of the whole and is not singled out, meaning it is then not separated from the whole by falsely identifying with it.

The statement here does not decry physicality – on the contrary – or the creation of abundance. The physical experience is a grand adventure. Adventures are experienced for the joy of it – not for the pain. However, pain is inevitable if the experience we call life is not balanced with Spirit. So the core-issue is balance in Self-identity – is to become God realized.

The insecurity of the individual is the lack of trust in his SELF. The man of society is prepared to eat its dust to be accepted by it. God is not particularly amused by his children making fools of themselves. It is when the Divine SELF is denied, that Self-images are created. This is when one is out of touch with SELF, when one is Clay-man and not God-man. Fear it is then which tries to uphold these images of a false Self. The greater the rift between SELF and Self-image, the more a person thinks of peril. Such a person will always tend to imitate and conform.

A Self-image is when Self operates still in survival mode. This is when a person identifies with its body and environment, its moneys, social status and achievements. It is here where role-playing is adopted to substitute SELF-identity, no matter how common or how unique the role is. It perceives itself as separate from the ongoing Isness of its own Soul. This is when man has lost his soul purpose, and this in a dual understanding. Lost in a state of 'limbo', the Self-image becomes the substitute for the Creator-SELF, the God I AM. The result is a society sworn to infidelity.

We pay tribute to the man of enterprise and worldly achievement, who, at closer inspection, is but a walking appetite. Our faith is in shares and bonds, in electronics and creature comforts, in warfare and science, but not in Divine sustenance. We hail monuments of beauty, works of art, a Michelangelo, a Mozart, a Rembrandt and yet, we never seem to come close enough; their beauty is suggestion only, creating more of an absence than a presence. We yearn for what we lost.

The disease of separation from the God within is the loss of identity. The compensation for this loss is, as we heard before, a

Self-image. What we did not hear as yet is that separation does not stop here. The process precipitates if not arrested, meaning the abyss we created between us and our Divine Source becomes larger (in our experience, not in actual reality). This is most clearly seen in the trend of our society to use this image as a marketable commodity. Even body language is studied in great detail, so as not to cause offence in the presentation of one's 'Self' in order to gain greater material favours. The Self now becomes any image the other would want it to be. This is true SELF-denial – it becomes the chameleon, adopting the colour of its environment, the image it is 'supposed' to have just to 'survive'. This, for example, results in the 'executive' look, with uniform briefcase, uniform suit, uniform plastic smile, uniform conduct, the end of diversity, the ultimate monotony, therefore the epitome of boredom – an altered state of mind proper. Being separated from its Source, from pure Being, a consciousness in a fallen state is impure Being, the root cause of woes on the physical plane. The Ego tends to cover its impure reality with pure images. Hence, for instance, the nature of intent of any military establishment in this world, which is destruction of life and property – chaos, however justified – is veiled by images of regulation and order.

The same inclination we witness in the world of commerce: the sterile, 'clean cut' images of the corporate sector with its sparkling glass palaces, immaculate executive exterior and dust-free office environments hide its effects, the world's garbage piles, the poisons industry pours into virgin waters and the fumes it spews into the atmosphere. However, it is not them who do this to us, there is no 'them' and 'us' – there is only US. We, as a society in an altered state of mind, will always project two faces.

This tendency to produce an image depicting the opposite of the Ego's debatable deeds culminates nowhere more than in the field of advertising. Society's sadness and emptiness is covered up then by projections of youth and happiness. The tar of cigarette smoking is veiled by pictures of freshness, emerald forests, pristine mountain streams and waterfalls; the very things we shave off the Earth and pollute. Alcohol does the same by project-ing images of merry crowds of (loving) people – all young, of course – having 'fun', the exact opposite of the effect it has on those consuming it. The death-cry of a sick society desperate for an image of itself as healthy, vibrant and energetic. Having thus robbed itself of all substance, this Self has to maintain itself by literally gluing itself to mainstream attitudes, else its identity would collapse.

True perception recognizes all this with a discerning mind, yet it does not judge, for if it would it would only judge itself. It sees it as part of the great dream, therefore stands apart from the dream and is no more in bondage to it. It recognizes its brothers as merely mistaken, to whatever degree of folly their conduct attains.

Experience of life through the eyes of the personality Self forces perception to contract. Time, space and matter we perceive in a linear fashion, unaware of their real properties as resonances of cosmic harmonies. For example, to perceive time as a measurable commodity only, is the same as if we assessed a symphony solely by its duration, disregarding its quality aspect as harmonics. Time is a reciprocal flow of cyclic movement, an ongoing now with its own adagios, allegros and fortes. We can illustrate this understanding even if only crudely: if we, instead of hearing a symphony and feeling its vibrations, only studied the sheets of musical notes on which this music is recorded, then we have a good example depicting our perception of life. All we read is symbols, yet one in tune with music, a musician, would hear the symphony clearly in his mind. So it is in life; in a state of separation from our Source we perceive life as symbols, and try to make sense of them. However, one in tune with life, that is one with True perception, would perceive the symphony of life, one in a state of Oneness would BE the symphony.

In our present perception of reality, we merely look at singular notes on the sheet, not even grasping the chord it is part of, or which octave is expressing the tone; not to mention that we miss out entirely on the colour which the single tone conveys, or the nuances of fluctuating background colours the chord expresses. Yet most of us pride ourselves as skilled 'musicians', although we deny the presence of the symphony's great Composer and Conductor altogether.

We plug our ears thoroughly, but claim we hear the symphony. This is social consciousness. To hear the grand symphony we have to listen. To listen we have to still the noise in our minds and lives. Should we succeed in doing this and the first faint cosmic harmonies reach our ear and soul, then our first enthusiasm tempts us into dissipating this precious sound by talking it loudly away, unaware of the fact that anything 'hatching' is tender and fragile. Thus it has to be nourished very gently and quietly into life. Only when our Being resonates unwaveringly to the frequencies of the grand symphony may we safely join the orchestra. The altered Ego would have no bar of this. To prevent the earplugs from falling out, we adhere to mainstream thinking, right down to the smallest details in our lives. This keeps us glued to the dream.

This thoughtform cements in us continuously the belief in 'fact'. In this worldly way of thinking we are so sure of certain 'facts'; for instance, what causes an illness, or why we cannot pay a bill. What is more, it suggests to us the 'done' things, right conduct in other words. Right conduct in a social sense is merely the attempt to display a behavioural pattern which finds the approval of those around us, covering that terrible yearning for acceptance, the cry of the heart to be loved. However, a closer look would reveal the truth: In the measure of seeking approval by others we disapprove of Self.

Consider this: it is 'just not done' to weep in public if an emotion demands such expression (especially when being of male gender), or to laugh out loud in a court room, because the sight of the Son of God dressed up in motheaten wigs and black bat coats is too hilarious to be taken seriously – this would be unthinkable. This would be regarded as being utterly disrespectful, notwithstanding that Human Law itself is the most disrespectful institution, for it sanctifies condemnation. Therefore it establishes guilt as real, where God only sees innocence. True perception sees here, as everywhere else, the Ego's reversal of truth. True perception is highly in tune; it could never not pay respect where respect is due. It would never hurt its brother's heart, but certainly sees the Ego's Law of reversal in action, where it encounters society's price tags. Society denounces common sense.

Why do we restrain ourselves in every walk of life to the extent of Self-denial? The answer is clear. As each individual adheres to the Ego's voice, the collective altered Ego, the Global Thoughtform can be no different, only amplified.

To end a boring conversation by expressing truthfully that one desires not to listen any more is unthinkable. Nobody enslaves us to this yoke but we ourselves, merely by allowing this thoughtform to keep a hold on us. In many a case we justify these behavioural patterns with the word consideration so as not to hurt our brother's feelings. There is a fine difference between conformity and tact. What we 'consider' in general is the other's Ego and thus conform to it.

To continue with the 'done' things: for instance, the idea of learning a profession and doing nothing else but this for one's entire life, is great if it brings joy. If boredom sets in, we know the soul extracted all the wisdom it possibly could from this experience and it is time to move on. But this is not the 'done thing', what would the 'people say'. Who cares what the people say – they do not live our life for us. They have to live their own. The bird cares not who listens to his song – his song is self-expression, therefore a jubilance of life, whatever form this expression assumes.

The purpose of this chapter is to make us consciously aware of the Global Thoughtform and simultaneously to clarify in part how to transcend it best. Firstly, we should be mindful of a fundamental truth: Nothing in the universe is ever lost. So it is with thoughts. Let us not, for one single moment, believe that our thoughts are not known. Being in truth of one universal SELF, this SELF knows each single one of its own thoughts.

Yeshua Ben Joseph expressed this very truth as this: 'Are not five sparrows sold for two farthings, and not one of them is forgotten before God?' [Luke 12:6]. This knowing should encourage us to take responsibility for our thoughts. Not in the sense that we should feel embarrassed for intimate or private thoughts, but as to their effect on others and the whole of humanity. Our Being becomes purified when our thoughts are purified. So it is not to invalidate fear – it has validity as an experience, therefore it is a teacher. However, when we entertain fear thoughts, such as hate, blame, guilt, greed, self-pity and the like, and they constitute our reality, our mind remains polluted and affects the minds around us adversely. The world outside of us only reflects the sum total of our minds. To transcend 'monkey-mind' is a prerequisite to coming to light. This may be uncomfortable at first, because we are so apt to succumb to the thoughtform surrounding us. And why? Because we allow each and every thing to distract us. To allow is a choice, however passive, and a choice is a decision. So, all that is required is a decision.

We clean our house, our car, wash our laundry, but when do we wash our mind? As much as we clean our bodies as part of our daily routine, even more so we should 'hose out' our mind on a daily basis, replenish it with the highest and purest of thoughts. Again – the understanding of purity in this context is the absence of fear and has nothing to do with 'blue nose' attitudes. (We shall elaborate on the 'how' of this cleansing process in the chapter on Self-Reliance). The greater consciousness always includes the lesser, therefore one who is in the process of awakening creates his own powerhouse of thought, which supersedes the Global Thoughtform. However, delays set in when we slip back in the initial period of coming to terms with True perception.

Looking at some typical encounters of succumbing to the thoughtform will assist us in developing a discerning awareness for the very now moment, enabling us to be very conscious of each of the altered Ego's attempts to lead us astray. We are bombarded every minute of the day with the Ego's propositions and slipping back into our old ways of thinking is very easy, especially at the beginning of our awakening. When we first learn a new skill, for example learning how to drive an automobile, we have to be very alert. However, as time goes by, we do all the right things automatically without any conscious effort on our behalf. And so it is with True perception – before long it is to us as natural as breathing.

A humanity denying its Source may be likened to a majestic eagle who believes his wings are clipped. He has forgotten how to fly and now pecks with the sparrows. He is grounded, although he can fly. All the human soul has to do is spread its forgotten wings and know it can fly. It is with a childlike spirit of adventure and expectancy that the soul will meet with newness and miracles in everything it encounters. Giving credence to the stupefying 'reality' of society, – the world of 'nine to five – must earn a living – cringe before officialdom – must not say a word, else I'll be noticed – protect against diseases – insure against loss – respect the law – no one can be trusted – I am a victim – must survive,' – clinging to this perversion of life we shall never depart from its suffocating staleness, but die of boredom instead.

When the eagle remembers, the sparrows will hush. It is when he dares to unfold his mighty wings that the winds of Spirit will lift him free. To help us with the takeoff an example from the field of aviation may make things clearer: The greatest amount of energy spent in the flight of an aeroplane is at the moment of its takeoff. To overcome the mass inertia, much energy is needed, and not only that, the energy for the takeoff has to be applied in a continuous flow without interruption of the forward motion, otherwise the takeoff would be no more than a series of pathetic hops leaving us exactly where we started: On the ground.

Eastern wisdom depicts this inertia principle so well in the idea of the Gunas, the three principal forms of energy: Tamas, Rajas and Sattvas which represent inertia, action and light.

So the 'takeoff' from separation to Oneness has to overcome much gravity. The Ego tries to pull us down again. We may be full of enthusiasm, for we have true hope for the first time, and step out to meet the world with a newly found zest. And this is how it should be. Yet immediately we find ourselves confronted with the idea of fear and lack. We may have changed or are in the process of it, but our environment still moves on its old momentum. Let us then not be tempted in changing the ways of the world. True perception changes the perception of a condition, not the condition. That conditions are but the mirror of perception we shall learn thoroughly a little later on.

It may not be easy, at first, to witness our fellowman surrendering his power to each and every thing. It is always fear we give our power to. The forms the principle of fear is worshipped in are infinite in number. The fact remains that what I fear, I must see as harmful, therefore I have given these forms the power to harm me. In truth we are so powerful, that we can actually give that very power away. It is strange that otherwise sane Gods – in matters of health, for example – should put their faith in no greater thing than green beans and carrots. The sick give it to pills, the antismokers to tobacco; some give their power to sugar or salt.

Others render up their power to a partner or an economical condition. Loss, age and death are feared, and sickness of any kind. We are held in the grip of fear in as much as taking precaution against it. We worship the tree of all fear and sickness, which is our separation from Oneness, yet we resent its fruit. We insist on wrestling guarantees from life to guard us against living – or the dangers thereof – notwithstanding the fact that life does not come with guarantees or warranties – life IS the guarantee.

Again and again we single out aspects of this illusion, focus on these and seek for answers within the illusion, the dream. Perhaps this will make it clearer: Any value we give to a condition within a dream, the state of separation, is still part of the dream, is therefore not real. However, the more we evaluate parts of the dream, the more we value the dream. It follows then that with every evaluation of the dream we make the dream more real to ourselves. This in itself is simple enough to comprehend. However, the difficulty is that we read these words from within the dream, not knowing it is a dream. If we dreamt in a nightmare a 'bogeyman' with a big knife chased us down a dark alleyway, we would most likely run for our life. We tremble, sweat and shake and think our end has come. We evaluate the event as one to be feared. On awakening we sigh with relief and realize it was all a dream. Had we known this fact while still running down the alley in our dream, we would have stopped and laughed, and the 'bogey man' would have simply dissolved into nothing. Yet this describes exactly our position here in what we call our life. It is an upside-down perception of reality.

The 'bogeyman' appears here in a million and one forms. Be it a terminal disease, financial lack, the passing of a dear one – it matters not. We evaluate our world by its form aspects, instead of evaluating that which caused these forms into existence in the first place. The result is a dream state and not a real state of Being. Our present consciousness dwells in the realm of effects, hence focuses on them and not on their cause, which is a Self separated from its Source. This attitude attempts to treat effects instead of itself, the cause, achieving no more than shifting effects around in preference to healing their cause.

We put values on these forms and therefore affirm their reality. How can one part of a dream have more value than another? It still

God \

remains a dream. You see, we made this experience we c
real to us, that it seems insane to even doubt its reality. W
all this while safely at home!

Take no offence: you, who reads these lines, read them in your
dream! They knock at the door of your dream to call you to
awaken. This we can only do by putting an end to judging parts
of the dream as more valuable than others. This is the main
purpose of the chapter concerning the Balance of Polarities – to
evaluate all as equally valid parts of one dream, enabling us to
release our judgment of it. As long as we cling to a part of the
illusion we are glued to the entire illusion and the likelihood of a
transcendence into light is virtually nil.

All that we hold dear in our hearts, the things our soul yearns
for – we do not have to give it up through the act of awakening!
Of course not, we receive it by awakening! This is the whole
point. Waking from this dream does not mean everything disap-
pears. It means everything appears as it really is. Life then is seen
as a unified Whole, as Oneness. Oneness knows only ONE. In
Oneness the puzzle has been made whole. In Oneness there is no
more good or bad, desirable or undesirable. It is absolute fulfillment,
completion, bliss, whatever we may call it. It is a state of Being
beyond hope, for all hope is fulfilled. We can not even faintly begin
to describe the Indescribable. It can only be experienced. Oneness
is the ALL-GOOD. In Oneness it is not that the tree, the mountain
and our brothers are not there. In Oneness they are there for the
first time as they really are. Our fellowman is no more our
fellowman, he then has become our fellow SELF. The I AM in me
then sees only the I AM in everything else. It is a shift from
perception to knowing. The tree is no more the tree, it still appears
as the tree, but is I looking at Me. It IS me. I AM Creation, I AM
humanity, I AM you, awakening as one single, unifying intelligence in my expressions. There is nothing outside I AM, for I AM
is All-There-Is. Therefore there is nothing opposing – this is
freedom. It is the merging of the true SELF with the body-Self,
the union with the crystal SELF – the Christ reborn.

Each time we ascribe a greater value to a certain aspect of life
than to another, we nail ourselves more and more to the cross of
separation. A certain aspect may be more desirable than another,

but to invalidate the undesirable means to separate. An awakening soul recognizes this as an upside-down perception of life, as false perception; sees the Ego's Law of Reversal in everything and so we are almost bursting to communicate, to tell there is a better way, that the Power Source is our Being. And this is alright and shall certainly educate our brother, if we are invited in!, if our communication is welcome. If not, if we feel resistance and still continue, then we are back in the midst of the war of opposites. Let us never forget this. We can only change the world by changing our own world, the heart within.

The moment we feel a fellowman's resistance to our communication and we, nevertheless, insist on changing his ways, we oppose. We learned resistance achieves the opposite of its intent. As we shall soon discover, opposition results in fixation and this means our brother becomes even more fixed in his old ways. Instead of helping him to unify his body Self with his real SELF we are isolating him even more. This certainly does not ease his mind, so an expansion of his thought is even less likely. In essence then, to stand on a soap box exclaiming great wisdom in order to sign up disciples, would testify to a misguided mind and not True perception.

So it happens that at times we may feel very alone because we do not feel understood in our new way of seeing. Of course, any one having uprighted his perception from False to True perception shall be seen as upside-down by false perception. It must be so, if false perception thinks it sees things upright.

We said before: the dreamer, believing his dream to be real, must see reality as the dream. So the position of an awakening soul is one of a mountaineer. One climbing a mountain must, of necessity, leave the valley with all its hustle and bustle behind. At best he shall have the company of a few fellow mountaineers. And the higher he climbs, the further the valley is left behind, but the greater his vista becomes. So it may be that for a while he feels very alone. But that is alright; all it means is he is learning to stand on his own, without the constant confirmation of his ways through the applause of his fellowman.

No one needs applause or a pat on the shoulder while he climbs a mountain, or while he learns how to fly. This only weakens the very strength we are gaining. We shall need every bit of this strength for the takeoff and to make our flight a full success. There shall be innumerable encounters with the wind gusts of illusion, while trying to take off. The Ego would prefer nothing more than a crash right on the runway, before we even lift off. For you see, being our passenger, it knows its rule is history, once we are airborne.

So temptations come and temptations go, as long as we recognize them as the Ego's attempts to keep us grounded. It will try time and time again to clip our wings – for those with little wings cannot soar with the eagles. This happens in the most ordinary and mundane situations of every day life.

What if a friend announced his birthday, expecting to be congratulated? What do we say? Will we say what True perception sees or will we conform? For True perception would say: 'I shall most certainly not reaffirm your belief in death. For affirming your belief in having become one year older, I shall only help to celebrate your aging!' For what the soul hears, be it from the Divine or altered Ego, it accepts as reality. And if 'getting older' is part of one's reality, the soul activates a certain hormone in the body and the body begins to degenerate in exact proportion to one's concept of aging.

True perception sees birthday celebrations as but the countdown of the race toward a coffin. With loud noise and hollow laughter we cheer the race and make the altered Ego's day. For it is then when it celebrates. If we forget concepts such as time and age we shall also forget how to age. True perception knows that body cells are subject to one's consciousness, renew themselves indefinitely if this be the body Self's reality. It would remember the average age of human beings before man invented the calendar. That age was five hundred years and more. The soul does not have wrinkles. If anything, to make the transition easier, True perception would count the birthdays in reverse. Now the direction points to birth – not death. Birth IS its direction, the birth from Dream into Reality. If you happen to perceive yourself as aging, then do not crucify yourself for it. It is alright. The very purpose of coming to this plane of third density, of physicality, is to experience limitation, although the time is now for flying and not crying. The cosmic season is of spring, of unfolding – of bursting forth new life.

The birthday example, depicting linear thinking, only illustrates the tides of illusion, an awakening one will have to face. If he be wise, he rides the crest of the wave – this way he does not resist and the very tide of illusion shall be the thermal wind enabling him to soar.

What if we find ourself in the midst of a group of business people and someone asks for the name of the insurance company we have insured our life with? What do we say if our only insurance is God? (This describes a personal encounter.) The Ego is quick to whisper: 'Don't make a fool of yourself'. But the assurance might be given here that one who quietly speaks his truth shall never ever make a fool of himself. So we say the truth and answer: 'God'. This is, of course, the end of questioning time. We might as well have dropped a bomb. But not for the reason one might assume. The eyes then looking at us told the truth. For the souls of those present recognized, if but for an instant only, that this is the only way to be.

Each encounter with the world of illusion then becomes a reminder of whom to serve: The I AM within. The ONE and only God. We then follow the SELF and not some dogma, guru, church or master of any kind. If there be one to proclaim: 'Follow me', then let it be known to the soul that he needs followers to mirror himself. Whosoever needs mirrors to confirm himself is still immersed within the dream. To follow the I AM in me is to follow God.

Now we look at another typical daily scene. A member of our family may be short-sighted and the suggestion is made to obtain glasses. We witness this and see the quest for spectacles as a perfectly normal reaction to the condition of short-sightedness. Thus we have already become subject to the altered Ego expressing through the Global Thoughtform, the globally accepted remedy of curing by treating the form aspect, the symptom. True perception would chuckle at this proposition. To obstruct eyes with a piece of matter, a piece of glass, in order to improve the eyesight of a Son of God seems ludicrous to it. True perception may chuckle, but it does not mock. It chuckles at the thought of treating the symptom, not at the man desiring glasses. There is a difference. Only an altered state of mind could come up with an idea as twisted as this. True perception would once more look at the form's content, that is, the cause and not the effect, which is the symptom (short-sightedness). It would clearly see the person suffering this condition as being what it says: Short-sighted. It would urge that person to lift his attention beyond its daily busyness and look at greater horizons. For obviously here must be a tendency prevalent to avoid the greater questions in life by busying oneself with matters at hand. If the person considered this advice in earnest, the symptom would dissipate, for the material reflection of the problem has succeeded in pointing to the cause. There would not be a need for it to materialize. For to avoid greater horizons, the mental sight was trained to only look at things at hand. So much the avoidance mattered that the mental attitude, the avoidance of greater horizons, projected itself into the mirror of matter – it materialized.

We see once more: True perception does not change a condition by manipulating it. It simply changes its perception of it and healing occurs. If the short-sighted person insisted on his glasses, we would see this: For a while, the condition improves, which only confirms the choice for glasses, (says the altered state of mind.) Yet, a few years hence a stronger pair of spectacles is needed. And so it goes. And if our person represents an extreme case of stubborn refusal to listen to his mirror, his body, blindness will eventually come to his rescue. Now the man is forced to look at greater things, for what greater horizons could there be but in the space within.

A farsighted person reflects an imbalance all the same. Perfect mental sight sees greater horizons and matters at hand in balance, therefore the physical sight is balanced. A farsighted person would most likely be reminded not to avoid matters at hand by 'running into things'.

This little illustration should point out the type of trap the surrounding thoughtform offers us on a daily basis. Adhering to the seeing which True perception offers, we create our own thoughtform and lift the frequencies of our own environment. Soon the frequencies of those near and dear to us affect their next of kin. And when the hundredth 'monkey' sees aright, the wave of their combined thought ripples around the globe. And thus we see: we heal the world by healing our own.

Illustrations such as the above could fill the libraries of the world. For what is there in our lives, individually or globally, that is not subject to false perception? There is one gauge by which we can measure if our actions are motivated by our altered Ego or not. Especially at the outset of our shift in perception from an Ego-based perception to a seeing guided by the Spirit within should we make use of this gauge as much as possible: we should ask ourselves if our motive for thought or deed is based on fear. If it is, then we are certainly listening to the voice of illusion. We then remind ourselves of the impersonal Global Thoughtform and dismiss it as a nothingness and correct our thinking.

Fear is ignorance and states, therefore, a lack of knowledge of one's true identity. Apprehension of any kind can only be experienced when we identify with the personality or body-Self, for this is the Ego's sole reality. To become aware of the true nature of our Being we must transcend the personality Self – clinging to it we cannot rise above it. The familiar statement 'let go – let God' holds this understanding. To let go is a choice and a choice is a decision. To consciously decide to let go of our false identity paves the way. Anything standing in our way will then make way, but it requires that conscious decision.

To apply practically the knowledge which comes with True perception liberates us from the Global Thoughtform and heals our personal altered Ego as well. This should not cause any strain, as this would only defeat its purpose. Impatience only acknowledges time, therefore introduces pressure. True perception perceives time as an ever present now. That is patience. It knows tomorrow as just another now. Yester-now is gone and tomorrow-now takes care of itself. In the now of today, between the rising of the sun and its setting, is all the now it needs to do its allotted task. To it, the thought of time running short is just another Ego thought of lack. We said before, once True perception is our sight, the altered Ego will make last attempts to drag us back into false perception. Knowing we now see through its tricks for the greater part, it now devises traps not so readily detected as fear. In a way, one cannot help but admire this part of one's Self for its inventiveness. It now supports our effort with vigour and with zest, convincing us it has finally been healed of its erroneous thinking. It even praises us for our noble effort – it whispers: 'You see, how great you are compared to all the rest still snoring in their sleep?'

And soon we begin to feel better than our fellowman who still grovels down there in the valley of false perception. The Ego sighs now with relief, for now we have set ourself apart from our brother and separate him once more in the subtle name of pride. Pride is just one of its tricks, there are a thousand more. However, awareness of the Ego's constant tendency to draw True perception back into its labyrinth of contradictive thought makes its attempts quickly transparent.

Deflation of our worth is another one of its games, subtler perhaps than inflation or pride. This one it calls humility, but it is nonetheless a game, the game of Self-belittling. 'Justified' anger is one of the more difficult hurdles to be seen in the right light. Suppression of it only turns it into a cancerous poison, so let us not force ourself to be peaceful when we are not. When we learn how to balance polarities we will also know how to deal with that particular energy.

These first steps into True perception may, at times, be very trying. However, there is one way with which we shall handle any situation in which we see ourselves slipping from True perception. That is, we let the situation be handled for us. How is this done? We define our problem and give it unto the God I AM, our real SELF, and then let go. Once we do this we must not interfere, however much the situation tempts us to manipulate and to 'pull strings'. What we really are doing by giving the problem to our SELF is this: we are handing it over by saying: 'Father/Mother God – I step aside – You lead the way'. To then let go, means we perfectly trust. There will not be one single case, if we truly let go after having given our problem away, in which the situation is not resolved. The manner in which this happens is always one which teaches us at the same time, and gently so. For remember: God is Love.

What we actually do by rendering up a problem to our SELF, is we establish contact with the Source, the I AM of us, and IT, which is love, can flow forth. As we shall learn in the Law of

Supply: love is convertible. There is not a thing in the entire universe it cannot supply. There is no degree of difficulty for it to supply. It gives and we receive, just that. To supply the solution to a difficult situation is as easy to it as the supply of a hug. This giving away does require trust. It is called faith. It is also termed 'letting go'. To be able to let go of all doubt and manipulation on behalf of the 'little' Self presupposes the understanding of Clay-man being nothing in and of itself. '...of myself I can do nothing – it is the Father within me, who doeth the work'.

Love, the SELF, is the universe and all that it contains. Therefore it only gives unto its SELF. Remember, if SELF or God is All-There-Is, then SELF must be absolute. What is absolute must be all-encompassing. Where does this statement put you and me? Where we belong: we breathe and move and have our Being within God. The SELF in us is God. If we cared to still our minds and sincerely endeavoured to listen to the still voice within, we would hear this:

I AM the I AM of you. We are ONE. There is but One Spirit permeating All. It is I, who am joy, love and peace. I, the Creator, in the on-going Isness of I AM, my Creation – tenderly touching myself in all through all in my forever sea of eternal Being – the dance of life. I am Creator and Creation – experiencing myself through you – my I AM. I AM you. We are ONE !

The full realization of this truth is the peace that passes all understanding, but if we only comprehended as little as a grain of this truth our life would change forever. There is no telling of the joy which comes with this understanding. It transforms Clay-man into God-man. If we considered in earnest how much time and energy we spend in a single day on trivialities, banal conversations or plainly busy ourself with trite activities, then to spend five or ten minutes a day in stilling 'monkey-mind' cannot possibly present an inadmissible suggestion. It is one of the first steps toward a realization of one's true identity and that realization is the sole reason for our sojourn through this physical plane. There is not one single act or labour in any man's life that has precedence over this one objective. This is where our investment should be. We are not here to amass material wealth or achieve health, have a cosy niche in life or seek forever the elusive companion – we are here to find God, which is the I AM of us. If we consecrate our energies to this one end, which is really a beginning, then our life-force is not dissipated. Peculiarly enough, if we do just that, all else is added on to us.

So, to return to our thought once more of surrendering a problem to the I AM in us: when we feel ourselves slipping from True perception, we refrain from manipulating things. Manipulation would be the fastest way of returning to false perception. We simply say: 'From the Almighty I AM Presence I call forth clarity, I step aside – You lead the way!', and let us mean every one of these words. This implies a profound decision. It portrays an attitude of surrender, gratitude and infinite trust in the Spirit that causes all things to be. Eventually we begin to discover that this Spirit is the very I AM of our Being, that it is Being and that there is nothing that it is not.

At the outset of our adventure, when we cease identifying with the personality Self, we tend to think of the I AM in us as being our personal identity only. It is much more than that: it is an individual expression of the universal I AM, it is the universal I AM. I AM the universe and all it contains. Think of a holograph. If we would cut off a corner of the holograph, it would still contain the entire picture of that holograph. We meet with the same principle in biology, where the tiniest cell contains the sum total of all the information of the entire body; and so it is with the individual expression of God. It contains the entire Godhood. The SELF is all-encompassing. This awareness dissolves the fences of the little body-Self and the Self, imprisoned for so long, is released into freedom. It merges with the Creator-Spirit and becomes it as the drop merging with the ocean becomes the ocean.

We see thus clearly how we dream within our Being, which is God, and think ourselves apart from SELF. Consequently we believe God's will to be different from our will, and if our will is different to God's then we cannot be doing God's will. This is where guilt originates. At the root level of our Being we feel guilty for denying that Being, which is the reason why we generally avoid to look within: for fear of being judged. This in turn is where the idea of God as a judge originates. Being that God we only judge ourself and as long as judgment is upheld our Being remains split, and so does the DNA in our physical body as a result of it. We heard the physical is but the mirror of consciousness. Being but an individual expression of this very Being we call God, we should begin to consider our awesome power, for whatever we decree, so is it unto us. We pray: 'Thy will shall be done.' If we would only awaken to reality and realize, what we are saying, for God, our SELF would answer: 'My will is Thine, for we are ONE!'.

So the next time we say: 'I am hopeless, I am miserable, I am a failure', we ought to think twice about what we are actually saying. With each of these words we make profound statements. With each of these we decree what we are, we determine our reality. Say not 'I am good' or 'I am bad', worthy or unworthy, righteous or wretched, but rather say I AM. For this is a state of Pure Being. Being is not this or that – it just is, and Pure Being is innocent! It is all that, because if it singled out one aspect of its Being it would be whole no more. It then would be back in the realm of the 'this' and 'thats', the realm of opposing opposites, where polarities are taken from their whole and therefore incomplete. I AM is All-There-Is, is God, the holiest of holies, the sacred spring of my Being, the fountain of life. I AM sees your I AM as my I AM, therefore we both are ONE I AM. There is not one I AM in all the universes that is greater, more worthy, more intelligent than yours. The reason for this is that there is only ONE I AM. The individual point of expression of this I AM may, temporarily, have lost awareness of this fact by dreaming a dream, but it is still the ONE I AM.

Each time we single one aspect out we constitute our identity. By saying 'I am this or that' we cast the shadow for our next now and when that now is here, we are surprised it is so boring or miserable or 'this and that.' It has to be that way, for we determined it to be so. There is no God outside of us designing our next moment. We do that! We are that God. The God who dreams he is not God.

Let us not say ' I am the victim of this or that.' There is no such thing as a victim. Although not consciously aware of the fact, inflictor and victim have nevertheless chosen to come together to afford each other a learning situation, whereby the Law of

Compensation claims its dues as well. Being all of one SELF it is a co-creation of the sleeping Son of God, appearing as many, separate, little Selves.

True perception sees all this with a calm and unveiled mind. When this is seen, one has risen above the thoughtform. The altered Ego knows now its ruling days have nigh come to an end. Trembling with fear that it might really now have to awaken to reality, it prepares for its last and grandest act in the strategy to defend its dream. It humbly steps out into the open, arms up, weapons on the ground, and says: 'I know, it was all a crazy dream – I surrender – I am sorry, I repent. You are so right. If I fall back into my old ways once more, you must resist my temptation with all your might, with all your strength – for God must not be denied ever again!'

Reconciled with its repentance, we embrace it lovingly and the next time it raises its head in opposition to the truth and tempts us into false perception, we resist following its suggestions with all our might, just as it had asked. For now our shield and sword carries the seal of its approval. This makes the battle so much easier and so we find ourselves right in the centre, from whence we started off: The war of opposites. Now we do not fight aspects within the realm of opposites. No – now we fight the realm itself, the dream of separation. This surely keeps us grounded on the runway forever, because repetitious resistance to the Ego strengthens it only further. Until one day, we sadly fold our wings, sit by the runway and try to fly no more. We think it impossible and bury our dreams of flying to heights of promise and hope. For a dream it must be and where we are must be reality. We weep for a while and think it would have been so nice if..., and accept the Ego's way as the only way there is. And if a Winged One calls on us, asking to fly with him into a new day, we think him to be a fool, because we know with certainty it does not work; that it is he who fell prey to a dream.

What we are saying here in so many words is this: This most honoured and respected statement 'resist temptation' is a twisted truth from the Ego's mouth. We said before that any truth coming from our crystal SELF is bent and distorted by the altered Ego. The original statement was 'do not resist Temptation.' By omitting st two words the meaning of it becomes reversed. Exactly ... ordance with the Ego's Law of Reversal. We have acquainted ourselves now thoroughly with the truth of resistance achieving the opposite of its intent. By resisting temptation, that is the altered Ego, we keep it alive. We can only resist something we acknowledge as real. Thus we keep it real and therefore never leave its realm – the dream.

The answer is, once more, to see it for what it really is, a mad dream, nothing more. This is what True perception does, if it is truly True perception. It does not fight or resist – it simply changes its perception of what it sees, and does not try to change what it sees. This way the sticky, heavy, ugly dream becomes light and sweet and from this awakening is easy – is a joy. The learning required is but the perfect trust in the now. For SELF is not in the past or future but in the now. This is where Being is. One cannot be tomorrow, one can only be now. Being contains all it is. This is the end of want. The end of want means one is complete – means to BE. Not to be this or that, just to BE. The only place to be is here, the only time to be is now. This knowing does away with planning for the future-nows. The now well-lived secures the future-now to be well worthy of its past. The instant we look into the past or future, we have projected our state of Being into the there and then and are no more here and now. By living in the here and now we enter the state of Being and say farewell to the state of survival. Now we see time for what it is. Future then is seen as just another now, not a now we have to provide for and plan for, but as the now I have my Being in which is now and that is always. As we learn to perfectly trust the SELF in us, we see all 'others' as we see SELF. Now we cannot help but trust our fellowman and having given him this gift, the gift returns increased. So trust calls forth trust, if trust is invested in Me, the God I AM of our brother and not in the personality image he has of himself or we of him. SELF gives trust to SELF – SELF gives love to SELF.

In summarizing, the formula for rising above the Global Thoughtform emerges crisp and clear: to retain the awareness of its existence as a cloud of make-believe and to adhere to the Principle of True perception. True perception changes its perception of a condition and not the condition!

A Global View.

The influence the Global Thoughtform has on our planet Earth should become self-evident once we fully comprehend the meaning of the world of matter as a canvas onto which human consciousness projects itself. If man is at war, the Earth is at war. The Earth is a mighty Being in her own rights and is subject to becoming, as much as human consciousness is. Together with the Sun and the rest of an unfolding universe, she prepares as much as man to move from third level to fourth level density. Earth is going through an initiation period, in fact, the process Earth is involved in concerns the alignment of entire galaxies.

The coming transition is a culmination of not only one but many cycles. There is a 44 year cycle (which began in 1965) within a 2,000 year cycle and that again is within a 26,000 year cycle which in turn is within a universal pulse of 50,000 years and that within an overall cosmic heartbeat of 206,000,000 years. The cycle mentioned last represents the midpoint of involution and evolution, marking a shift from third to fourth density.

So, if the transition concerns literally thousands and thousands of entire galaxies, what makes little Earth so important? Among the physical planets offering conscious life the opportunity to experience physicality, Earth happens to be not only the most beautiful, but also the most dense. For this reason souls became entrapped and allowed themselves to slip deeply into negativity. What once was supposed to beam love and delight into the universe, had become a rotten spot in the apple of creation, threatening to affect the rest of all life. The interest shown in Earth by our brothers in space and those of other dimensions – seen in this light – is then a natural one. A relatively smooth transition of Earth is in their interest, is in fact vital for their own growth. These brothers come from the Pleiades, the Orion constellation, Sirius in the system of Canis Major, Vega in the system of Lyra, Alpha and Beta Centauri, etc. Then we have the fourth density beings in our own solar system, from Earth herself – the inner Earth – and from Venus for example, for she prepares to take the place of Earth in aeons to come. So, the scale of the transition is magnanimous.

To bring the focus back to Earth we see that an ideal state would depict Earth and Man's consciousness in perfect alignment, therefore both engaged in an act of harmonious cooperation. We all know man does not keep his side of the contract. The Earth, in trying to stretch mentally, emotionally and physically, is hindered greatly in this process by the non-flow of Man's energies and vibratory patterns, the Global Thoughtform. The split in consciousness occurring in humanity as a whole creates blockages in the Earth's energy flow. These blockages result in enormous pressures, which Earth cannot release any more in a gradual process. Earthquakes, volcanic eruptions, floods, hurricanes etc. are her safety valves. The war in Man's consciousness – the clinging to the Old yet yearning for the New – finds its reflection in Mother Earth.

The hole in the ozone layer is the hole within ourself as Mankind – the void which aches to be filled by the God-SELF. Each awakening soul not only dispels all pain from its own life, but also helps Terra to smooth her transition into super-consciousness.

The Earth, as man and every other living thing, universes and galaxies, have multidimensional existence, therefore multidimensional bodies. The physical counterpart of these bodies, where they exist, are always the smallest in size, the densest. The physical body is contained within its blueprint, the etheric body and this in turn is within the astral body, each one subtler, larger and surrounding the denser form. The astral form is within the mental and this within the causal body. As we see, the physical form is but a tiny condensation of a much greater form and appearing as coagulated matter. Every atom of these bodies is connected and interconnected with every other atom anywhere in a cosmic sea of electromagnetic wave patterns. As our cells are part of a greater whole, the body, so are we the cells within a greater body, the Earth. She in turn is but a cell within a greater whole. Here we may recognize the connection between the energy of Man's thoughtform and the energy of the planet itself. If the two are not aligned, disharmony is the result. These bodies must be brought into perfect alignment as they stretch to prepare for an enormous expansion in consciousness. Any discord in the flow of energies results in man, for example in such diseases as cancer and AIDS. These are named specifically as they are purely attracted through fear-frequencies and are thus obvious reflections of love withheld. The entire universal process occurring at this time is an unfoldment into love, which is God. Anything resisting this process is not in accord with the Universal Intent and as such causes fixation.

To build a new house on the site of an old one, the old house obviously has to be destroyed first. This is the process we are witnessing at present. It is a necessary purification process. Before the New can move in, the Old has to be removed. Where the Old resists, its removal is implemented through destruction, yet no one is doing this to the Old but the Old itself. Wherever light or love moves in, the fearful elements – if they resist – destroy each other. In most avenues of life the removal of negativity need not be implemented through negative processes, it simply dissipates. Whatever adds value to life can only be added to – what does not add value, what is not conducive to the spiritual benefit of humanity, must go. Corruptive, oppressive and destructive systems – be they political, religious or financial – are crumbling.

To view this process negatively would be very foolish. It is a cleansing that is occurring – something every sane mind has been awaiting for aeons of time. When the destructive fires of separation are extinguished by the waters of love and truth, much hiss and steam is generated. When we sweep we create dust. Seeing the calamities and upheavals of our times in this light does away with fear and apprehension. There is true hope for the first time. There is a greater power at work, a light-force preparing a New Heaven and a New Earth. There is a unifying force emerging, a single intelligence, the God I AM, bringing Mankind together as One, transforming humanity into one diamond with billions of facets. The times of Self-gain, of lovelessness, of countless humans dashing aimlessly hither and thither, arriving nowhere – attaining nothing – is coming rapidly to an end. We have entered a new cosmic cycle of evolution – a New Age – lifting those souls ready for a quantum leap from a material to a spiritual understanding of life. In a last all-out effort of the impersonal altered Ego to cling to the Old, there are individuals short-sighted to the extent of endeavouring to use even this light-force for their own materialistic and oppressive ends, in the guise of benevolence – fear it not – it too will crumble. Fear only feeds these energies – let us be very aware of this last point.

Whenever a free-flowing energy meets with an inert or stationary one, a transformation takes place. As water changes its form to steam when heat is applied, so the light-force at this present time accelerates Man's consciousness from third to fourth density, that is, his reality expands from the material to the etheric realm.

Those not aligned at the moment of universal rebirth are of necessity not ready to make the transition into super-consciousness or Oneness. It is their choice. These souls are cherished and loved as all the rest, but must continue their evolution elsewhere, where they have opportunity to act out their destructive and self-destructive tendencies. Earth shall not offer this opportunity any more. They shall continue their growth in other universes, where the emanation of their thought patterns has no direct influence on this universe.

Every soul has free will, therefore makes its own choice. Now we may understand the underlying urgency in the universal call for an awakening of as many souls as possible, for many are just simply dawdling. With or without man – Earth is on the move. Where human consciousness is not in accord with the process of her expansion, the prophecies of dire circumstances must, of necessity, come to pass. It is Terra's only way of cleansing and realigning. Yet it need not be this way. A prophecy is not Law, it merely points at the most probable reality determined by our present choices. The transition of the Age of Fear into the Age of Love may take place without pain and suffering, if we become fully aware of what is actually occurring. This way we may choose consciously to flow with the universal energy and not against it, thus not only easing but assisting the Earth and humanity in the birthing of a new era.

To hear that calamities are not necessary if we align, is one thing – to understand why that is so and how it works, is another. There are two avenues for the alignment to take place: Through the upheavals and torment of catastrophes or through the gentle, harmonious birthing of Earth and humanity into a new era. By way of an example we may illustrate why and how it works: If a man would find himself in a situation of being aggravated by constant abuse and being taken advantage of by a fellowman, then pressure is building up and the day may come where our man has simply enough of the situation – he explodes, he vents his anger, he releases the pressure. Release is real ease. Our man is at ease again – he has aligned. So, by airing his frustration, by erupting his anger, he aligns. This is the avenue of calamity.

Mother Earth does the same. Calamities are not some sort of punishment, they are her safety valves. It is her way of releasing pressure via a volcanic eruption or an earthquake; or she may 'sulk', that is she withdraws and withholds her life-giving waters in form of a drought or she may weep and her tears may cause torrential floods. Whichever way she releases her pain – she aligns.

To continue with our angry man: If the abuser showed a change of heart and approached the man humbly, saying: 'Look – I am truly sorry, I did not realize my selfish conduct, I did not mean to hurt you. Forgive me, brother – I really do love you and I promise it will not occur again, I truly repent'. How do you imagine our man will respond? I will tell you: he will melt. His anger dissipates, it is aligned. He is at ease again. There is no more pressure. This is the avenue of love.

If this is our approach to Mother Earth, if we revere her in every blossom, every leaf, in her gentle breezes, in her bubbling brooks, then she melts! If we say: 'Mother, I took you for granted – I did not realize how much I have hurt you. I really do love you – I love you so very much – please, do not pain any more'. What do you think Mother Earth's response will be? She will weep tears of joy and they will replenish the land. She will rejoice for she is included once again in the magic of life, she is at ease again. She will embrace us, nourish us, delight in the dance of life with us, for we have embraced her with love. This is the alignment, the avenue of love, and in this same manner we align our brothers and sisters and our Self as well.

Any individual, having chosen the ways of love, shall find himself always at the right place at the right time. To fear the days to come would just indicate a relapse into false perception. Yet let there be no false sense of security. To transcend fear, that is choosing love, is a total commitment. It entails every aspect of one's life. It begins with the acknowledgement of the Divine Source within us and therefore acknowledges even the discordant and destructive elements as divine, for all is of One source. It extends to honouring our Great Mother, the Earth, in reverence and humility. To use her persistently for selfish ends shall bring increasingly conflicting circumstance to those who do so. An aware observer cannot fail to notice that calamities occur where ignorance runs most rampant. Dark consciousness attracts darkness.

To regard Earth as a host only to be used and eaten up makes anyone in that position like the cancer cell eating up the body, for it too regards the body as a host, instead of serving the greater whole of which it is but a part. Having read this last sentence with awareness, you will, as well, have discovered the true cause of all forms of cancer, for it is but Man's consciousness projected into matter.

Who is there among us who truly gives thanks to the animal whose flesh he eats? How few are there who realize that they feed themselves with the intense fear vibrations that very animal saturated its body with before and while being killed? It was slaughtered mechanically, in utter lovelessness – its Being unprepared, not respected, disregarded as a feeling Being. Well, consider this: The animal is not just an animal, but you yourself. It is another particle of consciousness of the Christ, exactly the same as you and I, who offered its consciousness to raise the animal body to higher frequencies. So it is for every single creature gracing the Earth with its presence. Is it so unthinkable for us 'Christians' to humble ourself and learn from the 'heathens'? The Mauri ask the tree's forgiveness and pray before they hew it down to build their boat. The native American did the same before he took the buffalo's life, he honoured its being, gave thanks and blessed its Spirit. So do the 'primitive' Bushmen in South Africa. These attitudes revere life. Obviously the suggestion is not to perform a thanksgiving dance each time we fetch a steak from the supermarket, but to have love and reverence for the Beings who give their lives to sustain our bodies – to treat them as feeling Beings and not as commodities. Hearts aligned with love cramp at the needless atrocities which are performed daily among the winged, furred, four-legged and finned of our brothers in the name of commerce, science, sport and progress. But it is not for much longer – Spirit heard their silent cry, it is soon coming to an end.

An awakening soul has the deepest love for his nourisher and sustainer, his Mother, the Earth. To rubbish and pollute her, hurts him as much as her. However, to fight the polluters is not the answer, but to change his own ways is. By changing ourselves, we change the world.

In fighting pollution, we only treat the symptom. The cause is the mental and emotional pollution of fear, expressing itself in its various forms such as hate, anger, greed, jealousy, pride and the rest of the Ego's children. Fear's task is contamination of purity – the voice against God. This creates an energy stench of global magnitude, condensing in the physical as pollution and diseases. So, to treat the effect – the physical impurities – though necessary, is not the answer at all. Healing is purification. By purifying ourselves, purification of our environment and that of the ecology of the Earth inevitably follows suit. It is very simple and obvious: A polluted mind generates actions which pollute. Whether we like it or not, a mind operating under the tutelage of the altered Ego is a polluted mind. As long as fear of any kind remains part of one's reality then the mind is still polluted, regardless of the nobility of motivation the Ego projects, because it is always a denial of Divinity. A pure mind can only manifest purity.

A true healing can only occur on a spiritual level. To believe in the impotence of oneself as a single individual in regard to the healing impact one has on the whole, is erroneous indeed. This is where our real responsibility and commitment lies. By healing ourselves, we heal the world. The efforts of the individual to release fear, the cause of all disease, cannot possibly be overestimated. If only we knew what absolutely stunning healing power we have as single individuals, we would not hesitate one second in wanting to change our ways from fear to love, from insanity to sanity, not to mention the sense of purpose which such choice brings with it in its trail. I urge you in deepest sincerity to consider these last sentences. Humanity is aching and the Earth is crying out in pain. Both need you and your cooperation. Both are craving for your love. Please, believe that you make a difference, not so much by joining the armies of helpers who work on the level of effects (however praiseworthy that may be), but by healing the attitude which makes these armies necessary from the very outset. And this one does best by healing one's own separation first.

A fact generally not known is that one's efforts are augmented, actually heavily reinforced, by our brothers in the unseen. They need our willingness to be able to help. The will to heal has to come from within humanity itself – only then can we expect to be aided in our efforts. By blaming our fellowman for his thoughtlessness in poisoning the planet, and thus himself and us, we do not heal. All we do with this act is accuse him of having succumbed to separation, as if we stood out as all-enlightened beings apart from him. The fact that we begin to see, and he does not, only states that we opened our eyes a little earlier in time than he. Accusation is not his need – education is.

The prophecies of destruction are attracted by those who cannot let go of their old ways. How else could Earth shake off the biting fleas? Those condemning society's treatment of the planet, without changing their own lives, are as much subject to the Law of Compensation as the actual doers. This is certainly not to judge, but to hold up a mirror. Those who let go of fear have nothing to fear. This urge to use Earth for selfish gain and plain greed is only based on fear of lack. To let go of fear is all that is ever required, for once fear has been released, the God I AM is found, and whosoever walks with God walks in harmony with the Earth.

Within the years 1990 to 2010 we shall witness the decline and disintegration of every institution, business and government that is fear-based. Each soul is given the chance to choose between war or peace, competition or cooperation, healing or attack, fear or love. With each choice for cooperation and love the collective frequency of the Global Thoughtform is pulsating at a faster rate and therefore aligning with the universal intent. To lose heart by wondering how the world could possibly ever rise beyond the

Global Thoughtform, and awaken to the truth, would indicate another doubt we place on life.

If we regard humanity in its upside-down perception of life as a sick patient desperately needing treatment, we may console ourselves with the assurance that the medicine has been applied already. The patient only needs much loving care and encouragement to get back on his feet. The patient swallowed his medicine a long time ago, when very loving healers diagnosed the disease and began the treatment. These healers – and not only Yeshua – saw man as innocent, no matter how deluded he was and is. Thus they saw in man their own true SELF, and demonstrated it too. This allowed the miracle in. True perception is the condition for the miracle.

The only obstacle that had to be overcome since then was the unbelievable mass inertia of humanity's altered Ego. Seen in cosmic terms, the healing process occurs at a stunning speed. The denial of reality, the Fall, occurred billions of years ago in our counting, long before we entered into physical matter. The few thousand years since the miracle's occurrence are but as fragments of a second, if we compressed the aeons of living in illusion into a day of our time. However, this does not mean that a healing takes place while we continue worshipping the Golden Calf. The healing of the body of humanity can only occur in the measure of its single cells healing themselves.

Each time a human being changes his or her mind from false to True perception, the effect on humanity is immeasurable, for we put into our service now the Hundredth Monkey syndrome and let it work 'in reverse'. Such a person has a tremendous healing effect without ever having to speak a word; this merely due to the fact that the high thought-frequency he emits raises the frequencies of his environment. We heard before: the greater consciousness always includes the lesser. The consciousness of True perception is infinitely more powerful than a mind still in illusion. Whereas man aims at possessing and yielding power and therefore can never own it, True perception IS power, it does not use power. If it would, it would not be True perception. It may be likened to the Sun. The rising Sun does not fight the night. It just

IS and by its very Being the night becomes a bright and promising day. Humanity is becoming.

With each awakening soul an impetus of such power is added to the momentum of the awakening of the whole of mankind, that its effects literally ripple to the farthest corners of the universe. We need not marvel then at sightings of spacecraft and the like, for our 'ripples' have been felt and called our brothers forth to witness an event of such magnitude the universe has never seen. The promise is given us that by the end of the first decade of the new century the era of Social consciousness is coming to an end, unfolding into the era of super-consciousness. To interpret this promise correctly, we shall look at it this way: say we are stranded in a strange land, but know of a jet-plane flying home. We still have to make our way to the plane and step inside it to be flown home. The plane flies with or without us. Although we know of the coming changes, we will not partake of that cosmic transmutation from third to fourth density if we do not transcend our own fear-based reality of separation to one of love and union with the Source. It is a choice we have to make. The approaching new era may be likened to a harvester gathering ripe souls. What is not ripe cannot be harvested, has to be put back into the earth to start the process of growth all over again.

You, who have made it this far, have stepped into the light of the rising sun. This statement can be made without the slightest hesitation, for this one reason alone: No one who has not doubted the Ego's reality could have read this material this far. It takes courage to do that. It takes an awakening soul.

Let us now move to the grand lesson of the Balance of Polarities, as this shall lay the foundation to the development of True perception.

Chapter 4
The Balance of Polarities

The Nature Of Polarities.

To define this world as the plane of polarities is, of course, correct. So is the term dualism. To describe it as the realm of opposing forces has, however, a more descriptive appeal as this illustration is in accordance with our perception of the world of opposites.

Positive and negative, male and female, peace and war – everything that is represents a polarity. For every yeah there is a nay. This applies to the whole of Creation, not merely to the physical plane. But are the forces of life really opposing each other as we perceive them? Let us see. Everything is universal energy in one form or another. This energy has a positive and negative charge. This charge ought not to be understood in terms of good or bad – these are human evaluations. The I AM is neither good nor bad, it just IS. It is the All-Good. Terms such as positive and negative should rather be interpreted as the principle of male and female.

Polarities are opposite reflections of one another, of the All-There-Is – the God I AM. This universal energy, if allowed to express itself freely, represents a harmonious interaction of these two charges. Although opposites, they do not oppose, but merely reflect one another. In different words – there is no conflict.

The Asclepius symbol in the field of medicine depicts this idea of unified polarities as the secret of healing. The serpent (female energy) embracing the sword (male energy). Any form we encounter, be it a thought, an emotion or a flower, is this energy made manifest in form. It always expresses as union and each expression is as valid as any other one, regardless of our preferences. However, to a mind in separation from Oneness this wholeness appears not as union, but as polarized aspects of itself, which we then value as wholes in themselves.

Day and night are the same continuum seen in their different facets. The night gives way to the day – there is no conflict. One be without the other. But we split the unified whole of polarities by way of unequal evaluation, which removes them from their whole. Anything not whole is unwhole, therefore sick. This depicts accurately the realm of human experience, the world of matter. Humanity as such is sick. Hardly anyone would argue with that.

Our entire perception of the physical realm exhausts itself in a rejection and acceptance game. We fight conditions, resist most currents of life and honestly believe we can make life function this way. We hardly encounter a situation which we do not manipulate in one way or another. Thus, as a result, there is barely a day in our lives without a problem surfacing somewhere, however minute. We have come to accept this as normal. 'That's life,' we say, unaware of the fact that this evaluation is born of a split mind. That same life seen with a unified consciousness would be pure bliss.

The very instant a polarity is singled out from its unified whole as being of greater or lesser value than its opposite, it develops into a problem. Life, however, functions perfectly without our interference. If we would only let life be, we would literally arrive at a paradisical state of Being. In fact, life can only function if we do not interfere with its seeming opposites. Interaction yes, but not interference.

Taking a closer look at life's manifestations we recognize in everything the rhythmic flow of harmonious interactions of polarities. Any attempt to interrupt this flow would inevitably result in fixation – things cease to function. If we robbed the ocean of one of its tides, the ocean would become fixed, all flow would cease – its life would stop. If we offered the particle flow of a rocket any resistance, the forward motion of the rocket would not be a success – because the flow of these particles could not escape freely in the reverse direction. Without dispersion there is no accumulation. To lift something up, we first have to bend down. To resist one of the polarities of movement involved here would fixate all movement. The harmonious blending of opposites can be observed in everything, from the tiniest cell to the grandest galaxy. As Above so Below.

It is not difficult to comprehend the underlying principle in the harmonious interchange of polarities. The idea of this principle is almost forcing itself into our awareness: Reconciliation, which is the Law of Compensation. Each movement or action of life reconciles with its opposite reflection. To balance polarities means to reconcile with the entire realm of polarities as such. The result of this is True perception, a consciousness which knows nothing of conflict, for here energies are unified and can flow harmoniously again. Where energies can flow unencumbered, fixation does not exist. The implication of this is salvation from fear, therefore from all lack.

The tree grows up yet simultaneously it grows down. As the branches spread so do its roots. Every vice is 'punished', every virtue 'rewarded'. The water closes behind the parting hand. An iron bar magnetized at one end will produce the opposite magnetism at its opposite end. Nature is always in perfect balance. It is when man upsets this balance through his false perception of reality, that imbalances occur. False perception only perceives one side of the coin, though every inside has an outside – every rope has two ends. The staircase leading up also leads down. God made weeds as well as vegetables.

Although any movement of energy consists of two charges, we single out one charge and evaluate it on its own merit. We are obsessed with the mistaken belief that the transformation of one polarity into its opposite would improve life. We continuously attempt to change bad to good – poor to rich – insecurity to security and so forth, impervious to reason which tells us that a polarity is but part of a whole, that negation of one negates the other – collapses the whole which consists of the two. A birth could never take place if we suppressed the contractions of the process of labour; expansion could not occur. Both are part of one movement. Interfering with one aspect of its rhythmic flow creates an imbalance, hence fixates the entire event, and this holds true for the smallest detail in our daily experience. This is when things do not function any more.

Two electric wires, plus and minus, when forced together create a short circuit. This is when sparks fly everywhere. What happens if we contemplate the harmonious union of these two polarities? We create Light!

To resist the inbreath makes breathing altogether impossible. This would result in death. Any malfunction in life is really a death by degree. We may recall the axiom: Resistance effects the opposite of its intent. We are, by now, well acquainted with the altered Ego's tendency to reverse all truth. It opposes opposites – instead of flowing with them. To flow with is to atone. To atone means to be at one. As opposites are but components of life itself, by opposing these, we oppose life itself. Passive resistance is resistance all the same, merely its passive expression – it is called dodging, but have we ever outwitted the Law? If I resist the movement of one leg, while walking, the walk becomes a limp. Our entire earthly experience reflects this limp.

Instead of liberating woman from man, her liberation from separation would be the answer. Emotion is thus released into motion – can flow freely once more. The moment we resist a situation, we oppose it, however minutely is of no relevance. This is not to say we shall not have our preferences, but resistance feeds that which is being resisted with its energy, therefore strengthens it and makes it even more real. The moment we learn how to go with the flow, we glow with the flow. We would never be too early – we would never be too late. But we insist on opposing life, the cohesive whole of opposites on every level – even time itself.

If time is judged as too short, as being in short supply, the shortest distance in space seems to expand, and it takes too long to get there. So resisting time by compressing it, that is by rushing, we achieve the opposite of our intention: we slow down. We rush so much until everything grinds to a halt (rush-hour), and this only because we assess time as not being in abundant supply. We single it out and put our stamp of evaluation on it.

If we evaluate space in one place as more valuable than in another, for example cities or 'real' estate, then it not only takes twice as long to get somewhere as in the open country, but we create as well an endless chain of problems which flows forth as a result of this evaluation. So what has been gained? Nothing. One is always at the price of the other. And why? Because in truth they are fragments of the same puzzle, reflections of one and the same whole. Space and time are in reality here and now, and that is ONE.

It is but the sequential appearance of the one here and now in the realm of matter.

Both are but two ends of one rope – two aspects of one whole. Whereas life reconciles the act of receiving with its polarity of giving, we reverse this fundamental law and get, that is receive, by taking, and then wonder why supply runs short. The polarity of receiving is evaluated as being of greater value than giving. Thus an imbalance has been created. Imbalances cause fixation and so the natural flow of abundance becomes blocked and supply cannot rush forth. Lack of any kind is the result.

This material world continuously reflects our misinterpretation of life, but through our complete loyalty to the altered Ego we refuse to see. The entire material plane is one gigantic mirror reflecting man – that is, his consciousness. We seek happiness in conditions, oblivious to the fact that such a condition is only the result – the manifestation – the reflection of a happy mind. Happiness cannot possibly be found on the level of effects, but a happy mind shall always manifest its own on the outer.

We are forever endeavouring to change symptoms instead of looking at their cause. We perceive a fragmented world because we are fragmented, meaning our consciousness is not unified. The outer is but the reflection of the inner. If it be an injury or disease or a war between nations, it is the same – the only difference here is that the first reflects an individual imbalance of polarities – the second reflects the imbalance of the collective consciousness of a nation. Initially the greatest difficulty for an awakening soul in transcending mass-thinking is in coming to terms with the understanding that one can only experience whatever is encompassed by one's own thought patterns. I am not miserable because I experience a miserable situation. I experience a miserable situation because misery is an accepted part of my reality.

If we stood before a mirror making a grimace and felt displeasure at the face looking at us, the intelligent thing to do would be to smile at the face and we would receive a smile in return. But in life we do not react intelligently to our reflection – we either take the mirror off the wall and hide it, or run from it, or destroy the mirror altogether.

Perhaps a little illustration is welcome at this point: we may have 'caught' an influenza and feel dis-ease. Immediately the blame is put on some innocent little virus, as the one having caused the condition. Now we fight it. Instead of looking at the real cause, which is our consciousness, we want to blame something or somebody – this induces guilt and therefore separates. The virus is not causal, the virus is instrumental – this statement reveals a world of difference. We caused the influenza by having created an imbalance, which resulted in an interruption of the harmonious flow of energies. And this is how the influenza manifests as a reflection of our act of interruption: viruses, bacteria, poisons etc. are flowing through our system every second of the day. They are not absent while we are healthy. They are right here and now with us and not on vacation somewhere. They flow through our bodies continuously – it is when they do not flow through any more, that we feel dis-ease. For now they become 'stuck'.

So it is our perception of a situation – the focus on the virus – and not the situation itself which is the problem. And this perception is false perception. Constipation, for example, indicates a blockage. Not realizing that the condition, the constipation, is a reflection of consciousness into matter, we single this condition out as something bad to be fought. That it is not the cause but a symptom only, we do not see. A disease is one of life's ways of pointing physically to a lesson not learned, or better, which we refused to learn otherwise. The constipation is in our mind. If we cared to look at the cause we may detect an attitude of not wanting to let go of past emotional luggage, or we might find some information there which we find hard to digest or assimilate. Therefore we create a blockage. If the assimilation is neglected, then it becomes an unresolved condition. It will now be projected into matter, the body. We have resisted the process of assimilation – the result is a problem. Now we interpret the constipation on its form level and that is only a symptom. The condition therefore is an effect only – not a cause. So what do we do? As usual, we reverse reason and treat the symptom, that is, resist the condition. We evaluate it as undesirable, as bad, although its only purpose was to point at the cause. Now we have singled out one polarity once more as being of different validity to the rest and at best the symptom shifts and appears elsewhere in a different form. It is really the same as if we looked in the mirror and discovered pimples in our reflection. To polish the mirror now, the reflection, would hardly dispense with the pimples.

If we looked at the cause of the pimples, the symptom, the pimples, would disappear. And what is the cause of these pimples, or for that matter any disease? – Consciousness. We may step in the right direction and read a hundred excellent books on the matter and shall find most certainly the mental condition which has caused our individual problem. The symptom then dissolves and we feel healthy again. And we really believe we have healed. All we really have done is to prune a tiny shoot off the Tree of Sickness. The tree is still there and very alive. What we have really performed here is another act of splitting polarities, because we have given health a greater value than sickness. These are only two sides of one cohesive whole. Sickness is valid, it has great healing power, for it always reflects the inner condition we neglected to look at. Instead of probing for the individual cause of a sickness, or any problem for that matter, we should look at the universal cause of all dis-eases and problems, which is the human sickness of separation from our Source.

Admittedly, in our example we have moved in the right direction. We did not treat the symptom, however we did not treat the true cause either. We chose the right direction but did not walk all the way. What we ought to do is look at the root cause of all problems – which includes sickness of any kind, and we would find our altered state of mind to be the culprit, and not the problems themselves, for these are only projections of imbalances, therefore symptoms only.

Seeing separation as the ultimate cause of all our 'pimples' would dissipate the pimples, for now the symptom has fulfilled its purpose, hence it is not needed any more. In the measure of realizing separation from Oneness as the root cause of all of life's 'pimples', they would vanish. Seeing separation as the cause, we evaluate the parts it contains as of equal value to one another. To deal with separation our focus must shift from an evaluation of individual conditions to an allowance of separation itself of which conditions are but a part. This allowance is in truth non-judgment, the alchemy transmuting agony into ecstasy, or separation into Oneness. Allowance may have its preferences but does not invalidate.

A good example illustrating our distorted seeing would be the intensive attention with which two lovers focus on one another. Each sees in the other his or her source of happiness. Female singles out male, seeks outside itself for fulfillment, and vice versa. Each gives its own Self less value than the other and fixation sets in. The energy of love becomes blocked and broken hearts are inevitable. If each evaluated its own Self as equal to the other, both would see their own Self as the Source of happiness and their love would result in true union. Each seeing their own Being as the Source, they would become ONE BEING.

Such union, if sustained, would impress a lasting effect on the rest of the world, for they as ONE create a vortex of such power and energy that they eventually draw literally thousands of souls into the ever expanding whirlpool of their union. As long as we identify with the body or our gender – male or female – and thus judge, that is, invalidate, our Self, such union remains an impossibility. Our SELF is both male and female, it only projects itself as such into the physical realm and therefore stands in truth above polarities.

The Cross Of Separation.

A mind in the state of separation, in essence, wants to split, divide – wants to make unwhole, therefore wants to make sick. It does this by breaking the whole into its parts and then gives each of these parts a different value. It justifies this with the concept of usefulness. One part or thing in life becomes more 'useful' than another. Life is not to be useful – life is to BE. The ultimate simplicity is the ultimate truth.

However, a mind whose sole aim it is to oppose simplicity, God, to make complex, to contradict, to veil truth, does not tend to take very kindly to a reversal of its own reversal. Simplicity is the last thing it will look at. True perception is the bridge to Oneness, and True perception is achieved by balancing polarities, which is, in essence, the surrender of judgment.

To do this is very, very easy. What is not so easy is to bring this simplicity to a state of mind in separation which is in itself a complex jungle of contradictions within contradictions. To just superimpose simplicity onto complexity would only result in further confusion. So a 'house cleaning' is required first. We must first recognize illusion before we can exchange it for reality. The rendering up of judgment has to be born of the right reason. To attempt this merely because it is the trend or because we have heard that to judge brings no gain in return will rather suppress than release. Once we obtain an in-depth understanding of the utter insanity of any form of judgment, then it is not a great effort – it only requires attention. Anyone who sincerely sets out to learn this final major lesson receives an unexpected bonus, whether aware of it initially or not – and that is this: He will have at his command the entire forces of the unseen to help him in this task. His God-SELF will be the wind beneath his wings and he shall learn how to fly. The reason for this is that anyone learning this lesson is for the first time in aeons fulfilling his only purpose here: to unify his separated Self with All-There-Is, his God-SELF. The healing of the altered state of mind is the most sacred task for any human being. For one doing this in earnest, this promise is given: all obstacles hindering this process shall be removed from his life. We need not marvel, at this stage, how this can be done. It is an absolute fact.

Although initially the obstacles created by the individual are used to teach him, they fade in the measure of his learning. Towards the end of this chapter we shall understand why this must be so. When we read about the cessation of all sorrow we shall know.

In this world of polarities we seem to have a choice. The maxim we are all familiar with is freedom of choice. On closer inspection, the freedom of this choice reveals itself as rather limited. We may only choose between two of any aspects, between minus or plus, male or female, hot or cold, rich or poor, good or bad, likes or dislikes, advantage or disadvantage, etcetera. The instant we decide for any one polarity, the choice has to be made for the next polarity contained within the first. If we dotted a graph, representing the progression of each choice leading to a number of further choices, we would recognize the quantity of each set of choices being the square of the previous number of choices. It may be easier to imagine us travelling on a river, the direction is upstream. At each tributary junction we have a choice as to which way to take. This, of course, will never lead us to the river's source. The tributaries become narrower as their number increases. Not even the sum total of these brooks, streams and springs are the river's source.

Science, for example, characterizes this upstream motion into the maze of choices best. It dissects a given whole into its parts for the purpose of analysis, only to repeat this process now with each further part. These are then split again, and the graphic curve depicting this search for knowledge would draw a forever expanding labyrinth of choices, an endless process, which never can nor will lead to knowledge – shall never find the river's source. The focus on parts of a whole (the upstream direction) leads to contraction – not expansion. Now, contraction ought not to be evaluated as of lesser value than its polarity. Although the wrong direction, it is of equal value to life itself of which it is but a part. As we saw in the example of a birthing process, contraction precedes expansion – both are equally valid aspects of one energy.

To continue with the river analogy: the simple solution to this problem offers itself. Instead of exerting strenuous efforts in rowing upstream, a little attention in observing the river's direction would show the way: to let go of the oars and allow our boat to flow with the current of the river. This way the water carries us safely to its source, the ocean.

It does not require a trained observer to interpret this analogy correctly. For man to find his Source he must let go of his old ways, his oars. For these are based on an erroneous assessment of his situation, are based on fear. He must reverse his direction as our river boat did. This is the only true choice he ever has – to row against the current of life or to flow with it. To solve all of his problems at once, he will have to lay aside his oars of fear.

Now we will move to another paradigm in order to present us, together with the river example, with a mental scaffolding to bring the overall picture into better focus. We imagine a vertical pole, the vertical pole representing God, or reality. This symbolizes a unified whole. We split this pole lengthwise, thus we have two poles. We take the one we have split off away and lay it across the vertical pole to create a horizontal or lateral pole. Now we have the picture of a cross. By splitting the vertical pole and laying one pole across we have laid one half of the unified whole in exact opposition to the vertical or God pole. All the lateral pole contains must now, of necessity, as well be opposed to God, or the vertical pole. This lateral pole depicts our world – our view of reality. A reality which is no more real, for it is no more whole. It depicts our separation from Oneness. What is not real must be unreal, as a dream is unreal from the vista of one in the waking state. So this lateral pole describes the world in which we express. This is the world we know, in which we breathe and live – a world split from its whole. It is this lateral pole we misinterpret. If we did not see it falsely, then the lateral pole would upright itself in our perception, would realign itself with the vertical pole and become One with it again. But being as it is, our perception of reality is at cross purposes with reality, so we see it as separate from it and across. So the lateral pole becomes the world of illusion or altered state of mind – the altered Ego. This point needs to be clearly understood: The lateral axis itself is not the illusion, only its lateral position is; that is, our perception of it as being separate from the vertical pole. We have thus formed a cross to which we nailed ourselves. We crucified ourselves. Nobody else did this to us.

The point where the two poles intersect, hence the crossing point, we shall term the bridge. We could have called the vertical pole love and the lateral pole fear, it is all the same, as long as we keep in mind the underlying nature of the lateral pole's position, which is our perception of a split reality – the dream. In our present perception of life, we move within the lateral pole, the world of illusion. Regardless of which emotions are experienced within this dream pole, they are all based on the concept of fear.

It follows then that our perception of reality has to be reversed. Now, the only point of contact with reality is at the pivoting point of the lateral pole, the point of perfect balance – the bridge. For only here may we walk across to the real world.

The river analogy showed us the illusion of finding the river's source by rowing upstream. The cross analogy shall serve as a structure helping us to understand the purpose and goal of balancing polarities. Keeping these two pictures, the river and the cross analogy, in the back of our mind as we read on will help us considerably to understand the simplicity of arriving at the bridge. It is simplicity which we find difficult to comprehend in an altered state of mind.

To bring the next point successfully across, the reader is asked to give his utmost and undivided attention. For the words to follow aim at recalling a feeling, a subtle knowing. If we imagine the intensity of activities within the lateral pole or the state of separation to increase, as we move away from its middle point, then we shall have no difficulty in seeing the centre or bridge of this lateral axis as the one with the least activity. Meaning, here the least emphasis is put on opposites. It is a point of stillness.

Now to the feeling we want to recall, an hour in our life which looks something like this: we are lying in the shade of a tree somewhere, perhaps on some beach in the warmth of a beautiful day, or remember one of those timeless summer days we spent on grandpa's farm when we were little; where birdsong and the hum of bees only intensified the stillness of the moment. There was Spirit in the air, the scent of rosehip and fresh hay and the promise of greater things to come. We somehow sensed our possibilities and knew that all was well. We retrace such a moment now. Everything seems so still. We become a little drowsy and the distant laughter of playing children barely seems to reach us and only adds to the peace and stillness we feel. It is as if time stood still, we feel very content. There is no resistance in us to anything. We are completely removed from the noise of the world – we are highly aware and yet we seem to float in a sea of peace and have merged with its eternal rhythm of tides. We feel we could lie like this forever. We are at peace with All-There-Is.

We have reached a point of stillness. What it really means is that we simply feel without evaluating, that is judging the feeling, and are therefore close to standing on the bridge, the still-point of the lateral axis. It is here where we come closest to True perception. True perception may find itself in the midst of noise and activity, yet is completely at peace with All-There-Is. It knows and it trusts. And this is why: all Ego activity has come to a rest, which means here is a state of mind wholly unconcerned with judging conditions. There is no attempt of the mind to evaluate one aspect of life as better than another. One simply sees any situation or condition as an expression of the Source – else it would not be – hence it is valid. This is the allowance of the state of separation. This is what balances opposites. It is a state of Being, a state of equilibrium. A state of mind where everything has an equal right to be.

The essence of this feeling is the non-judgment of any expression of life, therefore an embrace of life. This stillness is not inactivity – it is activity with the voice of the altered Ego stilled. One not only may, but shall, celebrate life in a dance of delight. This dance celebrates all of life and not only parts of it, rejecting parts of life. Life desires to be embraced – all of it. Much in the way the dolphin ploughs the ocean with punch and vivacity, splashing in the waters of life, without evaluating the ocean's different currents as being of lesser or greater worth. The dolphin cares not for applause of his friskiness or prankish games. He does it for the 'heck' of it. He loves life – all, all, all of it. So it does not matter how much we love or emphasize parts of the lateral pole – as long as we grant all parts equal validity, an equal right to be. The instant we can accept the entire lateral pole with all its seeming opposites, we have reunified the lateral with the vertical pole. It is then that we become ONE. It is then that we live. To balance polarities does not mean to give up desires or reduce living to a point where life is 'stilled' or dead, but to equalize, that is not to reject parts of life. Then the parts which do not resonate to our signature frequency, to our particular flavour, shall not manifest as our experience. This consciousness releases all suppressed emotions such as hate, jealousy and greed, into the All-There-Is. It grants each an equal right to be and sees these only as fragments separated from the union of their being. Therefore to such a mind they are no more. In this understanding of the balance we arrive at its bottom-line: to not even see judgment as wrong, but merely as a mistaken way of seeing life.

This is our concern here. Let us relive this feeling of stillness, for if we can, we have a solid base for understanding the rest. Now we shall proceed: One polarity cannot be without the other. They represent One whole, a pair. The instant we split the wholeness of a pair of opposites, we des-pair, for we have made unwhole, made two where there was only ONE. This is the picture of our world, a split world, therefore in despair.

The Balance.

Polarities in themselves are innocent and harmless. Our perception of polarities is not. The falsity of this perception is that we see them on their own merit, as things on their own. For instance, if we examine the single pieces of a puzzle – removed from the puzzle as a whole – we find them devoid of any meaning.

Yet this is accurately representative of our perception. We somehow feel the lack of progress in creating a meaningful picture. However, having denied the existence of a complete picture in the first place, we keep looking at our single fragment and expect it, by some miracle, to take on some meaning. And what makes matters worse, our fellowman has found another fragment and insists that his fragment is the only one with real meaning as well. We do not agree and begin to defend our tiny fragment and, in accordance with the law of polarities, we call for attack. This causes a split. And now we have the world we see. Fragmented, disunited – a far cry from harmony and peace.

We witness this process in every aspect of living. Every human being sees another as a separate being from itself and each 'separate' person slices life into further parts, dogmas, convictions and claims his slice to be the answer to Man's woes. One political denomination insists on being God's answer to all problems – so does the other. Many religions do the same. On a family level we find the same reflection of separation. Father believes in organization and rigid discipline, mother compensates her lost reality with soap operas, the fourteen-year-old son thinks of both as mothballs, because he just invented living – and the teenage daughter prays to her rock star to forgive all of these heathens, for they see not that he is God come to Earth.

Each has a fragment of the puzzle and thinks it to be the whole picture. Instead of allowing one another's diversity, disgruntlement sets in as each defends his piece of the puzzle. This is done at first with the tools of compromise and conformity. But nevertheless the underlying intent is to run the world one's own way. By evaluating one's own fragment of the puzzle, the fragments of the others are at best less valuable, in most cases they are plainly rubbish. Now we experience friction and fixation. This escalates and our puzzle piece does not do as it was told. So we know it must be somebody's fault, and now we hunt the guilty party and hell breaks loose. At the most we achieve a truce which is like walking on thin ice, for this can give at any moment.

To reassemble all the puzzle's fragments we require a conscious, intelligent reorganization of thought, yet without limiting oneself to such thought structure. If the sound of this rouses images of strain, then we may say it differently: We must look at our belief structures, those certainties without competence, with awareness, and not look away as we usually do, vaguely hoping for things to improve somehow. Once we begin to suspect that most of the values we believe in have 'no foot to stand on', have been adopted through conditioning, we can begin to reassemble the fragments of the puzzle into a cohesive whole. And how is this done? Simply by seeing the Divinity in all things. It is called love – giving each condition, person or situation absolute validity.

If not, then we create an imbalance. Not realizing this as an imbalance, we nevertheless feel urged, by the very nature of the situation, to create a balance. Having misconceived the nature of polarities initially, any attempt to balance these with a misunderstanding mind leads naturally to further misconceptions. So we find ourselves constantly under the crossfire of conflicting forces, opinions, currents, options, interpretations, which leave us – if we face our situation honestly – in a rather bewildered state of mind.

Perception of conflicting forces makes for a perception of a world in conflict. Of course, outwardly we cover up and reassure ourselves of our motives to justify our actions and intents. The reassurance, however, and reinforcement of an error does not make it right. Relying on our unquestioned ability to judge a situation we set out to rectify, repair, make good. To do this, we utilize a set of 'proven' tools which help us deal with any situation: conformity, compromise, resistance, defence (which is attack) and if need be outright murder. This we call 'dealing' with a

...on, any imbalance, that is, we confront ourselves with. At best, with these tools we achieve truce, which is as far removed from peace as heaven is from hell.

In this world, this reliance on our judgment is regarded as a virtue, a thing of maturity. Indeed – for how could it be otherwise in a world where every single truth became subjected to the altered Ego's Law of Reversal, became turned upside down. Yet the SELF in us which still remains wholly Spirit, would have us lay down our judgment and judge the situation for us instead, if we only cared to listen – but we don't, for this we feel as personally insulting. The mere mention of such a proposition scratches the fine polish of our Ego's dignity.

Any invalidating emphasis on one polarity will separate it from its unity and call forth the opposite of unity, which is separation and which always appears as some form of fear.

In the seventeenth century, Isaac Newton discovered a Law of Physics which is known as the Balance of Forces. (Newton's third axiom: actio = reactio). Being matter orientated, we readily accept physical laws, but physical laws merely reflect universal principles on the material plane. As Above so Below. Let us recall in our minds the picture of grandma's kitchen scales, two bowls at each side pivoting around one central point. If we pressed our finger on one bowl, this one would travel down, yet simultaneously the opposite bowl would rise up. In simple terms: pressure creates counter-pressure. This, mind you, we accept as being in the perfect order of things. And so it is. Surprisingly, when it comes to understanding life we abort this understanding entirely.

Our lives are mirror to the continuous imbalance we incur. Any judgment we lay on one polarity will make the other raise its head. Judging Good as better than Bad immediately calls Bad onto the stage to perform. This, in all probability, is a 'hard cookie' for many to chew. The very instant we think of one aspect as being of greater value than the rest we give birth to its opposite as a reality to be experienced.

We may remember a lesson we learned in the discourse on the altered Ego: resistance creates the opposite of its intent. We must not be tempted now into concluding that if emphasis is put on Bad, that its polarity Good would come up to rescue the scene. It comes into the scene, most certainly, but not as the All-Good of the vertical pole. The Good in the world of polarities is only the antipode of Bad. It is as much based on fear as is Bad. So what good will Good do? It will fight Bad! Thus the battle of polarities is in full swing, defence calls for attack – attack calls for defence. It is here at this point that we must indulge in some 'nitty-gritty' homework. We either begin to understand the balancing of polarities here or most likely not at all. So let us indulge then as much as necessary.

Our aim is to unify the entire lateral pole with the vertical pole. Life within the lateral pole is fear motivated, because the entire realm of the lateral pole has been set up by our Ego as an opposite to God. As the Absolute cannot have an opposite – if it would it would not be the Absolute – the Ego's reality of being apart and separate from the Absolute must of necessity be of illusory nature. Consequently fear is a make-believe state of mind. So far this reasoning is a logical deduction intending to provoke thought, yet any individual in a unified consciousness owns this knowing as an incontestable truth. Truth is not instructable but a mind can be provoked to search his soul for it. The truth he finds there is the truth for all of Mankind.

As the Ego's reality is solely based on fear, emphasis on values within its reality must then, by compulsion, focus on fear, and fear not released must manifest as an experience.

Now, to bring this understanding from the realm of ideas to a concrete level, we need illustrating examples. We imagine a person having a certain fantasy. The nature of it is totally irrelevant. The fantasy might aim at the detriment of a business party or be of sexual character or even dwell on attack of some sort.

This fantasy keeps 'popping up' from time to time. It wants to be faced and acknowledged. Through social conditioning our person is convinced that one is not supposed to have such notions. In fact he feels quite guilty for having such thoughts. Now they are 'put under the carpet' so to speak. These very real desires and feelings are now suppressed. If anybody knew about his secret desire – so our person feels – he would be judged for such immoral or bad or antisocial thoughts. So, what is taking place here? One aspect of life, a certain desire, wants to be experienced, it urges

sion, and there is absolutely nothing abnormal about it
erfectly normal event. After all – if God is All-There-Is
of life's expressions must be an expression of Divinity,
of God. The very reason for being here is to experience. The
experience and embrace of all emotions is required to consciously
reintegrate them with their Source. The 'holier than thou' attitude
of sitting on a mountain top, avoiding participation in life, is living
death. This would reflect a mind thoroughly misled by his altered
Ego. True perception may very well choose to do the same thing,
if it owns all emotions, thus it does not deprive itself of anything.

This is not to taint the path of the sanctimonious and the pious,
for it leads them to their highway too. It is not to deduct from its
validity, but whilst the pious speaks his litany I rather draw my
inspiration from the wind.

When the coward finds his courage – let him speak of courage.
When the warrior finds his peace – let him speak of peace. Their
truth, however gently voiced, carries spice and scent and is
thunder in my ear – the sermon of a man who is 'so good' is stale.
If he has not passed through the fires of life, if he never blundered,
never laughed and wept, never been in love or hated, doubted,
never suffered, never roared his anger and never trembled at the
softness of a woman's breast, if his loins were never aflame with
passion – then he never lived. If he never stood in awe before the
giants of the forest or felt the pain of a gentle woman's broken
heart – if never he stumbled, was proud or humbled, if never he
crawled he never danced – then he is dead.

But men and women unafraid of living, true to themselves,
radiate a freshness, an attraction that commands, that fires the
heart, and the nectar of their words invigorates the soul.

Emotion always precedes wisdom, for it affords experience,
without which, thought would not mature into truth. Hence the
necessity to embrace one's emotions in preference to suppressing
them.

Back to our person. If he would understand that the very
reason for his experience in physicality, for being here, is to
embellish these feelings, then judgment would be impossible.
Now judgment takes place, because he does not accept his
feelings as equally valid as any other feeling or thought. He makes

his feelings 'wrong'. This point must be clearly understood. The singling out occurs when we fear something to the extent that it has to be resisted, suppressed, despised – in short, if we invalidate it – if we judge it instead of making it 'okay'. This judgment of an aspect of life begins to show its effects now in our person's life. Guilt and self-accusation breed further separation, because now he entertains these thoughts in a sealed-off environment within himself, where no one can look in. Or he suppresses these feelings so thoroughly that they seem to have disappeared. But as we know, pressure creates counter-pressure. This counter-pressure must be released in one form or another. It could express itself as aggression, frustration, depression or some form of an infinite number of neuroses.

If our person entertains his fantasy, but evaluates it as being of a lesser value than other emotions or thoughts, say for instance as bad or immoral, it will have to manifest as his experience. So once more: emphasis on a polarity, the singling out of it, occurs through rejection or over-evaluation of it, because we value it less or more than other facets of life. That it only comes to us to be experienced, to instruct our soul with its wisdom, we cannot see – the blinkers of judgment prevent this seeing. So what is the remedy? The remedy is to reintegrate this particular polarity into its whole, by granting it an equal right to be as anything else.

And this is how our person should have proceeded. The moment his fantasies haunt him, he should not judge them as 'this or that'. He should wholeheartedly welcome, embrace and enjoy them. If his fantasy be one of murder, the suppression and judgment of it would eventually result in murder. To release this thought from the dark place in his mind, where he had hidden it – to bring it welcomingly into the light of his awareness – is the embrace. And this is how it works: If he murders the hated person in his fantasy without the slightest Self-judgment for this mental and emotional act – without making it wrong – simply releasing his pent-up emotions, a transformation ensues: The very attainment of a non-evaluation of his own emotions as negative or immoral persuades him of the impossibility to judge the hated person for whatever it may have been that this one was hated for.

For you see, the instant we release Self-judgment, we are incapable of judging anyone else. Hence, the hated person is not hated any more, because the emotion of hate has been unified. Now the murder can never manifest.

If he is not ready to have his fantasy without being accompanied by Self-judgment, than the murder must manifest. Having judged himself, he remains part of the Ego's reality, which is condemnation, and as such he subjects himself to its pitiless laws. Now he will be incarcerated for many years and this gives him an opportunity to look within himself. If not – he will have to repeat his act until he learns.

Let us not evaluate the thought of murder then as bad or immoral. If the fantasy could have been lived out in thought without any evaluation of it, the feeling of hate would have been released, unified with the All-there-is, and the murder would have never happened. It was a thought which wanted to be experienced without being judged as good or bad.

To judge crime as despicable will only call forth more crime. For what we judge we empower. What is justice? It has nothing whatsoever to do with justice, but is only our perspective of seeing things. The murderer condemned for his crime would have received a medal if he had committed the same crime in uniform. As we shall see further on when we speak of starvation, the altered Ego is diverting our attention from the illusion of death to the justification of it. This way death remains a certainty. True justice is the allowance of all that is. Once we are able to do this any discordant energy is transmuted into harmonious energy. This allowance does not mean we pretend everyone is a 'sweety-pie', regardless of the malice of conduct. On the contrary – we become more discerning than ever before. But what it means is that we see it all as part of the outworking of a humanity struggling for light. It means we see every individual as a fellow student in the university called Earth. We do not punish the little child for the lack of feeling it demonstrates when pulling out the wings of a butterfly, but we educate it instead. The suggestion then is that we see every experience as an equally valid expression of life and as such we simply cannot judge it.

In this realm of separation we are teaching ourselves from separation to unity. Who are we to deprive anyone of his right to enrich his soul with whatever experience he chooses. True non-judgment sees any condition, any act or person as being in its rightful place for learning purposes and that – in truth – is the forgiveness of separation. An altered state of mind may now climb onto barricades and proclaim loudly, that our world would result in chaos if we allowed everybody to do what he wants to do. To him I say: forgive yourself for your blindness, for you do not see that this world IS chaos. Not one single crime would occur if the world released judgment, for polarities would be unified. Remember the Ego's Law of Reversal. It speaks of hell and what goes with it, projects this image into the future and another place. This way we do not see that we have already arrived. We shall not judge the Ego either, for through its 'reality' we learn that its reality is not.

To judge health as better than sickness will call forth sickness, because judgment is born of fear and what we fear we empower, therefore we attract. Health may be our preference but to invalidate sickness only demonstrates our misunderstanding of its cause. It comes for a reason. It is always a reflection of an emotional imbalance. Therefore it is in its place – it is valid – it points to its cause.

As our perception of the whole lateral axis is based on fear, any reaction to an act of fear must bring forth more fear. Knowing our way of singling out events, things and persons as but a false way of seeing, we now begin to evaluate them all as being of equal value to one another. This way we embrace our feelings, we welcome them, of whatever nature they may be. We simply make them 'okay'. What I embrace I have to face, and eventually all invalidated polarities are seen as equal parts of one misunderstanding, as parts of separation.

To welcome means to receive with love. With this act we unify polarities and release them into the ALL-there-is. As such, the person in our illustration has made whole. And to the same extent he has become more whole. Once these feelings are released, they shall never haunt him again, for now he owns the experience, the feeling, in his soul – that is why the fantasies came in the first place. Life wanted to enrich the soul with this experience. Simultaneously, this particular polarity called for acceptance, wanted to be confirmed as an equal part of life – therefore it was a call for love.

The emotion of guilt, if singled out and invalidated, serves as an excellent example for the precipitation of sorrow. Guilt always indicates a lesson not learned. The boomerang effect of judgment becomes nowhere more apparent than through the act of inducing guilt. This keeps our brother separated from us, and us from him. For here we condemn by establishing sin as real. If sin is real, then God is not. To see sin but as error – for this is what it really is – means it can be corrected. This would set our brother free again, and this the altered Ego cannot allow. This urge to blame, to lay guilt on our fellowman, may be observed in our most mundane daily activities.

That this act of separation separates us as well escapes our notice. Thus we are drawn, together with the one we blame, into the vortex of sorrow. If we could see but for an instant what implications even the slightest blame holds in store for us, we would shy away from it as if it were lethal poison – for this is what it is. It poisons our lives, and eats the happiness of both away – the inducer of guilt and the 'guilty' alike. Who is served by this destructive energy – the God I AM or the altered Ego? To blame at all, to induce guilt, is to attack.

Let us put this knowledge to practical use –
let us seek brotherly concord;
the tongue bringing forth abuse
cannot converse with God.

Once we have lost the power to harm,
we have gained the strength to enter the Calm,
where God is all and the Ego is not –
finally bearing witness to God.

Where God is living reality, no more personified;
the glorious, grand totality –
not in shallow abstraction indignified.
(For man – when put to the test –
pictures God as man at his best.)

A tyrant's God is a tyrant. A judging man's God will always be a judge. God does not know of judgment, hence knows nothing of guilt – only in the state of a fallen consciousness is the Ego altered, and tries to maintain the status of wholeness split through unequal evaluation of polarities. We live in a self-created prison cell – the force holding the bars in place is judgment. The instant we release judgment the bars collapse and we step out into freedom.

Guilt is always an acceptance of judgment. It may, for example, be experienced when partnerships collapse. That such a bond only dissolves because the partners involved have afforded each other all the learning opportunities they could, and that these are now exhausted, is rarely understood.

At once we have the case of the inflictor and the inflicted, for one is always the 'victim'. It is the ill fate of the inflicted to become now the inflictor, because he or she immediately points a finger – induces guilt.

So far – so good. Remember, the situation is a co-creation to embellish emotions. It is not about 'right' or 'wrong' but about feeling. The emotion of guilt is of equal value to any other emotion. It is just another facet of the spectrum of emotions wanting to be experienced.

Where we 'get off the track' is when we repeat the experience lifetime after lifetime after lifetime. To own an emotion it only needs to be experienced once. Repetitions are not necessary. They are simply caused by our fixed way of seeing things which is stabilized perception, which in turn is judgment and that is invalidation of conduct.

The conduct is of perfect value for it generated the emotion.

If this is not understood then Self-judgment raises its head again and again. The other hears the accusation often enough, not knowing that he only listens to the altered Ego's voice and condemns himself for his 'despicable' act. Now he wriggles like a worm in the cancerous emotion of guilt, and literally consumes himself in the process. Being the exact opposite of the acknowledgment of the SELF as innocence, the Ego feasts in its 'victory' over God.

Guilt can only occur where sin is seen as real. True perception witnesses here once more the altered Ego's singling out of one polarity to raise its voice against God. It knows sin as but an error. Errors are corrected by learning from them. Sin would have us chained forever to separation. The error in this case is not the form aspect, the 'breaking away' from one's partner, the error is to believe in the altered Ego's reality of sin.

So we see how such a situation comes to teach us. The inducer of guilt evaluates the act of the 'guilty' as contemptible, hence singling it out from life as something to be condemned. The 'guilty' believes he has committed an unforgivable act, therefore condemns himself, meaning he deflates his Self-worth, which is the perfect denial of the God I AM. Thus both draw each other into such a dark hole of the Ego's mire, that at best it may take decades to climb out again, or at its worst they destroy each other altogether. A perfect example illustrating how we lay sacrifices down at the Ego's altar, because the guilty party's entire focus is on restitution; all energies are concentrated on the form level and not the form's content.

True repentance would not attempt to repair the form level but embrace the emotion of guilt as the principle it stands for: SELF-denial, induced by the voice against God. This, it knows, is a necessary experience in the soul's learning process. For this reason it cannot invalidate the invalidation of conduct either, which created the emotion of guilt in the first place. In other words: it cannot judge the judgment. It sees all as being in its rightful place and therefore of equal value. Now we own the emotion and are not compelled to ever repeat the experience again.

In the light of True perception we see that as the hatching chicken leaves its shell behind to enter a new expanded state of being, so do partners shed their existing bond like one takes off an old garment in order to put on a new one. It enriched both partners for the experience and as such served its purpose, but then it became limiting. That each now goes his separate way to seek new adventures, which are in truth but learning opportunities, is part of the natural unfolding of life. Now healing occurs. True perception would see both partners view each other with love and dignity, and release one another with gratitude and appreciation in the knowing that each has to climb to greater heights.

If both partners know, at the outset of their relationship, that neither can be possessed, that neither owes the other a thing, that the entire event is a co-creation for learning purposes, then their experience will be a harmonious one. If not, and both partners' learning curves are parallel, then both still may experience hostile confrontations but afford each other learning opportunities which may last an entire life. Otherwise new horizons have to be pioneered, else further learning would be stifled. Every single break-up of a relationship signifies a new learning epoch for both partners involved. Hence we see that the act of tenaciously holding on to a partner, although that one feels driven to move on, only delays that partner's learning process. This, naturally, is easier said than done. One's conduct in such a situation depends entirely on the degree of attachment to one another. By depending our happiness on a thing or person we are depending on a condition. Conditional happiness is not happiness. It is a deal, whereby one partner really says: 'On my own I am a miserable sod. In order for me to be happy you must stay with me.' What a terrific 'deal' the other one made, and what is worse, if he does not live up to it he is made to feel guilty. However, in the rarest of cases do we admit to our love being but conditional love. We rather accuse the other of not loving us, although we show so much love. What we do not know in such a case is that the only love is unconditional love. All else is make-believe, deception. If we truly loved that partner, we would wish him to be happy, whatever that entails, for we would be happy with or without him. Peculiarly enough, once we reach that stage then whatever contributes to our happiness is added on to us and in that case our partner would never leave us in the first place.

To truly love someone we have to know first what love is and this can only occur when we discover our own true SELF. This we cannot help but love. Only then can it be extended. To love oneself one has to know one's SELF first, which IS love – we cannot love what we do not know. To know my SELF I have to know the God I AM. Unconditional love loves because it IS love and does not depend the bestowal of its benediction on conditions. It loves the 'deserving' and 'undeserving' alike. It has to do so for love's nature is to love.

Thus we see in our partnership example that the repetitious experience of guilt – lifetime after lifetime – was based on erroneous thinking, was based on judgment. Yet it was in its place, therefore the judgment itself is not to be judged either. As the emotion of regret – when accompanied by guilt – falls under the same heading, it seems worth mentioning at this point that whatever act of the past we regret we will have to repeat at some time or other. The reason for this is the non-release of Self-judgment. We are still singling it out and as such we still judge ourself. If we could view our 'bad deed' as an equally valid part of our life, admitting to ourself, no matter how right or wrong, that we did it for the experience of it to garner the emotion, then we would be freed of this emotional weight. Repentance recognizes an error but does not crucify itself for it.

This 'hanging on' to a past event is merely an attachment to Self-judgment. The story, the form, through which this attachment expresses itself matters not. Attachment is the forerunner of blame and this in turn induces guilt, hence attachment leads to pain. Even if blame as such is not involved, attachment still brings pain in its trail because it identifies with what we attach ourself to. A person attached to another identifies his happiness with that person, meaning he projects the cause of his happiness outside himself. This always indicates lack of Self-worth which is SELF-denial. It is not that True perception is ignorant of attachment – the difference is that it does not depend its happiness on any one person or condition. This takes the sting out of attachment when the one we feel attached to is 'lost', be this loss in the form of the passing of a loved one or in any other form. Genuine detachment is not indifference.

This principle may be observed with material objects all the same. We are all familiar with the image of the young man and his dented new sports-car: the man is in pain, because he identifies with his car. A mind unconcerned with his possessions wholeheartedly enjoys what he owns, but stirs little should these things leave him. Detachment does not advocate emotional aloofness or coldness. On the contrary – only when we are freed from this bondage can our care and tenderness express truly and freely.

As soon as we look with awareness at anything we normally judge, we must arrive at the conclusion that any form of judgment is of necessity born of ignorance. We are simply not in the position to judge.

For example, we judge a brother for the colour of his skin. He dared not only to look different from us, but also chose a completely unlike cultural background. This generates in us a feeling of insecurity. To overcome this, we devalue him – this puts him in his place and secures ours. Now we have 'dealt' with the situation as only false perception can. What a dull world, if it were populated with clones of oneself! The moment we understand the reason for diversity, the appearance of different forms and cultures, in that moment we transcend judgment as naturally as we breathe.

Seeing that my brother chose his particular skin and what cultural background goes with it for the learning of his particular lesson in this lifestream eliminates all evaluation of his appearance and characteristics. The knowing that any circumstance a person finds himself in is consciously chosen to supply him with the necessary environment conducive to the specific lesson he needs to learn, MUST do away with all judgment.

Should he choose a green, striped, or neon-pink skin, who cares? If that is what he needs, then that is what he needs. If price tags have to be handed out at all, then his and mine must read the same value.

To compare anyone with anyone only demonstrates ignorance of the fact that no-one can be compared. Each soul is unique, hence each precious beyond words. The Almond tree and the Banyan tree are both trees, but not comparable to one another. Both serve as a different expression of the One life. Both are God appearing as different fragrances. To judge one fragrance as better than the other is judging one aspect of God as being of greater value than another.

Should it so happen that a brother comes from what we term a primitive society, then an invalidation of his social standing would be the same as if a high school student looked with contempt at a first grade toddler. All the high school student's behaviour demonstrates is amnesia – the fact that he forgot he was once a toddler himself. If anything, the toddler is deserving of the high school student's gift of dignity and guidance. Parents may be reluctant to give their toddler control over the household budget – and rightly so – but they certainly find him equally deserving of their love and of equal right to be as they themselves.

We may assess the giggly maiden, who is lost for a time in trendy substitutes, and dismiss her as shallow and not worth the minute of our day, or we may see who stands behind her – counting the hour to take her place: a selfless mother of children yet unborn, serene womanhood lending her strength to those in need.

The pimply face that did not make it quite as yet from jackfruit to peach – did it not humble me in my hour of pain with its finely honed sensitivity, its peachlike gentleness and empathy?

The scruffy looking beach bum at Coconut Bay, who, hour after hour with untiring patience, holds the preying terns at bay until the very last turtle has hatched and finds its way into the surf – is he a lesser God for venturing where I venture not? Do I not meet in each one of these my master in some quality of character?

To validate, to judge at all, is to say I am ignorant. We usually measure the other by our own limited standards. If that person does not measure up to our yardstick, we assess him negatively. That he has to live by his own yardstick rarely occurs to us. If you are a mother, then this is all your child will see in you, but is it all of you? Should the role of motherhood be denied to the child, it would evaluate you as a pretty useless person, for its evaluation is based on your usefulness for itself. This is its criteria for assessment, its yardstick. To your own mother you will always be the child, regardless if you happen to be a grandma yourself. Your husband will most likely limit his awareness of you to your facet as a lover, companion and partner. Should you fail in that role your popularity would slump to nil – you would be judged. Your lady friend's evaluation of yourself will, in all likelihood, exhaust itself in your ability to converse on topics of her interest. Your boss, if you have one, estimates your worth by the weight of the plough you pull, in other words how good a work horse you are. To your cat you are the supplier of goodies – to the man you pass on the sidewalk you simply represent a body, either spunky or not worth a second glance. All see facets of you only – all evaluate you, but none has seen you as you really are – not even you yourself. We mistake the rings on the water's surface for the stone that causes them. We do not judge the sun by the play of light and shadow on the wall. The sun remains poised in space untouched by the effects of its light, it does not forget itself and think it is its light pattern.

So it is with the God I AM. The roles we act out in our lives are but as the patterns of shadow and light. The pattern is not me – it is an effect of me. The more illusion I put between the God-light of my SELF and my plane of manifestation the darker the shadow I manifest. As all the light patterns on this Earth are projections of the one Sun so are the billions of soul patterns merely projections of the one God I AM. As each Sun ray is an emanation of the one Sun so is each soul an emanation of one Being, the God I AM. Not a single ray of light would judge the other, for all know their common Source.

Shadows fall where light is obscured. So it is with our identity. When our identity is in the dark, then something must be obscuring the light which would reveal it. This something is the cloud of judgment. To release this cloud we have to face it and facing is embracing.

This is how we balance polarities – by embracing them! At this point some questions may be raised. For example, what if we disliked a situation or person? How can we embrace an adversary, how can we love the unlovable ? How can we reconcile with an antagonizer? Firstly everyone is lovable – any person's mother would agree with that statement. As we saw a little further back: what we generally call love is merely acceptance on condition. A mother in contrast to this attitude loves without imposing a condition on her love. This is unconditional love. What it really means is that she does not judge. On this plane it is the closest to God's love. In the understanding of a mother looking upon her child as part of her Being, so should we look upon our fellowman as being part of our Being. This attitude can be practised – this attitude heals. Try to pierce the surface of these words and recognize the enormity of their implication, for herein lies the secret to a transformation from darkness to light. It is this which leads to Oneness.

Understanding that my antagonizer came here not to learn to be 'so good', but to feel feelings, justifies not only his feelings but those of my reaction as well, hence neither experience can be judged. It is merely a co-creation – another sightseeing stop on our journey through the vast spectrum of emotions. Obviously, once this is understood, adverse conditions become experiences of the past – are not possible any more – because the lesson has been learned. Judgment has been transcended.

In the same manner in which we can only receive the radio or television station we are tuned into, we can only perceive in another person what we see in our own make-up. A thief will unfailingly recognize another thief. We have to be on his 'wave-length' to see him at all. To say it differently: what we reject in a fellowman is what we dislike in ourself, which really indicates Self-judgment. And we can only judge ourself if we have not accepted ourself unconditionally. This recognition points to the root cause of judgment: lack of Self-love, which can only occur if the Self we identify with is a Self-image only and not the true God-SELF, the I AM. As a Self-image is not real, only an image, it cannot be loved. We can identify with it but it shall never please us. A consciousness separated from its true, divine SELF can only substitute the lacking identity with an image of itself and this cannot be loved. We cannot love what is not real, what is nonexistent. What we cannot love we cannot accept. Thus we see that being in a state of separation from our true SELF we cannot accept ourself. As such we are compelled to judge.

A person unified with his Source knows the I AM, the God-SELF to be his SELF. This he cannot help but love unconditionally. There is nothing in pure Being, or God, that can be rejected or disliked, therefore judged. Seeing himself thus, whatever such a person beholds he sees as himself. This is the end of judgment. On a personality level he may be fully cognizant of his own shortcomings and those of his fellow humans, but as he does not identify with his own personality Self he does likewise with his brother.

It is easy now to falsely conclude that the entire situation is a vicious circle: We judge because we lack true identity and to achieve true identity we have to surrender judgment. But fortunately this is not so. We can release judgment, the singling out of polarities, before we realize our true SELF, simply because we understand now the cause of judgment. Knowing the cause, realizing why we judge, it becomes obvious that any form of judgment is a senseless act, not to be judged either but simply to be accepted as a distorted way of seeing. This then leads us to a to a release of judgment and therefore to the realization of our real SELF, because the instant we release judgment we find ourself on the bridge spanning the abyss between the horizontal and vertical pole of our cross analogy. Once there – in that state of consciousness – we cannot ever encounter adversaries any more, because they only come to teach us non-judgment in the first place.

Everything about us is a mirror reflecting ourself. The moment we point a finger at a part in the mirror we only identify it as a part within us, because we are pointing at a reflection of ourself. If we strolled along a crowded side-walk in a city, stepped aside for a moment and pretended we were some visitor from outer space, seeing the human species on planet Earth for the first time, what would we observe? We would notice a sea of faces passing by, each one absorbed in its own personal miniature dream – much like sleepwalkers – oblivious to their cosmic destiny and grander purpose. We would be looking at the Gods who suffer amnesia.

Yet, even this state of spiritual stagnation cannot prevent a Son of God from being a perfect mirror to his brother. For if we picked out a face, any – it matters not which one – and let our eyes meet, then for the most transient of moments we know we are looking at ourself, at just another aspect of our own Being. The One appearing as many. That sacred instant gone, the other becomes a stranger once more. Could we but hold the awareness of that instant and carry it into our day, then pointing a finger at our brother would be inconceivable.

To say: 'You have done unto me great injustice, you caused me to suffer', indicates our search for happiness outside ourselves. It shall never come this way. 'The kingdom of heaven is within.' Archaic words for an eternal truth. Happiness flows forth from one's own Source, the I AM in us, when not denied. Then happiness is reflected back onto us through each and every thing. Happiness is a choice of every moment. Thus the now moment casts its shadow onto the next now moment, which then, of need, must be a happy one as well. Let us never, never forget that we are the masters of our destiny. No one in all the universes writes our script. We do that, in co-creation with our brothers. As we rewrite our script, our brother must do likewise or leave the stage of our drama, for the shift is now (to borrow a term from an ascended Master) from tragic into magic. For this is all it is – a shift in consciousness. This knowledge calls for responsibility. So we shall respond to our ability to design our next now. We can start by discarding the separators of our verbiage which are 'Good – bad – better – best'. These divide and slice life into sections, some to be despised – others to be glorified.

So the moment we feel antagonized by someone let us rather cast our bread upon the waters, which means we spread a consciousness of divine support and as we spread it freely, it returns to us manifold. Ancient Sanskrit tells us: 'Those who sing have songs sung unto them.'

Who is to judge one flower to be a weed and another to be a delight? The weed was a delight unto itself before judgment arrived. Now it is rejected, deprived of love and must spread to be noticed, to make its call heard. It is all one movement of life, regardless if it be a thunderstorm or an august night. To acknowledge my brother's sovereignty, to allow him the right to be however he wishes to be, is to set him free. So, the answer to the question, how to embrace my adversary, is always: embrace what you feel. This brings us back to our own attitude. If it is hate we feel or hate's milder form, which is dislike, then we embrace this emotion all the same – and without judgment. If the person's conduct is so unpleasant that his presence becomes intolerable we can remove ourself. If this is not possible, then we take action not in the form of attack but rather as a mother corrects a misbehaving child. This can be done without any judgment. The essence of this learning is this: we only experience the person or situation as unlovable because polarities were singled out and judged. We see but ourself in the other person, hence judging him is judging ourself. We would never experience an unlovable person or condition if we embraced every person or condition and welcomed them without judgment.

Again we see: True perception changes its percep' condition and not the condition. This way, these feelin; be released into the ALL, therefore allowed to be reunified with the whole of their origin. For this reason alone they could never ever 'pop up' again. Only what we press down – as the bowls of grandma's kitchen scale – must 'pop up' some way or another. By allowing ourselves to embrace all these emotions, which we reject or suppress, therefore judge, we free ourselves from their weight – we become lighter. We become enlightened. Each time we do this, the lateral pole of our cross becomes shorter and thinner. Its parts become reunified with the vertical pole.

This 'embracing' is the key to the understanding of how to balance polarities. The waters of a brook do not accuse the rock of being in its path. The water does not say: 'Rock, I hate you, do not stand in my way or I wash you away.' The water says: 'Hi there, Rock, I grant you the right to be there, but I desire to create my energies elsewhere' – and now the water giggles around the rock. We can learn from the water. It does not fear or hate the rock, it does not resist it either. In this sense the act of embracing should be understood.

To fear the entertainment of fearful thoughts is just another fear. To embrace what we fear, we must first learn to see the true nature of fear. The same applies to hate or aversion. It is fear all the same. We cannot pretend to ourself and embrace what we hate or fear without understanding the real nature of fear as being but the Ego's finger pointing against life. To force oneself to do this is plain hypocrisy. Yet, once the principle of fear itself is recognized as the altered Ego's veil of illusion, we can embrace the person, situation or feeling, grant it the same right to be as anything else and 'giggle' around it as the water does. If we, in this spirit of gaiety and laughter, remove ourself from the scene and decide to go elsewhere, this scene shall never follow us. If we choose to remain with the scene, or if we are not in a position to remove ourselves, we reconcile with its energy as having an equal right to be as anything else and this we do by making our own fear alright first.

To do this we have to admit to our fears in the first place. This is the embrace. It is called 'dropping the front', it is vulnerability – it is also ultimate strength.

Now the polarity of discordant energy becomes unified and thus released and things go well for us and it. Now we can get on with living, instead of dissipating our precious life-force by focusing on unprofitable emotions.

To embrace then is to love whatever we face back into life. This is an act of light-heartedness – there is nothing heavy about it. The giggling of the water expresses laughter, being of a light heart. Laughter aligns, shows a heart full of light. Laughter sees an unlovable person or situation as the altered Ego's interpretation of life. It faces it and says: 'You have a right to be however you wish – it is your choice – but you have certainly the same right to be here as I. Your choice of how to play in the game of life is of equal value to mine. Your flavour may not be my choice, but I grant it the same right to be as mine. I acknowledge your Divinity as I acknowledge mine.' The rejected 'flavour' not only feels accepted, it is accepted, thus it is reunified. It now can unfold into its own blossoming, whereas before it was resisted, rejected, 'cut out' from life and as such was in a state of stagnation. In essence, the message is this: embrace and welcome, therefore face, any emotion, however fearful it seems, and it shall be released into the ALL.

The experience then of that which was feared shall never manifest. Any polarity not balanced, that is any fear not unified, must always, always, always manifest as an actual experience in our life. If not in this, then in the next life, but it will always manifest. It has to, for its appearance is a call for love, a call for being reunified. Life does not allow itself to be split. Every imbalance is compensated, however much we plot against it. The eastern idea of Karma is the Law of Compensation. As long as polarities remain polarities in our perception, differently expressed, as long as we perceive with false perception, we are subject to the effects of divisive thinking. Our understanding of the balance of polarities sheds a different light on Karma: Karma in the traditional eastern understanding does not exist. There is no element of punishment, neither is there ever a debt to be repaid. If all occurs in an everpresent now, for which 'past' act should a person be 'punished' – and by whom if all is One?

128

It is simply a balance which we normally understand as the workings of the Law of Cause and Effect. It is still cause causing an effect, however the true cause is the singling out of any movement of life which causes an imbalance, a fixation – which is the effect. It follows from this understanding that any condition we encounter is exactly what we deserve, it is the balance of what we handed out. But it also follows that anyone can set himself free from the chains of his or her 'Karma' by unifying polarities. As much as my slave is chained to me, I am chained to him, how else could I chain him. By setting free the slave, I release myself into freedom. It is not fear that holds us prisoner – it is we who hold fear prisoner. By releasing the prisoner the jailer may walk free.

Returning to the clarification of the thought of 'embrace', the thought might creep in that a joyous desire for a partner or a home shall not manifest, because we welcome the thought, embrace it and hence release it to be unified. This would indicate a misunderstanding.

This will clarify: unification is inclusive and not exclusive. Every desire we have is known to our Source before the personality Self is even aware of it. We enhance the fulfillment of these desires by giving them equal value to anything else. This way our happiness does not depend on them. Now they are freed and can gush forth and embrace us in return with their lushness.

Applying The Balance Of Polarities.

Anything that would not add value to life could then not manifest as our experience, for any discordant energy having been unified, has become harmonious energy. Only what is NOT valued equally wants to be given equal value. If we do not want the experience, it will never come. Nevertheless, it wants to be valued as an equal part of life.

Our altered Ego is an absolute master at this labelling game. We may just succeed in seeing life in all its variants as innocent and of equal value to one another, when it introduces self-inflation. 'Look how good I am – so much better than the others who are still dashing about, putting price tags on everything!' Let us look evenly at this last 'price tag' and remove it without further comment. For it too is in its place. All is in its place. All things work toward a high end.

Instead of judging a grinding situation as bad or worse than others, we should rather remember that the oyster's irritation becomes its pearl. The irritation thus is an equally valid part of life, as it forms in us the pearls of wisdom. When experiencing a 'bad' day, we have the choice of seeing it with True perception, for this would see the day as the polarity of contraction. Not to be opposed or resisted, but to be seen together with its counterpart, which is expansion. Now we have made whole, for we see contraction and expansion as part of a birthing process. The birth into a new consciousness.

To resist the bad day would only lead us astray once more, but to see it in its true light frees our experience of the day of any vestige of disharmonious energy. The desire for a certain polarity need not entail invalidation of its opposite. It is then a preference only. It is the intention behind preference that changes it into a judgment!

No emotion must ever be resisted, but welcomed. If it does not add value to life, if it is of destructive energy, it will never manifest once it is embraced as equally valid, therefore unified. Resisting, or judging it as less valid than any other part of life shall always result in the experience of that which is feared, suppressed or despised.

Now, the sentence 'resistance achieves the opposite of its intent' could be easily misinterpreted. It does not mean we should allow a mosquito to suck our blood and we look on while we suffer. The mosquito may be understood in a metaphorical sense. It means that if we welcome the thought 'mosquito' and embrace it and see it as an equally valid part of life, and do not judge it as a nuisance, the mosquito will never enter our experience in its capacity as a blood sucking insect. We can practise this embrace in every walk of life and thus we demonstrate this truth to ourselves. After all, this principle would be useless if it could not be applied in life. It must be applied to be able to transform our life.

Remaining with the mosquito for another moment will reveal another Ego trap. To embrace it as equally lovable as any other manifestation of life means just that. The mosquito is just being a good mosquito, meaning no harm. Sucking blood is part of being a mosquito. It is not aware that its own being is motivated by fear. Its form of feeding is essentially an attack, therefore fear based. With this thought we grant it an equal right to be and release it as something to be feared.

Now we sit on our front porch, sip a glass of wine and hear the buzz of the mosquito we just accepted as having an equal right to be. Our altered Ego, knowing only fear, sees its chance and whispers its 'What if...' So we ponder and think: 'I wonder if it really works.' What we are really doing here is doubting that life is safe and thus we shrink from it, resist and have to start all over again. A little trust in one's maker would come in handy here – it is called faith. As long as we have not given trust a chance, we should not pretend to ourselves. If it sucks, and we cannot remove ourselves from its presence, we must squash it. Doing this in a spirit of hate or disgust for the insect will attract hordes of them, so we better squash it dispassionately in the understanding that we have not yet learned our lesson.

Once we succeed in learning this lesson, that is trusting – and therefore accepting – life with all its variants, the frequency of our auric field is accelerated from a fear-vibration to one of love. Any being or situation vibrating at a fear-frequency is then not attracted by our auric field. It follows then that these things avoid us because we are not pulsating at a like frequency. We do not have to consciously think 'mosquito' and fear it. Our auric frequency advertises our fear if we are still vibrating at that frequency. Differently expressed, we attract fear, and all its children, when still in an altered state of mind. The biting insect is our consciousness projected into matter, and thus becomes the reflection of our attitude.

True perception once again does not alter the condition – does not squash the insect – it changes its perception of the condition. To practice True perception is not a boring task, for while we practice we discover an entirely new world. It can be quite exciting. We can start with small things. Without losing ourselves in details we shall take a quick look at another example of 'target practice'.

We imagine being attacked by a dog. In this example we are, of course, concerned with the idea of attack and not its vessel, through which the idea expresses (the dog). We could imagine, in its place, the overpowering attack of a thought of financial or emotional loss. So let us face the dog, for it stands for all these things. A vicious looking dog, perhaps, say, a Doberman, charges toward us, growling and snarling. Our blood seems to freeze, adrenaline shoots into our system, the overall feeling is one of panic, therefore fear. Be it a four-legged creature or our fellowman: attack of any kind is always a call for love! Twisted, perhaps – distorted – but still a call for love. In fact, the harsher the attack, the more desperate the soul's cry for love. So we face the dog.

With True perception there is a correct interpretation of the scene. True perception in its learning stage is no stranger to succumbing to fear. However, it 'owns up' to it, knowing it is alright to be fearful. It makes the shivers of fright 'okay', makes the lump in the stomach valid, it feels it. What is more it knows it has not only created the situation to present itself with a choice but knows it has created this very fear itself. How can it fear its own creation? With this understanding it does not run from fear or resist it, but it does not give it credibility either. It desires a greater reality than forever tiptoeing through life. And now it approaches the real secret in transmuting fear to love: Knowing that fear is no 'outsider' but its own creation, it surrenders all defences! It may still say: 'I know intellectually there is nothing to fear for all is God but I am still scared silly. I have heard all the wise words but my heart is still trembling.' Yet it also says: 'It is my choice to either continue living in fear or to claim a greater reality. So it is all or nothing. For once I shall trust in my SELF – I surrender – I drop all defences. I rather not live at all than live in fear.' This is called vulnerability. It is the ultimate strength, the ultimate safety, however, it is also the hardest thing for any human being ever to do – to surrender one's defences; and this for one reason only: for fear of being hurt yet again. This is where the real fear lies, the fear containing all others, the fear that life is not safe.

This is True perception's embrace of the situation, meaning it faces and welcomes it as an opportunity to choose a greater reality. It does this by realizing the illusory nature of fear. Knowing that it can only – ever – experience what its own thoughts encompass, it also knows the solution: Not to deal with the dog, but with the 'reality' of its own thoughts. Fear, to it, is always the call to deny reality or God. It looks past the form through which the 'threat' expresses. It is not fooled by it. The outward appearance of the scene it sees as but the Ego's suggestion to see fear as real. The 'threat' is not the dog, but fear as such. Resisting this temptation would make fear real. So True perception embraces the situation, it does not evaluate the dog as of lesser value than any other being. Any thought such as 'kill' or 'run' would reject the dog's being, hence devalue it. True perception's embrace accepts the dog's being as equally valid, thus releases it as unified into the ALL of God. It calmly understands – just that – and knows the being of the dog as part of its own, and that is God's. With this understanding it can drop its defences, for what would it defend itself against but itself?

Now there is no fear, because fear to it is part of the dream; how can it fear what is not real? It simply acknowledges the dog's being as its own. The dog still approaches, threatening to rip us apart, yet two feet in front of us his charge comes to an abrupt halt. His snarl gives way to a whimpering – we pat him a little, approvingly – his being now content because it is accepted and acknowledged for what it really is, the dog now strolls away with a wagging tail. If this sort of practice sounds too severe, then let us try spiders first, or return to mosquitoes. True perception evaluates equally, this unifies. Unified life is love. Love is void of fear. It is essential to understand love not as asserting itself in the face of fear but as being void of it altogether.

What we fear we empower. An example: the more an antismoking campaigner fights for his cause, the more he will be irritated by smoking, the more the smoking scene will play a role and have importance in his experience, his life. In truth, his campaign represents a smoke-screen to hide the real pollution, his own veiled mind, which is in ignorance of truth. The real motive here, the underlying Ego's intent, is not to rid the world of smokers, but to fight against, to oppose. The anti-smoker is, most likely, not consciously aware of this fact. The physical 'pollution' caused by the smoker is the reflection of the anti-smoker's mental pollution.

We may recall that everything we perceive as worthy of our judgment is a reflection of the projection of our consciousness into matter.

In defending any part of separation as the anti-smoker does, we are defending, thus affirming, separation. In affirming separation we are rejecting reality or Oneness and we do this best by 'picking' on someone, pointing a finger at our brother, for this keeps him separate. The smoker in this case just happens to be the pick of the bunch. The altered Ego has to oppose life in every way, the above illustration only exemplifies one of literally millions of such forms our Ego uses in its effort to remain separate. It will do this in the guise of the most noble intentions. Anti-war, anti-hunger, anti-cruelty ...where is the end of the list? The world is full of campaigners. Every campaigner is anti some body! The form his attack is directed at is always a body, some-body. First the body is created to house a separate 'Self', the very thing the altered Ego identifies with, then this Self is attacked. What could more clearly demonstrate the madness of the altered Ego's Law of Reversal. Where God is equipoised, where cosmic order leaves nothing to chance, the Ego, to be the 'opposite' of God (a contradiction in itself), had to turn this state of being into chaos. To screen this madness, this chaotic state, the emphasis on law and order in this world certainly comes as no surprise. And for the rest of us who deem ourselves apart from the campaigners, let us not cower behind such pious thought, for every single soul on Earth is for something and therefore simultaneously against its opposite, which makes us all campaigners. The degree of intensity with which we defend our stand for and against something is irrelevant, the singling out of aspects of life worthy of defending is what counts, not its degree.

If I am for something, then somewhere out there must be somebody who is against it, hence I am against this somebody, no matter how subtle the degree, the intensity of opposition, and to be against is to separate. Let us not misinterpret this as advocating a wishy-washy mind. We certainly shall be discerning and have our preferences, but invalidating the unpreferred lays judgment upon it, hence it becomes singled out and therefore a cause for fixation.

Returning to our illustration of the anti-smoker, we would see that the minute he could unify the polarities involved, smoking would not be part of his experience. But how is this balance achieved? The balance, in essence, in our example of smoking, is achieved by seeing the option of smoking as of equal validity to the option for not smoking. If we can see both options as having an equal right to exist and as being of equal value to one another, then they must be of equal value to us. My left thumb has an equal right to be and is of equal value to my right thumb. They do not fight each other and I do not fight either of them, they are part of a greater whole, my body. If one option is of equal value to the other, then it matters not which option is chosen. It now becomes only a question of personal preference.

So we can safely extract some wisdom from this: if neither option matters to the extent of being feared or of being an irritation, then the option of smoking does not matter either. And what does not matter in this understanding will not materialize as an experience! Resistance to the smoker will achieve the opposite of its intent: it will attract smokers, for these want to be accepted and not rejected. So each smoker appearing to the anti-smoker is in truth calling for love. Once smokers as such are embraced and seen as equally valid in their option for smoking, their emergence as an irritating factor in the anti-smoker's life would serve no purpose. If the smoker's smoke had been embraced and welcomed as merely another variable of life's vapours, equally valid to anything else, the smoke – whenever encountered – would drift the other way. A fairy tale? Try it!

The anti-smoker's fear of lung cancer for the smoker will become the anti-smoker's experience, because it is his fear. The fear I have for my brother shall manifest in my own life as my experience, for it is I who fears. If the smoker allows himself to be brainwashed and succumbs to the anti-smoker's thoughtform to the extent that this thought constitutes a reality for him, then, naturally, he will manifest the feared disease as well. Whatever I fear must manifest as my experience. Thus, we see that the anti-smoker achieves the opposite of his intent, merely by resisting the option of smoking.

If sickness is evaluated as of lesser value than health, then we have separated it from the unified whole. Any emphasis now on health, its opposite polarity, is emphasis on separation itself, with the result that the polarity we singled out, that is sickness, will surface more and more. It is being resisted, therefore it is empowered. If emphasis (other than a simple preference) is on health, we call forth its opposite, disease. Monumental efforts are made in this world to fight disease and the world, as a result of this effort, has never before been so sick. If sickness matters enough to be feared, then it has to materialize.

This process is in exact obedience to the law of polarities. As long as the destruction of the world's rainforests matters, their destruction must materialize. As long as starving children somewhere in the world matter, their starvation must materialize. On the surface this thought seems outrageous and many will say: 'Up to this point I could accept it, but this is not funny any more!'. And you are correct, it is not funny at all. Truth does not want to be funny, truth wants to set free!

Before we look at this statement properly, we should face one fact honestly, lest True perception is clouded by self-deceit: first we weep for hungry children, so we feed them until they are fat and strong, only to push them onto some unknown battlefield and slaughter them in the name of dogmas, whose number is legion, or for self-gain. Now their death is justified! So it is evidently not death itself that counts, for death, the altered Ego's only aim, is the only certainty for one who dreams, the rest he is allowed to doubt, this way he stays confused. No – it is not death itself by which our outrage is sparked but the justification of it, for the Ego would have you see your one-and-only certainty justified at times, and at other times not.

There is a purpose behind this madness, for you see this way death itself is never questioned, only its seeming cause; and this assures death remains a certainty for one who dreams, and he will never look at its true cause. Ponder this subtle, but most 'vital' point, for around this hinge alone pivots the altered Ego's sole 'reality'. The intent here is most certainly not to induce guilt, to make the heart heavy. Human hearts are heavy enough as it is. The intent is to confront ourselves in all sincerity with the real reason for our behavioural patterns. This way the answer can be found; enlightenment is not enheavyment. The ultimate intent then is to make our hearts light again and bubbling with radiant life and joy, to see naught but innocence where before was naught but guilt.

We better pause here and look at it again from another angle: the One who remains whole in us uses the Ego's very mistakes as a means for their correction – these things come for a reason, remember! They teach us. Without the starving children, how could compassion be raised in Man's heart for his fellowman? Without the rainforests being raped, how could love for our beautiful mother Earth, the great nourisher and sustainer, be awakened in our hearts? So the purpose of these things is to open the heart-aspect of man, who until a short while ago only used his fellowman to gain, used his great Mother Earth as a host to get. Until then, the emphasis was all on 'have' and 'get'. Now for the first time in millennia he contemplates the act of giving.

In the above case, man is not asked to feed his own children; this would be easy. He is not asked to spend money to fix his back-garden; no, he is asked to donate to some faraway cause to save some forest he has never seen, and feed some children he does not even know. Doing this indicates a readiness to identify with the greater whole, indicates an expansion beyond the little fenced-off Self the Ego deems itself to be. It means he is moving toward Oneness.

A further, much more subtle point, concerning the illustration of the starving children: in most cases the initial motive of upset and indignation at the sight of starvation is nothing else but once again the Ego's finger pointing, this time not so generally against life, but most specifically against his brother for allowing such horrifying shame. For this, the Ego knows makes guilty and condemns his brother to be sinful, exactly what the Ego would have him be, for this states him as separate; the Ego's sole intent. And if the Ego had full reign, compassion for the little children could not enter our hearts, love would not be. But by the grace of One who remains wholly Spirit within ourselves, this is not so. This One uses the Ego's creations to make whole, uses its errors to correct. So giving is wonderful, but the spirit of fighting a condition is a misguided one.

Refraining from fighting a condition does not advocate the attitude of indifference to what we perceive. All it asks of us is to give each side equal validity, equal right to be. Seeing each side, each polarity as having a purpose, each side's purpose of equal value to the other, we can step out and feed the children.

Now we have reconciled with starvation and the statement 'as long as starving children matter' translates itself into: 'as long as starvation matters as a polarity to be opposed and fought..'. Now the spirit of giving is not one of fighting the condition of starvation but one of calm understanding and dispassionate compassion, and to our surprise, the condition dematerializes. It has to do so in obedience to the law of polarities, for we have granted the polarity of starvation an equal purpose to be. Furthermore, True perception would recognize the starving children as fellow souls who chose starvation as an experience, to extract its wisdom from it and simultaneously afford the rest of the world an opportunity to open their hearts.

In the above example we did not judge starvation, but saw it as an equally valid, necessary experience, chosen by certain souls for learning purposes. Just stop here and consider: What need would drive us on to a greater reality if all would be sugar and honey, if this physical experience would be devoid of contrast? Resisting contrast shall generate more contrast, but seeing it as a tutorial we rather learn our lesson swiftly and rise thus above contrast.

In the starvation illustration we made use of our only freedom of choice, we ignored the illusion of separation and chose to unify. Until this is clear to us, we see our freedom of choice as one between polarities. The real choice is one between illusion and reality. But we still believe we have freedom of choice within this world as we perceive it to be.

This, of course, is what the altered Ego would have us believe, for this sort of choice is the substitute for freedom. Where life or God created absolute freedom, the altered Ego, or voice against God, had to set up an opposite, total limitation. We have heard it had to leave some Good, so a substitute was offered instead, the illusion of freedom. As the balance of polarities is the most crucial point in Man's awakening, our true SELF presses toward us the awareness of the need to balance these opposites within ourselves. Yet by the time this message passes through the 'little' Self, this crystal awareness becomes diluted, dim and distorted as any other truth.

The voice against God now says: of course, these polarities must be balanced. Here are the tools I give you for this task, see? And so conformity, compromise and resistance take the place of balance, and, by their very nature only confirm polarities in their divisiveness, act on a lateral plane and push unity into oblivion. Let us, for example, put a little spotlight on conformity. Society hates nothing more than nonconformity. Everybody must conform, must pull in line, must become uniform (and how the world loves uniforms). This leads to uniformity, the Ego's answer to unity, whereas reality is diversity in Oneness.

A second look at the word itself reveals once more the pregnancy of wisdom in the language. To be uniform (and uniformed) means to be un-informed. The word itself carries the message ever so clearly.

Problems Are Not Problems.

To conform is to deny my SELF; precisely what the altered Ego stands for: SELF denial, the denial of the ONE crystal SELF, which is God. Recalling the picture of the cross, we may visualize extreme resistance to polarities as activities taking place within the extreme ends of the horizontal pole, meaning one involved in these activities is furthest removed from the point of contact, the bridge. As resistance decreases, the movement is toward the centre, the point of contact with the vertical axis. Should one succeed in seeing both ends of the lateral pole as equally valid, then one has arrived at the centre-point, the point of equilibrium. One has set foot on the bridge, and from here to reality it is only a step.

Any choices ever being made between polarities themselves remain within the lateral axis and lead nowhere, remain a motion of to-and-fro. Anything taken or singled out from a whole is functional no more, and thus blocks the flow of life – in simpler terms, creates a problem. Within this lateral axis, the world of polarities, we meet only with problems. Polarities seen apart from the whole become problems. When encountering a problem, we again seem to have the choice between two options: avoidance or confrontation. If we avoid it, it follows us. If we confront it we say: 'No good' and immediately set out to replace the problem with its opposite, a no-problem, a condition void of this problem, blinded to the fact that the problem is NOT the problem. The problem is the lateral axis, the polarities as we perceive them.

Remember: 'As we perceive them' – not the polarities themselves. For example: we may feel disadvantaged in a business venture. The immediate perception is one of 'bad', and the party having disadvantaged us is now to be crucified. So vengeance is added to the perception. The focus is now on the other party and no efforts are shunned to compensate the perceived loss. This, in short, is our remedy to heal the perceived problem of loss. This, in short, is false perception.

Now, True perception would not focus at all on the other party. True perception does not even see the loss as the problem. True perception sees the idea of loss as the problem. It would contemplate the idea of loss and not the form aspect of the problem, the loss. True perception would realize that abandoning the idea of loss abandons at once all losses contained within the idea. What else is the idea of loss but the idea of separation?

And having stated this, we see at once: the problem not only carries the answer within itself, but the problem is the answer, that is the reason for the problem's appearance in the first place. It comes to teach us. To recognize the answer within the problem, we need to look past the problem's form and probe the principle its content stands for. This is the gift the problem offers us. Yet, each time we are confronted with a problem, our instinctive reaction is to 'shoot it into orbit', to get rid of it. A problem does not even want to be solved. In truth a problem is not a problem at all, it is a condition, exquisitely tailored to our learning needs. It is a teacher, a friend, an opportunity offering us the correction of mistakes. The ultimate purpose of any problem aims at healing the illness of separation.

A problem on its form level is only a symptom! Trying to deal with the symptom at best shifts the symptom and leaves its cause untouched. Now the problem has to come again, most likely in a slightly different form, most certainly with more impact as its previous appearance did not succeed in teaching us, and now the symptom appears elsewhere. Another look at form level interpretation should reveal the error of such perception further: the disadvantaged party saw monetary loss as the problem. Another error is added to the first, if the loss of a large sum is perceived as a greater loss than the loss of a small sum. The lost sum of money is the form. The idea behind the form is loss. The idea loss concerns itself not with degrees of quantity or quality. Loss is loss. Therefore the party perceiving the loss should concern itself with the idea, not the loss itself which is merely the symptom. Once it is seen that the idea of loss as such is the fear of lack of supply, and thus the denial of reality, or God, the lesson can be learned and implemented. Thus the symptom, the loss of money, dissipates as it has now served its purpose and has become obsolete, it dissolves without manipulation on our behalf. The moment the real, the true cause of any imbalance, or problem, is recognized and faced, the symptom has served its function and ceases to be. The facing of the polarity of fear then is not resistance to it, but the embrace of welcome and understanding as to its true nature: wholeness split. Now it can be released into unification with its whole and it shall not be part of our experience again.

In truth there is but one problem and therefore only one answer. The intelligent approach to be expected then would be the attempt to define the problem containing all problems, which is, as we now know, separation. Once we have defined the root problem, we can look at the idea it stands for. Having understood the idea, not only intellectually but with our hearts, all problems vanish, for the root problem containing all its parts, all individual problems, is understood, and that is separation. Once we understand separation we cannot judge it or its individual appearances. With this understanding the only road open for us to take is to allow it in all its manifestations, and to transcend it. Allowing ourself and our brother the illusion of separation means to forgive. This delivers us to the bridge of the cross. As the last remnants of separation thus reunify with the vertical pole of the cross, the lateral pole dissolves, together with the very bridge we stand upon and merges into Oneness. We know we have returned home.

At this particular point we ought to be very, very aware of the 'Repair My Dream' syndrome. We are not repairing dreams – we are awakening from the stickiest of all dreams. So let us not fall prey to the notion that all this wonderful knowledge is designed to fix dream problems. It certainly 'fixes' the dream in the sense that we shall dream no more, after it has been 'fixed'. So we better keep in mind that our aim is awakening. If doubts are raised once more as to what we exchange our dream for, then we know we listen to the Ego's whisperings. For this reason, let the assurance be given again: there are no words to express the feeling and reality of completeness, our natural state of Being. It can only be experienced. If it helps, then this much shall suffice: the state of Oneness compared to Man's present collective consciousness is as Man's consciousness is in relation to that of an earthworm. Whosoever insists on fixing his dream insists on remaining an earthworm. Our doubts are understood, but we are urged to offer our trust. The knowing conveyed here shall never mislead us, for it comes from the Source. The caterpillar trusts his maker that all is well. He does not cling to his old garment and thus is transformed into a magnificent butterfly. There is no pain, it is a natural transmutation. So it is with us. As the chrysalis is the bridge between caterpillar and butterfly, so is True perception the bridge between separation and Oneness. We are transmuting into a new state of Being. Clinging to our caterpillar stage, our old ways of judgment, we shall never learn to fly into the dawn of a new day.

Embracing separation back into Oneness and not fighting or resisting parts of separation dissolves the root problem of separation. Thus the only real choice available to us is the choice between Oneness and separation, between illusion and reality.

To leave illusion behind, or to heal separation, polarities must be reconciled and not be fought or evaluated unequally. This is the healing of the disease of separation. Hence, all diseases contained within separation are healed along with it.

As long as the world of polarities is perceived as a world of opposing forces, as opposites to be resisted, a healing cannot occur. Preferences there may be. Preference of one polarity over its opposite need not entail judgment of the unpreferred, and thus leaves them as part of one great whole, where they belong, as two parts of equal value of One whole.

Preference in an ideal state is merely one's own resonance with a condition of like frequency. Preference without resistance to the non-preferred does not evaluate unequally, does not divide. We have seen at the beginning of this chapter, with the example of influenza, how the interaction of polarities reacts if its smooth flow is disturbed. Everything must be allowed to flow freely without blockage, even if it is an indirect blockage as in the case of a common cold. We have our 'nose full' of a particular situation and so this mental condition is reflected on the mirror of our immediate material environment, which is our body. This feeling of having one's 'nose full' is but a misinterpretation of our situation. Certain aspects are resisted as undesirable. If we had seen them as equally valid to the desirable ones, then they would not have mattered enough for us to evaluate them unequally and what does not matter in this manner, does not materialize.

At this point we have learned to 'deal the deck of cards' properly in this world. We do not manipulate the cards, we give each card equal value. For where we go there are no winners and no losers, a rather alien thought to worldly consciousness. We have learned to value each card the same. That is the first step toward unification.

To heal is to change the perception of a condition – not the condition! This is True perception.

This is standing on the bridge of the cross. The very concept of opposites is a concept of division, of split seeing. We only see one side of the whole at a time. If someone paid us with a coin we most certainly would not say: 'I dislike the tail side of the coin, give me the head side only'. A coin comes with two sides, so does life in the temporal world. We accept the two sides of the coin as one coin. Yet we do not accept the two sides of life as ONE life.

Obviously, there is a conflict here and that is our way of seeing. True perception always sets free from conflict because it does not perceive conflict. 'Ah,' I hear someone say, 'Wise words, indeed. But what if I lie dying of thirst in the desert. How could True perception give me water?' Remember the principle of stabilized perception? We recall: it is a fact that we believe what we see. It is equally a fact that we do not see what we do not believe. Another way of putting it is: we only experience what we hold possible. What we do not hold possible we do not experience. In the case of the thirsty man it means he holds it possible to die of thirst. He sees what he believes.

True perception sees not lack of water as the man's problem. It sees fear of death as the underlying principle of the problem – this is the idea the problem contains. Lack of water in this case is the form through which the idea of fear of death expresses. Giving the man water may quench his thirst but cannot quench his fear. The next time around the man shall fear again. This means he has not understood the principle fear represents. Now he needs more contrast again to help him remove his 'blinkers' to learn to look past the form aspect of his problem, the lack of water. True perception would now look at (fear of) death and recognize it for what it really is, a perverted way of seeing life, the Ego's answer to life. Once again it would see the idea of death as nothing but the voice against God, a shadow of life. A shadow is an appearance, is absence of light. Absence of light cannot be, for light, or love or God, is All-There-Is. Therefore this shadow must be an imagined appearance. Imagined appearances are dreams. In other words, True perception recognizes any experience which offers the temptation to doubt life as part of the great dream, and dissociates itself from such madness. What it cannot see as real it cannot believe in. What I cannot believe, I cannot experience.

This is the reason for the answer to the thirsty fellow, for to him I say: 'With True perception you would not be in that situation in the first place!'. True perception needs not the contrast of such an experience, for contrast only comes to teach True perception!

The keyword here is contrast. We remember what was said in the discourse on Metempsychosis: we are here to learn by contrast.

The Cessation Of Sorrow.

But what are we to learn by contrast? The answer to this is: to learn what to avoid and what to seek. That part of our SELF which is deluded, the separate Self, knows this only too well. So, in line with every other truth, it was turned into a farce. The seeking now becomes not one between dream and reality but one between polarities themselves, which are but part of the dream. Thus the choice, the freedom of choice the Ego offers, is the choice between a dream and a dream. A rock and a hard place.

So, now the picture looks like this: we religiously avoid the Bad and seek the Good or avoid what is Good and seek the Bad. As long as we 'avoid' and 'seek'! It does not really matter which way the pendulum swings, as long as it remains within 'opposing forces', within polarities; this way escape is made impossible, illusion reassured. As long as we are guided by false perception, we see the contrast as the contrast between polarities themselves and believe we must choose between polarities.

This is one level of learning by contrast. But this is the altered Ego's distortion of the true meaning of it. The Ego would have us bounce back and forth between polarities forever. Guided by True perception we learn from the contrast between Oneness and the world of polarities as we perceive them. Sure, the contrast of opposites becomes a 'school of hard knocks' until we are exhausted, badly bruised, and only then look at the contrast we were supposed to look at from the start (as the thirsty man in the desert), which is the contrast between reality and dream.

Caught up in an altered state of consciousness we bounce like helpless little yo-yos back and forth, yet feel quite righteous in our deeds. For we believe we are truly aiming at improving things.

The altered Ego wholeheartedly supports the action of 'avoid and seek'. What to avoid and what to seek, however, to this, it gives its own meaning. ONE, who dwarfed the greatest thinkers of all times, said: 'Seek and Ye shall find.' The altered Ego says: 'Oh yes, seek, for seek you must and spare no effort in this task, but, oh – for My sake – do not find!'

True perception would condense all problems into one root problem: separation from Oneness, separation from our Source! So, contrast within polarities is a teaching aid and, being that and only that, the message it carries with it should be clear: its task is to show what to avoid and what to seek. In the measure in which we turn towards what we should seek, the contrast lessens. Of course, for each time polarities are embraced they are unified and for this reason alone cannot present a contrast any more.

The moment we genuinely realize what to seek, the purpose of contrast is fulfilled, we have no need for it again. Do you realize the magnitude of this statement? Do you realize the colossal impact of this truth? It does not say all contrast ends when you have found what you searched for. It does say all contrast ends when you have found what to seek. In short, its purpose is outlived as soon as we are unwaveringly headed in the right direction. It is then that we align, as soon as we leave the lateral axis and move onto the bridge leading to reality, instead of deepening the 'grooves' within illusion. In practical everyday life on this physical plane, its implication represents the greatest consolation we can possibly wish for. In real terms it means the CESSATION OF SORROW for one who truly seeks to exchange illusion for reality. And so it is!

A word of caution seems appropriate here. It is one thing to seek and it is another to pretend to oneself that one seeks. In the latter version seeking perverts into a trip. It then becomes the altered Ego's version: seek but make sure you do not find. The tempter whispering this message is our travel companion along the entire road of search. Only when the total realm of separation is healed, that is allowed without judgment, is the altered Ego healed, for it is the separation. It is then when it merges, that it reunifies with the true SELF.

So the secret is: change of perception of conditions, not conditions. This is why the thirsty man in the desert would not find himself in the lacking position in the first place; this is what was meant by it. He would not be in need of the polarity contrast of lack if he were guided by True perception.

Once we experience a taste of reality we can never revert back to a fear-based perception again. Relapses there may be, particularly during the initial period of beginning to trust in the safety of life. The general direction, however, is now known and literally nothing can stop the Self from joining with its Source. Even if our initial motive to seek was to escape from woes, the motive now is to seek reality for reality's sake. To seek God for God's sake, and nothing else.

The seeker who succeeded in rising from False to True perception, who balanced within himself the war of opposing forces still stands in the world, but is not of it. This thought is so beautifully expressed in the Bhagavad Gita, that classic spiritual epic of India (approx. 500 B.C.). We hear Krishna say to Arjuna: 'Stand Thou in the midst of the battlefield, but be Thou not the warrior.'

Such a man stands in the midst of life and, from an onlooker's perspective acts almost like any other man, yet the motive for his action is diametrically opposed to the motive of one who still acts from within the dream. So anyone in this position may still witness the sorrow of his fellowman, the battle of forces, the teachings by contrast – but he abdicated the spirit of a warrior and therefore does not receive the warrior's just wages.

The Balance Of Male And Female.

In principle we should understand now how to reconcile with the realm of separation, and, as a result of this, change our life from mediocrity to the song of the morning bird: the celebration of life.

The principal energy of life is love, in its state of union appearing as equilibrium, and that is harmony. On the physical plane this same energy appears polarized, split into its opposite reflections, masculine and feminine. Neither is better than the other, but both all-good. To finalize this grand lesson of seeing life's innocence in all its appearances, we shall take one last look at life in its most profound polarization – male and female.

That the altered state of mind, the separation from Oneness, is a necessary part in our growth, we must have certainly recognized. It has its place in the natural unfolding of life. Thus, we do not judge it or condemn it, but this does not oblige us to remain slaves to its madness. The more we understand, the less we are able to judge. For this reason we shall shed some more light on the dominating aspects of separation, which are male and female energy.

To learn to recognize our innocence, and thus the innocence of everything that lives, is the one and only objective of the process of balancing opposites.

In the realm of polarities male and female are seen as in different bodies. Yet each has both energy-principles within itself. It is here where they need to be embraced and therefore balanced. Each energy is beautiful beyond measure, yet as polarities, that is, as energies not unified, represent themselves as discordant energies yearning for union. We take a closer look.

Some among us may be familiar with the thought of the Piscean era coming to an end and unfolding into the Aquarian age. It is not of much bearing what we call the age to come, however it is not the Aquarian Age, but the thirteenth sign, the unified sum total of all that was before, which is to come.

The mark of the Piscean era is male energy, which is now to merge with its opposite reflection – to unify into ONE, extending beyond the two. Male energy (the Piscean) is thrust and organization. On its own, taken from the union of its whole, it fixates and the natural flow of life ceases to be a flow. The waters of life thus become stale.

Intellect in our world reflects male energy, this mad urge to cut life into slices, like a loaf of bread, and label each slice only to file it away, as if life now suddenly had identity. The slices existed before they were labelled and were quite happy just being themselves. In the process of organizing, sorting and filing, man filed himself away.

As a singled-out polarity male energy seeks desperately for fulfillment. The altered Ego offers its version and so man has to fill every hole quite literally. Each void he encounters in his knowledge has to be filled with some theory, be it right or wrong, as long as it is filled. Everything must receive a label – only now does it exist to him, for now he has given it identity. Once this is done it can be safely filed away. The young boy roaming the woods has a greater comprehension of the butterfly and its place in nature than the entomologist who names it Papilio Ulysses joe sa, robs it of its joyous dance and pins it to a glass coffin. For you see, this one only values the form and its appearance, and not its Spirit, which is the real butterfly.

Measuring and labelling the temporal world in its linear dimension is the religion of the male.

His Self, seeking identification,
goes out to numerate God's Creation
in search for conditions to which to relate –
a Self-created delusive state.

How big the world is – or how small –
does not add stability.
It has no relevance at all to his divine identity.
How can we span and limit
what is fundamentally infinite?

Cosmic weight and space combined
are but specks in the spheres of the mind.
Weight and volume – far or near –
are justified only as an idea,
for imagination can easily dwindle
the vast universe into a thimble.

Is not a distant star as near as it is far?

The ultimate value cannot be found
within the dualistic bounds.
To find what is no more comparable,
the ultimate invariable –
the final measuring rod –
is to find reality in God.

By dissecting the dream man seeks for answers within his
dream. To leave his vicious circle he has to unify his energy with
that of his reflection, the female, for her gender wields the energy
of sustenance and that is love.

Those of us who are of male gender would do well to re-
evaluate our most valued, dissecting and analysing intellect, and
look toward womankind as such for some answers. Intellect
splits – intuition unifies. When woman comes into the knowledge
of her Power-Source, we shall stand speechless before her awesome power. She represents the nourishing and sustaining aspect
of God, and what is more, she knows of magic. She unifies, she
does not dissect. Her energy can be likened to an aquarium,
displaying clarity, yet having mysterious depths with iridescent
fish dashing in the sparkling rays of sunlight piercing the water –
an entrancing scene of hues of dark greens and blues. Male energy

is the one which drains the water from this bewitching world and finishes up with a salad of indefinable algae. But at least he went to the 'bottom of things', now he can file it away. That it lost its life in the process does not matter – another hole in his curiosity is filled.

This is the altered Ego's world. Yet it is of equal value to the female energy, therefore it must be embraced as such, then it can look toward woman with open eyes and unify with her energy. The answer is to embrace one's Self first, with all its seeming shortcomings, and know it is alright. This is forgiveness of one's own state of separation – not to fight it, but to know it is in its place. It enriches the soul for the experience, but now it is time to move to unity. The first step is to look to woman with acceptance and not reject or evaluate her as incapable of doing certain things, this is invalidating her. If allowed to be herself she will humble man and he will discover all the 'things' he cannot do but which she can. The two are not in competition with each other, instead should compensate each other, for in truth they are but two parts of ONE whole.

For each polarity to unite with its opposite reflection neither must be resisted but embraced for what it is – and that is God. For man to evaluate woman as not being capable of this or that and for woman to believe that she must be capable of this or that is utter blindness on both their parts. Each has its own flow of energy and therefore tasks. To evaluate each in its state of separation from union is madness indeed. Neither is functional on its own. As it is, the serpent tries to become the sword, instead of enveloping the sword. Only union will heal. To resist each other's movement is the malady – to forgive each other's movement is the remedy.

Woman hears an ancient song in her breast and remembers what man has long forgotten. She still knows where Santa lives. She can still lead her little ones to where the unicorn and undine play with gnome and elf, where the water-gods enchant fairyfolk – she knows the poetry of life. She knows things of eternity and where the rainbow ends, and when she walks alone, she tells her secrets to the spirit of the wind. She is a sorceress and as she passes by, fauns begin to whisper to the leprechauns that she can still tell the tale of the moon goddess on a full moon night. Blessed be she – indeed – for she is mystery, she knows the magic of God. A world only beknown to her and little children. The world of love.

Male gender in its merciless pursuit of an analytical approach to life dissects it and robs it of its spice. Woman shall be the one healing the wound. In different terms, it is the female energy man has to balance within himself. Life did not ask to be dissected and sliced into meaningless pieces, but to be lived. Reason must be balanced with intuition and vice versa.

However, woman too must come to terms with the task allotted to her by her altered Ego. For too long she looked to man for answers, denying her own nature in the process of it; she felt the pressure, so she took a stand. We learned the Ego encourages us to do just that, for this means resistance, and by taking a stand we become firmly grounded. So woman arose and proclaimed 'enough is enough – we shall no more be enslaved.' This seemed only fair – so she went out and mimicked man. The altered Ego celebrated until very late that night.

To prove to herself she can perform any task as well as her enslaver does, she now even ends up in uniform on battle fields. Hearth and cradle are now exchanged for conference tables and filing desks, man's world of 'getting', the world of hierarchy and stress, the proud world of career. Here she can busy herself from morn to night, for here the noise is loud enough to silence the cry of her heart for true liberation. The liberation from the separation of her true SELF.

Her Ego misdirects her and as such she becomes the hireling of her enslaver and plays his game. She need not prove a thing, neither need man. If each gender would just let the other be, embrace each other's nature as wondrous in their own right and honour one another's diversity – union would occur. If man allowed woman to weave her poetry into his geometry we would have a tapestry of such beauty as humanity has never seen.

As man must balance both creative energies within himself, so must woman as well. This does not entail resistance nor copying of each other's traits, but what it means is the wholehearted embrace of the other in the knowing that each is alright as it is. This changes separation to union. This attitude welcomes, therefore embraces, thus unifies.

As long as man sees woman as a desirable body only, false perception is stabilized. Woman in her yearning for acceptance and love complies with man's request and focuses on the beauty of her body, on things of youth, to lure man into union. But as we heard, the union of two disunited individuals does not make a union. The union must first occur within each one of them with their own SELF. Then the outer, the body, will be eternally youthful, for it is but the mirror of the SELF as it perceives itself.

The union resulting from the merging of such two becomes the ecstasy of the soul. For God embraces God. As long as man invalidates his other half, as long as woman invalidates herself, union cannot occur. The same holds true if man puts woman on a pedestal or woman sees in man the 'enemy', as the one enslaving her. Both must learn to see each other's innocence and this starts with one's SELF.

To let the other be according to his or her desire, and to look within oneself, is the step to take. The Ego whispers not to look, because it is afraid. It says: 'Don't look, for what you find is guilt,' so we look away. But if we laugh at its suggestions and dive into the depth of our soul we find the jewel of our SELF. Brilliant, sparkling, diamondlike – the Source of light. And what we see is complete innocence. Thus we look 'outside' of us and all we see is but the same innocence. We know it to be God. This is True perception, for it sees aright.

The Condition For A Miracle.

In closing this grand lesson we shall imagine now two people, amiable fellows, each one defending his own viewpoints in a discussion. Remember, emphasis on one polarity indicates resistance to its opposite polarity, therefore calling it forth. Defence thus becomes attack. One viewpoint is defended against the other, born of fear – the underlying subconscious fear that one's own viewpoint, the fragment of the puzzle, might not have any meaning after all.

The discussion heats up, emotions run high and before long a fully fledged argument is in the making. Harsh words are hurled at each other, insults exchanged with the aim to belittle, which really means to make smaller, to take away, to devalue. Thus we have a short circuit proper. Sparks fly everywhere. Our two friends are just about ready to consume one another.

We will now use the torch of True perception to shine a light into this darkness. What went wrong here from the very start? Each party valued one polarity more than another, had singled one viewpoint out to be the truth.

Aspects within the dream were accepted as wholes in themselves, each party devaluing the other's viewpoint, creating an imbalance and fixation set in. Energies could not flow freely because they were split. True perception sees the Law of Reversal here in full bloom: where Oneness has one truth for all, false perception claims a different truth for each single soul, a puzzle fragment for each soul and not an assembled, unified picture, which would express an intelligent meaning.

This imbalance caused a confrontation, whereas an acceptance of each other's viewpoint as equally valid would have achieved unification. Agreement is not required, but acknowledgment of equal right to be is. Our two friends did not make this choice and as false perception's God is death (in any form), war is declared. Defence, we know, calls for attack. To end the war the 'enemy' has to be killed and here we have arrived at false perception's central theme. Death. The Ego justifies its action and calls this madness by a different name: Survival. And rightly so, for to such turpitude it has reduced what sanity calls radiant life.

True perception would look upon a scene so different from one still in the dream that it would seem to this one as sheer lunacy. For if we believe illusion to be true, then truth must be madness. So madness is kept alive by the belief that it is true!

If only one of our friends would perceive with True perception, the battle could have never occurred. But how would an onlooker with a healed consciousness perceive the actual scene? Remember, he knows only of a unified plane of polarities – polarities reconciled. He knows the lateral pole of the cross as not being at cross purposes, but as realigned with the vertical pole. He knows the two to be ONE. He stands on the bridge, thus he knows only of ONE BEING, of ONE SELF. He sees his own crystal SELF, his own Christ-SELF, the Son of God, deluded in a dream, attack his own image in a mirror with the intent to kill.

True perception sees both as what they really are: ONE SELF in the disguise of bodies, pretending to be separate, to be two. Only a dreaming God could dream a nightmare such as this and believe it to be real. This sketch we draw of our friends in conflict is not a play of words to entertain. The intent here is to depict a 'real' life situation and to show an answer ending any conflict anywhere, if the answer is applied.

True perception is the answer for it remembers truth for our battling friends, sees past the error of separation, sees only ONE where there seem to be two and therefore it forgives, because it gives away separation. There is no way our friends can continue their battle, the battle dissolves. The miracle rushed in and healed. The wisdom extracted: *True perception is the condition for a miracle!*

We do not influence or alter a condition, we simply see it aright. When a condition is seen in this light, its existence as an appearance of the state of separation is revealed. That alone is enough to heal any condition. That is the miracle.

The question might be asked then, if True perception heals with certainty, then healing the conflict of our warring friends would heal all conflict anywhere at the same time. And it does, contrary to all appearances. The fact that it heals all conflict is the reason why you, the reader, are reading this material. To understand this thoroughly, we should remind ourself of the principle of the Global Thoughtform, which explains how the healing process is snowballing. The rise beyond judgment allows love to enter. This highest of frequencies changes our physical bodies by way of a restored DNA. Thus each individual in that position becomes a transmitter of the most powerful electromagnetic frequency, affecting everything and everyone around him.

In summarizing this discourse on the balance of polarities, we say: God is All-There-Is, therefore God is ALL-encompassing. Whatever enters my realm of experience, must, of need, be God. How can I put different price tags on the various appearances of God? For the I AM in me is God. Thus I only judge myself by judging God. God is Pure Being, therefore innocent and so am I. Now I look 'out' into the mirror of Creation and see but myself, and that is innocent, hence all of equal value. If witnessing destructive or discordant energy, I do not have to condone it, but I evaluate it as of equal worth to any other expression of life.

Any experience, no matter how fearful it seems, when seen as of equal validity to any other manifestation, faced and embraced as of equal right to be, shall unify and thus release this fear in to the All-There-Is. This way it shall never manifest.

This chapter on the balance of polarities showed us a step by step approach to unify the lateral pole of the cross – our state of separation from reality – with life, the vertical pole. The vertical pole without the lateral represents an I. This also is a 1. The I AM is ONE.

To bring this knowledge into our daily lives, we shall move to the chapter on the Law of Supply. Nothing unfolds this knowledge more in us than the actual demonstration of it in our daily affairs.

Chapter 5
The Law Of Supply

Clarification.

Each learning, as we see, expands into the next, unfolding a greater understanding, much in the way a rose unfolds its petals.

By now we should have arrived at a rather clear understanding of what the altered Ego really is: our very own consciousness deeming itself to be a separate Self, an altered state of mind.

It is nothing but a misunderstanding – the mistaken way of seeing ourselves as a separate being over here and life, opposing us, over there. What we perceive we can only see as we see ourself, which then, of course, results in the perception of a world filled with separate, little Selves. We see our brothers as separate Selves; as having their Being as a Self apart from our Self. This is the illusion, the dream, the altered Ego, Social Consciousness, false perception.

Whichever term we may prefer, it is irrelevant. They are only different names for one and the same altered state of mind. In contrast to this, alternative names for reality are: Oneness, super-consciousness, I AM consciousness, Christ consciousness. The term True perception is not applicable here, because this term applies to a special function. True perception we may see as being below actual Oneness. Oneness is knowledge, it does not perceive. To perceive I must still see myself as apart from the perceived. Perception as such is only one half of a process. The other half is articulation. We have not lost this ability entirely; we hear, thus we perceive – we speak, thus we articulate. Yet, each of our 5 senses can articulate. Perception is intake – articulation is output, hence it is the principle of Giving and Receiving.

In a state of Oneness or super-consciousness, the perceiver and the perceived become ONE. The wholeness of the process is restored, therefore, in Oneness, (if we still choose to have a body) we can articulate on every sensory level. Not only with our 5 senses, but also with the rest of them. However, in this dimension of third density we are not aware of all of our senses, only of five.

The understanding of articulation throws a different light on so-called miracles. To see, taste, touch and smell a loaf of bread is the perception side of the process – to manifest a loaf of bread is the articulation side of it. The feeding of the five thousand by Yeshua, seen in this light, frees the event of its supernatural flavour.

There is more to this, too. Our bodies, for example, have the ability to transform, that is to articulate, the photons of starlight, or sunlight, into the sustenance required by the body. It is a process similar to photosynthesis. This ability will surface on a collective level when man enters super-consciousness. It may already be developed in the state of True perception. This 'developing' is not a conscious process. It occurs on a soul-essence level, meaning this ability to feed the internal combustion of the physical body from the electrums of the ether directly – without the detour via carbon-based matter – shall surface naturally. It comes in the measure of our awakening. (We remember the implied possibilities of a healed DNA). The process goes further: in a state of super-consciousness we shall cease drawing energy (e.g. fossil fuels, minerals, etc.) from the Earth, but transform light directly into the forms required by our day to day needs. But let us return to True perception.

Without this bridge we cannot bridge the abyss we created, which separates us from our true state of Being. Another term for True perception we find in the Christian terminology: Holy Spirit, the Whole-I-Spirit, that which is still wholly Spirit. It is that part of our Divine SELF which is aware of both, the Dream and Reality.

One who would know of only ONE life would know himself to be that very life. Because he can only see wholeness – that which is wholly Spirit – he sees the God I AM in everything that is and everything becomes a pure reflection of his SELF, withstanding the fact that the reflection might see itself as having a life of its own and thus seeing itself as separate. If such a Self – in a body, still perceiving itself as separate – met with a Self-realized One, his own separation becomes healed merely by virtue of the Self-realized One not seeing his brother's separation, but only his SELF.

This is what is meant by remembering God, or t
one's brother. He gives his brother's separation aw
he for-gives! This is the true and only meaning of
Forgiveness, as it is commonly seen, first establishes guilt and
then pardons it. Again perverted truth, twisted by the Ego's Law
of Reversal.

Now True perception has the exact same effect, although it is
still a step away from Oneness. It still is cognizant of separation,
but is no more part of it. It stands apart from the dream. It
recognizes separation for what it is: only error, not sin – therefore
it cannot see any guilt whatsoever. Not seeing guilt, it sees only
innocence. This is True perception's way of giving away, of
forgiving separation. This is where the miracle rushes in to heal.
Those who fail to see, at this point, the relation of this to the Law
of Supply are kindly asked to bear with us for a little while.

To understand the utter simplicity of that Law, a thorough
'spring cleaning' in our thinking is a prerequisite. Worldly thinking
is such a labyrinth of contradictive mishmash that simplicity could
not stand out against its background. The simplicity of truth needs
as clean a background as possible against which it can be recognized.

A good way to illustrate the difference between the three
stages of awareness is to imagine the dreamer as being in the state
of Separation. The one who opens his eyes, but is not fully awake
as yet, is the person in a state of True perception. He stands at the
midpoint between separation and Oneness, at the point of balance.
He realizes the dream as being just that – a dream. And who would
not want to awaken from a dream, if he knows he is dreaming.

The fully awakened, or enlightened One is not a person in that
sense at all any more. He has transcended his identity on the
personality level. He is the Sun's ray identifying with the Sun once
again and not with the pattern of light on the wall. He is in the state
of Oneness, he is All-There-Is. He may be in a body, but he is the
Christ, one who is in Christ consciousness. His I AM is All-There-
Is and it is all encompassing. His I AM is your and my I AM. He
is the Son of God. The Christ resurrected. That is the one and only
meaning of resurrection. The 'Second coming of Christ' and
'Spiritual Rebirth' are only different labels for one and the same

process: the union of the separated Self with the I AM, the universal SELF. Let us be reminded here that this union was in truth never severed, only our cognisance of it was.

There is a belief commonly held among the few who know Oneness to be the coronation of spiritual evolution: that its attainment results in the surrender and loss of all they hold dear. The total nonsense of this notion cannot be stressed enough. One simple logical thought should put an end for good to this claim: Oneness is inclusive – separation exclusive! Therefore lack of any kind can only be experienced in separation, because it separates Self from SELF, it excludes Self from abundance. Oneness includes, therefore includes Self in SELF and Self finds itself home again, back where it always belonged, in abundance.

However, our focus is on True perception, for this is what we are concerned with here. This is the step we have to take, Oneness follows without our effort. One with True perception, we said, still perceives. But he perceives the true state of affairs, he has realized the dream for what it is, and because of this, he sees two things at once: His brother becomes a mirror to himself. He does not see a different Self in him, but his SELF. By the same token, he is very aware of his reflection deeming itself separate from him.

That is why one in the state of True perception is a healer. He remembers God for his brother, being in truth of One Being only, his memory becomes his brother's. How could he possibly be afraid of his very own reflection? This is the Truth that sets free. This is the miracle. It means fear is absent, therefore love is present and where love is, there is abundance. The process of arriving at True perception and Oneness is termed atonement. Atonement realigns, makes at-ONE. So this mistaken Ego, our consciousness mistaking its Self for what it is not, must not be fought or judged in any way, but must be healed.

At this point we may have comprehended in depth already what this material is trying to bring to our awareness: our experience of life on Earth can be Heaven on Earth, if we allow it to be so. To allow means not to resist but to see life as a whole and not single out parts and value these as wholes in themselves. If we insist on our upside-down perception we fail our mission. Our brothers and the Earth itself with all its beauty are not the Illusion.

But our perception of it is. Truth is not absent here, make no mistake, but it is certainly obscured.

The Ego permits truth, oh yes, but wherever it is seen it adds an opposite. Where Good attracts, it must prevent that only Good is seen. If only Good is seen, it knows its ruling days are numbered, so some Bad is added to the scene – now doubt is reassured and two, instead of one, masters are served. My brother is not the Illusion, but how I see him is.

We should not lose heart when we are told this world is an illusion. The tree, the lake, the lark and the sky or a crisp mountain morning – the delight of little ones chasing clumsily through meadows after butterflies – they are not the illusion we speak of here – no – they lift our hearts and thus point the way. The truth becomes reversed when these are seen as being apart from us.

There is beauty here, indeed – in fact, the elation at the sight of creation seen as my Being, and not perceiving myself as being separate from it, reverses the known picture to the extent of beauty being All-There-Is. Nothing outwardly may have changed, but one's seeing is now knowledge, not perception any more. In an instant one is transported into a higher dimension. One has come into one's own. That now the outward scene adapts itself to one's reality should not come as a surprise.

This is the awakening. One now sees all as it really is and the memory of one's 'normal' state of mind in Social Consciousness seems like death itself. One has come home. And it is so natural. One experiencing this knows this to be the natural heritage of every soul on Earth. The thrill of joy, the excitation, and yet the absolute peace one IS, is too far beyond words. One is complete.

Such sight would be at a loss for words, for words for this have not been coined. One with such sight would weep with joy and utter only this: thank you God for being God! Thank you for being the ME of me. Such one would see his brother as he truly is, as God created him. And if his brother be the meanest the world has known, capable of horrifying deeds – this one sees with eyes unveiled and what does He behold? He cannot share his sight in words, for there are none. In speechless wonder he beholds a radiant jewel, a beauty so divine, – his crystal SELF. He becomes witness to the living God. To him who sees with such sight, the ning of the Last Judgment is revealed. And truly, there is ~~..~~ a thing as this. And He who speaks it, says: Behold – My Son is innocent! What else, I ask, could Love say to its own SELF?

To see past the error in our fellowman – and see but innocence – is fearful indeed. For this would state we ourselves are innocent and this the Ego would not want us to believe. Attack could then no more be justified, trust in our brother re-established, and altered state of mind would then be dispensed with for all time.

To Be All Is To Have All.

The purpose of Being is to Be and not to Have. The concept of 'Have' was established by survival thinking in opposition to our natural state of Being. To 'have' means to be incomplete. Why else the desire to have something, if not for the reason of adding it to oneself. Only a state of incompleteness can feel want. To be All is to have All that the All Being contains. It is so simple! But with all our might we refuse to even look in the direction of reality. Having denied the only reality there is, we find ourselves in want of one.

So we created our own. Now it is real for us and anything other than that must now be, of necessity, unreal. Our sole purpose here is joy, not disenchantment. Yet we experience life in an upside-down fashion. Literally! These discourses try to tell us how to upright this picture again, how to live here, on Earth, in separate bodies, as long as we find necessary, and in complete joy. Death is truly an illusion. It is this certainty of death we are most reluctant to release. We made it our God and therefore worship it.

Fear experienced in any way is but death by degree. We are shown here – with this understanding – a way of living this life, where fear of lack of any kind, indeed, this very fear itself, has no place at all – where sorrow, guilt, sin and loss become but fleeting memories.

The statement of Yeshua, referring to the surrender of possessions as a prerogative to enter the Kingdom of Heaven has been, as so much else, sadly misunderstood: the possessions in question are our belief systems, which oppose the Truth. Fear is the major 'possession' we are so reluctant to give up. If we probed our hearts, who be there who would not find himself in want of a life lived in exuberance and joy. A life where every brother is seen as innocent – a life lived in the certainty that the ME of me is always, and death a mad reversal of the truth. Not to acknowledge the Spirit that causes all things to be is plainly unintelligent.

Be not offended by this statement, for one who dreams and believes the dream to be true must, logically, believe Truth to be a dream. We would do well in reading this last sentence twice.

The purpose of this chapter is to clarify the cosmic principle governing prosperity, or differently expressed, the Law of Supply. Prosperity means having sufficient supply to meet our needs; that these may, at times, include some 'unnecessary' needs is quite in the order of things. There is nobody keeping tabs on us as to what we should or should not have. We can have everything. To prosper is to flourish in all walks of one's life. The Law of Supply then concerns our entire life, not merely financial affairs, as these are but a minute part of supply as such. Ultimate prosperity translates into ultimate happiness and vice versa.

With this in mind, we shall now benefit from some more contrast, the contrast of fear and lack versus safety and abundance. Fear and our reality of lack are really one and the same. What else is lack but the fear of supply, whatever we deem supply to be. We look at this contrast for a purpose, without mockery, but to create a contrasting backdrop against which True perception shall be better understood.

The meaning we assigned to life in this world is to 'HAVE', and not to 'BE'. Every single soul on this planet is on the hunt to get, to add something to itself it obviously has not – or has and wants more of. Our days are spent in the pursuit of trivia, meaningless to one who knows his SELF. We want a house, a car, career, a social standing of some sort, a man, a woman, child, power, fame, an affair, – this is where happiness must be, fulfillment, to be sure – it has to be somewhere out there.

And if there be a thing we do not want – then we are told we do. We hear it long enough and so we want this too. Should it be so that we have all we possibly could need, then we are told supply runs short, get it while you can. So we go out, grab this and more – hoarding is the name. We toil and sweat, worry and fret, tread on those who dare stand in our way, and those of us who have mastered the art a little better than the rest let others do their toil. Defence, attack, lies and deceit, fair weapons in this game, are justified and if, in the course of this, our brother bleeds to death, – well, hard luck – the battle of survival do we name this game.

Some find the race too fast and hard, these contend with little. But they too take part, all the same, in the great game of finger-pointing against life, to show that really no One cares. The proof of this is the unilaterally accepted 'truth', that we have to go out and earn a living. The same expressed in different words says: we must make sure, take care of our well being, because no one else does.

Let us not resent this statement before we hear the rest. The advocation to replace this attitude is not one of sitting back and twiddling thumbs. God does not work for us. He works through us and must do so if He BE us. The game of survival has rules. It must have, because nobody can be trusted. We write them down in books, in words no sane mind can understand. We call these Laws, for all to be obeyed. To every Law we need to add another one, to explicitly explain the first. These need interpretation too, in detail, to be sure, and so we add some more to this until a thousand books are filled – now we are satisfied.

Hence we need learned minds, who spend half their precious lives in learning their way through this maze and interpret these important words for those who do not understand and do not want to hear them anyway. On our legal tender, the thing life 'is all about', we print the lofty words: In God We Trust. This is to offset the first rule in the book of laws, which says: no one can be trusted, therefore the need for laws. But nonetheless, proud of the monster we created, we now give it a name. We call it a system of some sort, juridical, to be exact, for this carries an air of trustworthiness, honour and respectability.

The executors of these rules we dress in pious robes, thus looking very honourable we call them so. The structure for the game complete, the game may now begin – we are prepared. This is the time again for the Ego's grand Law of Reversal to come into full swing. The law that states a different truth for each and every soul, while God has only one truth for all.

The savage game begins and there are those who do not play exactly by the rules. The Ego never having heard of error, knowing only sin, applies its Law, hands out just punishment, and correctly so, for did they not know the game has rules? The reason for the many laws becomes apparent now. The rich need some, the poor need some and those who hover in between, they need again some other ones. For the influential, there is a special book of rules – it happens to be very thin. And those of us who wrote the rules forgot to write some for themselves. Chaos successfully disguised as law and order, justice to be precise, madness is now sanctified and woe unto its servant who dares disloyalty or pays not due respect.

A world gone mad, where the ONE SELF, deeming itself as many little Selves, – denying its own SELF – is acting out its dream.

Our little ones, who still carry a memory of sanity, of God, who still know how to laugh, whose eyes still shine with joy, we put into schools. Here we indoctrinate them, show them 'the ropes', the rules of this grim game, make sure they know what life is 'all about'. If they do not accept this game as their reality, they might wake up to its sheer idiocy, and this we cannot possibly permit. For this means that our game be spoiled.

In short, we teach them well – to prepare them for this hell. This assures that madness does not die. For this is the altered Ego's only fear, that it may lose its autonomy, that God Is and it is not and all was but a dream. For this reason, no effort is spared to make this world a tombstone so large to constantly remind itself of God's demise. And the inscription reads, for every one to see: See! God is not.

What else could the altered Ego possibly be but our own deluded little Self, thinking itself as separate, fenced off, vulnerable and tossed into this world by the whim of some unloving God. A world in which each and every living thing looms as a threat, cannot be trusted, must be feared.

The game of 'getting' we designed to keep us constantly immersed in a battle of gain and loss. This keeps fear alive and well, fear of losing what we have, fear of not getting what we do not have as yet. We defend our lean bit with lock and bolt; this not enough – we insure and reinsure to be assured of what we call security, the Ego's substitute for God, our very SELF, the only real security there ever is. We lie awake at nights, designing plans against some future loss we fear, events which have not even yet occurred. But fear tells us that these will come and come they shall, for we decree it to be so. So fear keeps us on the run, keeps us well occupied, for fear we must – if we did not, we might just stop, lift our eyes but for an instant and, lo! see all as a dream. And if it just so happened that there be one of us who did this very thing, and spoke to us:

'Brothers, awaken from your dream – there is no thing to fear. Life is not toil, nothing to get, for all that is, is YOU. And if you be All-There-Is then you have ALL as YOU.

Stand straight, walk tall, discard your burdens, fly. For fly you can, but if you dream your wings be small, how can you lift to heights where eagles soar?

Do not compensate your dream of lack with things within the dream. Your Being is your sustenance. Do not disavow your heritage, for it is yours to take. Come, and leave your battlefields, their harvest is but fruits of fear with further seeds of fear.

The ONE who loves you more than you can love yourself, who knows you but as children having lost their way, He calls you home. He sees only innocence where you see guilt and sin. Counsel not your dream for answers, cling to it no more, for that is all you lose, just disenchantment, broken dreams. Awaken now and dream no more!'

If thus he spoke in earnestness appealing to our hearts, what would we say, what would we do? In all probability, most of us would smile with pity in our hearts for such a deluded one, for he – we know – must certainly be dreaming while seeming wide awake. 'Another dreamer', we then say, sigh with relief, and attend again to our fields and toil. And our Ego is content, it knows it has escaped once more the dread of waking up to happiness and joy, of putting madness to an end.

This game is tough, to say the least, 'getting', to most does not come light. So some of us shrink from the vine promising the grapes. They, somehow, seem to be hanging far too high. These ones say: we ask not for much, a roof, a bed, some food will do. And as they ask, so is it unto them. Yet this it seems does not exactly suit them either, for now they say: 'We only asked life for the least and even this is hard to get'. And this is why they change their tune and ask for even less – and as they ask so they receive.

These are no different from the ones who cannot get enough, for while they ask for less and less the others ask for more and more. The game they play is just the same.

What miserable beggars that we are. Life has prepared a banquet, has laid a table for its children overflowing with the best it can give – its very SELF. Yet we do not partake of this abundance, we do not sit down at the table of life, give thanks, and accept its gifts. No – instead we are crawling beneath, contending for the most meagre of crumbs. This way we are justified in our cry that we missed out, that no One cares. Truth once more reversed. What we are really doing here is what we do so well – we deny God and accuse our brother for not sharing with us what he calls his own. This keeps him guilty, and apart from us, thus testifying to the fact that we are too (and two). The ones whose spoil of crumbs outweighs that of their brothers, we call the wealthy and the rich. Beggars all the same. For they too believe that to get is the highway to fulfillment.

If there is anything I have to get and must add on to me, then surely does this indicate I am not whole, am incomplete. And to complete myself I must add to myself that which I think I lack. This, of course, 'hits the nail on its head'. Having separated ourselves from life, from God, we are apart, unwhole and therefore incomplete. To be complete again, reason would simply join with what was lost, would join with God. Not being governed by reason, but by our altered state of mind, we immediately reverse the only remedy there is. We know the answer lies in joining, but with what to join, is what we reverse.

The view is misdirected and so we seek for that we wish to join with, within the dream. That is the Ego's version of seeking 'within'. The Ego's name for this game is universally accepted – survival. What arrogance; the arrogance of claiming God is not.

167

For if he IS, we say, he certainly would care. For arrogance springs from ignorance, and this means not to know.

This is precisely our state of affairs – we do not know our true SELF. This is, of course, why we find ourselves wanting. The true want here is one for SELF, yet receiving this would definitely put an end to separate existence. So this want, like all else, has to be reversed. SELF we can only find within. SELF is ONE. The Ego, just having directed us to look within the dream, adds more to the confusion now and says: 'it is not within you, but outside and not One, but many, that you need'. So we seek outside to get the many, instead of within where we could find the ONE.

Now the Ego knows this keeps us occupied for all eternity – this way we cannot find.

To say God does not care because he allows suffering shows the Ego at its best. We, as God's Sons, are One with Him. The Father and we are One and the Same. To say God cares not is to say we do not care, which is precisely how it is. Being ONE with the Father we have the same free will as the Father. For the Father aspect to interfere with its very SELF, the Son aspect, would necessitate the end of free will. Such interference would rob us of the wisdom we extract from our experience. After all, we design our experiences in the first place for the purpose of learning from these. Because God, our Father-Mother cares, we are urged to awaken from the dream.

To claim to be helpless, to claim we are alone and have to fend for ourselves and have no God to take care of us – to claim we are exposed to the mean forces of life – to claim we are now forced to survive in this hostile environment – to claim this, is the epitome of arrogance.

How dare the Son of God reduce himself to a petty imp. We should give thanks that it is but a dream in which we act the role of paupers, in which we claim we have no home. Instead of settling for the crumbs of Life's bounty we should ask for nothing less than everything – the very Source itself.

We will return now to our daily lives and see how we can implement the truth best. A hungry belly cannot contemplate reality. The very lack we feel, for so many things, shall begin to teach us another way.

The Source Of Supply.

There is much we learned already in the discourse on the Balance of Polarities – now we shall extend this knowledge a little further.

If we asked a friend, or for that matter, anyone, about the source of his or her income, the answer would most likely state an employment, a business or the sale of some sort as the source. And this seems right, besides everybody else in this wide world believes it to be so. Yet again, truth is obscured, because truth would see the source elsewhere. And here is why: One who fetches a pail of water from a river would certainly decree the river to be the source.

But is it really? Is not the river rather the channel, through which his supply, the water, flows? The true source in this case is the almighty ocean.

What this analogy shall depict should be clear. The job or business can never be the source of my supply. My Being is. The job is instrumental, is the channel only, through which this supply flows. The job is not causal. This knowing, condensed in one simple sentence, reads: My Being is my sustenance.

There may be some who hoped the Law of Supply consisted of a magical incantation, or a mysterious formula, to invoke some unseen powers to shower Life's goodies upon them. This then should set their thinking straight. The secret of this all-powerful statement: My Being is my sustenance, is the reclaiming of our power Source, which we have given away to each and every thing. Only a mind in fear, fickle and uncertain, can rest his security in outward things and conditions. A mind voicing this statement, with true comprehension of its meaning, has released the veil of make-believe. The universe will bend to come to his aid. His is the power of God and it must be so, for he has withdrawn power from the outside and given it back to his own crystal SELF, his Christ-SELF, the Son of God. And He is ONE with the Father. Therefore, what is his Father's must be His. We can see this truth as clearly being in line with everything else which we have learned so far: this statement does not attempt to alter outer conditions or manipulate affairs of man. It simply changes its perception of these conditions and affairs, and above all, the source of power.

Anyone saying this with meaning, trusts in his SELF, which is God, for he knows nothing outside God. So in what else could he possibly put his trust? His needs are known to his SELF before his personality Self is even aware of them, and as a tree draws nourishment from the Earth without toil, so does he. And if there be some disciple of the Ego, wanting to doubt this last analogy, by saying: 'There are trees which die from lack of water or are uprooted by mean winds', to him I say: The very Earth is subject to Man's mass consciousness and reflects his torn mind with hurricanes, droughts, quakers and shakers. Let man change his mind about life and be once more at ease, then nature, too, will be at peace.

My Being is my sustenance. This is true security, here is a mind at peace.

A man with this understanding is given work he enjoys doing. Labour, stress and toil will be to him but feeble memories. He does not 'make sure' any more, because he IS sure. He has no need for plans, as these are to him defences based on conjecture. And should a project enthuse him enough, he may be seen to work harder than ever before, but will enjoy every single moment of it, though to an onlooker he may well seem to toil. He measures not his achievements by the accumulation of things.

Whatever such a man does, makes, produces or creates, he does it for the joy of it and not for its reward. He knows he could not even prevent his own from gravitating towards him. He knows himself as being perfectly taken care of. The thought of holding on to the fruits of his labour would seem very, very alien to him.

The Apple tree does not look for apples outside itself, intending to glue them to its branches. It brings the apples forth from within its own Self. The Apple tree holds not on to its apples, neither does it decree who be deserving of them. No, the Apple tree knows how to give, for it gives indiscriminately – this way, next year, there will be more. The Apple Tree seems to have so much more wisdom than man. It cares not for the fruits of its labour, but rejoices in the bringing forth of these. A man, working in this spirit, knows giving IS receiving.

Such a state of mind knows all manifested form as having sprung forth from the Source. As the thought of a house comes before the erection of its structure, he takes the thought of whatsoever he desires and knows it into Isness. Matter and circumstances coagulate around his thought energy to manifest his thought into Being. He knows its Source to be his very own Being. Observing those individuals who delight in their work, we cannot fail to notice that their needs are always met. The focus on their undertaking is for the joy of it and not its remuneration.

There is this special groove in the mind of Man, stabilized perception made sure of that. This groove says, there is only limited supply. How can the Creator deprive Himself of his own Creation?. How can God be limited when Unlimitedness is what He is? Only by dreaming a little dream that He is not God.

The denial of the Creator-Spirit in us as the Source of all supply and prosperity results in the want for possessions. This is merely the Ego's attempt to substitute completion through union with SELF with the misdirected view that completion can be achieved by adding objects and images to Self.

It is for want of true identity that we need things. The infirmity of the soul is compensated by material riches. A solitary hour in the fields, by a brook, with the sparrow-hawk circling high in the skies as our companion, is solace to the heart – inspires. A material thing does not. For the first we pay no price – for the latter we pay with our soul. Knowledge is Man's victory over his possessions, for these are for slaves. Instead of a means to an end, possessions have become an end in themselves. The value of a material thing lies in a man's ability to make it, or to bring it about, not in the thing itself, neither in its form nor its possession. The boy who makes his own kite can laugh heartily as the South-wind carries it mischievously away. His friend, whose kite has been given to him, laments for he feels loss – he lacks the ability to replace it. The first is master – the second is slave. If only a fraction of the energy and attention spent on the body and its comfort zone would be redirected toward our spiritual Source, we would find that material objectives would sort themselves out under a cosmic lawfulness the ignorant would term miraculous. This applies to any walk of life. Those of us, for instance, who dread their 'nine to five' existence would do well in pondering this thought as they only live – or feel – this way because their attention is focused on the outer and not toward within.

Unaware that possession's nature is to possess the possessor, in our desire to possess we enslave ourselves to objects, persons, dogmas, concepts, and power. The urge to possess shall always bring sorrow in its trail – regardless of its degree. The principle behind possession is known as attachment. The degree of detachment determines the free flow of the fulfillment of these desires. Without attachment to our possessions we may enjoy these things thoroughly without becoming enslaved to them. It is a wise man who regards himself as caretaker only and not as owner. Any person identifying with the I AM, the Creator SELF, cannot find himself in want of anything, because his SELF *is* everything. Whatsoever his needs require is available to him. In contrast to this anyone identifying with the personality Self has literally cut himself off from his Source. The mark of this is limitation because he has limited himself to an image of his Self which is an imagined Self, therefore not real. It is not him. Everything perceived now must of necessity be limited and this includes supply. And let no rich man rise and say: 'My supply is not limited – yet I know of no God'. For to him I say: 'Are you free of want?'

However, the Law of Supply serves this man all the same and that is this: There is nothing the universe would withhold from itself, meaning man; be it a sickness or riches, whatever it is that constitutes the reality of our thoughts is precisely mirrored by our physical life as our physical reality. As this man is very, very clear about what he desires, his entire focus is on money and therefore it is this that he receives, not as a gift but as an actualization of his mind. He simply experiences his own thought pattern as a physical reality. By contrast one who focuses on experiencing his SELF moves of necessity towards unlimitedness and therefore experiences the unrestricted flow of money as a mere by-product of that unlimitedness.

We will call another example to our aid and see how this knowledge could be applied: if claim would be issued forth on us to pay one thousand Dollars, Marks, Francs, Roubles – it matters not the name – we would look at our bank account and find one hundred as all it contains. False perception sees supply as insufficient now, because it firmly believes in limited supply as such. This is the belief which states: I have only one hundred in the bank, how could I possibly pay out one thousand?

The reason why false perception sees supply as limited is because it sees two fundamental aspects in a totally distorted way: the supplier and supply's form! Once this perception has been corrected, the payment of a bill, or any act of giving, becomes a matter of ease and does away with the petty clinging to the little we seem to have. And here is why (firstly in regard to the supplier): We identify the supplier with our personality Self, assuming, we give from ourself. As limited as the altered Ego is so is its supply. What else can we expect? Clay-man has nothing because he is nothing. The unwise 'set up' for their personal ends. The instant we direct our view beyond the little Self and see with a greater perspective, we will also take in grander horizons, that is we see the true giver of All-There-Is. In this frame of knowing we merely pass on the supply which comes from the universal Source, the I AM – in short, we let God pay the bill. He 'pays' everything else anyway, for what is there that does not originate from the infinite storehouse of the universal Source? The air we breathe, the body we have, the water we drink – where is the end? We think we are so terribly smart, but have we ever created a drop of water or an ounce of air? All we ever do is convert God's grain of wheat into dough and that into bread and there our abilities end already. So, seeing that everything, and that means precisely that – absolutely every thing – is supplied by God, we might as well let him pay our rent too. This way the landlord receives his money on time. Yet this shall remain mere wishful thinking if this God is conceived as being outside ourself. Such a God does not exist, hence cannot bring forth any supply. When the I AM is understood as the Source and not the personality Self, then the floodgates open, and not only for money, remember, for this is but a tiny aspect of prosperity. So, the answer is not to effect supply through the personality Self but to pass the claim on to the God I AM. Yet even then there is something lowly in our approach as it intimates a sentiment of begging. I come as no beggar unto my Father but stand tall as heir to his estate.

Many have no qualms about giving a material thing or rendering a service to their neighbour, are even desirous to do so, but stand perplexed when faced with the same situation when reversed. Now they have considerable difficulty in receiving as graciously as they give. Why should this be so? Because they split polarities in as much as esteeming the act of giving in preference to the act of receiving, for neither assumes a greater place in the hierarchy of qualities. Both acts ought to be accorded to the God I AM, then we can receive as liberally as we give, but incur no debt.

Now to the second error: supply's form. If we looked just past the form at its content, we would recognize the form as being instrumental only – and not as the source of supply. Remember the axiom: As Above – so Below. We can illustrate this in two ways, we shall examine the first: we have said, a physical law is a reflection of a cosmic principle on the physical level. The moment we create a vacuum and do not seal it well, mother nature rushes in and fills it instantly. Nature must do this to remain in balance. If we create an imbalance in our money supply – or in any aspect of our lives for that matter – life must rush in and fill the vacuum we create. We create a need, life fulfils the need. If we allow it. But this is precisely the crux of the matter: having turned every truth one hundred and eighty degrees around, we have sealed off the vacuum too well with our attitudes and thinking. If we just stopped and pondered what money really is, the scales would certainly fall from our eyes. As usual, we do not see the forest, because of too many trees being in the way.

The form of money as such catches all our attention and we miss the grand idea behind its form. So we land right in the midst of polarities once more and choose between two of them: we despise money or worship it, and those seeing it as a necessary evil feel contempt all the same, only to a lesser degree.

The second 'As Above so Below' illustration should help us to recognize legal tender's REAL nature: a mother gives her child a hearty hug and should the child desire more – the mother gives, the child receives, even if the child wishes for ten thousand more. To check her bag of warm and fuzzy hugs, to see if their supply is running short – this she would regard as sheer lunacy. The more love she gives, the more love she has. Yet to the delivery man at the door who claims the same of her in the form of paper and a few pieces of silver, she cannot give what he is wishing for. She finds these materials lacking. And what is astounding here, to say the least, she finds this way of thinking quite in order.

It is most interesting to observe the Ego's hand in this, how subtly it leads us astray again. Love given freely in form of a warm hug is quite in order with its mad philosophy. But the same energy dressed in material form, the Ego's sole identity, becomes reversed. Now its supply is limited. The man at her door – or any other receiver of our legal tender, for that matter – does not deserve a warm and fuzzy hug, and when he finally gets his hug, we give it reluctantly and all the love has drained from it. Now it is cold and prickly. This he 'deserves'.

Surely, if we are reluctant to part with a hug, then love and warmth have left the hug – the hug becomes cold, if not prickly now. The whole message we thus convey to the receiver is: You are not deserving of my love. And if pieces of paper and some little metal discs are eventually handed to the man at our door, he looks at them and reads: In God we trust. That now supply runs short must come as no surprise, – the result of universal laws turned upside down. The energy we give can only be fear or love, regardless of the form we wrap it in. Withholding love immediately withholds supply. Many find it hard to give love, for to these it means 'to part' with, as if love were now less. It then becomes painful to part with love, especially when in material form and most specifically when in the form of money. We moan and groan when it comes to paying bills.

The meaning of giving dropped from the verb 'pay'. We pay respect, homage, a compliment etc. The word there carries the meaning of giving, to please. As if giving money differed from any other giving. Giving is giving. Its form matters not. Why giving IS receiving, we shall see later on.

To Bargain Is To Bar Gain.

We bargain prices, another word for haggling. Some of us even take great pride in being thrifty bargainers.

How would it strike us if we substituted hugs for Dollars and overheard two men bargaining? The shopper asks: 'How much are these goods?' The vendor replies: 'One dozen hugs, Sir, but if you hug me now (cash) I will give you a discount of two hugs.' – 'No, thank you, I only want to hug you eight times for these goods. If you settled for eight, I would be agreeable.' The vendor agrees, receives eight prickly hugs and smugly rubs his hands behind the parting shopper, congratulating himself for his splendid sales talents, because the goods given away for eight hugs, he valued at only six. The man, once outside, meets with his wife and delights: 'Imagine, I succeeded in obtaining one dozen hugs worth, for only eight.' And she, the wife, congratulates herself for having such an extremely smart husband.

The act of bargaining reflects the clearest form of worldly giving: the withholding of love. It should give cause for contemplation, when we consider the world's poorest nations as being the ones where bargaining has become a way of life. More poignantly: where withholding love from one's brother has become the accepted norm and thus the cause of poverty.

Our use of credit cards shows clearly how we withhold love. 'Give me some love now – I shall return it later'. 'That's fine,' says the finance company, 'as long as you give us quite a bit of extra love (interest) on top'.

Facing our real attitudes courageously may not be very palatable, but it nonetheless remains a fact that we make deals and bargains with love. What about our ability to give love with love when we must repay a debt to some impersonal financial institution or pay our taxes? Then this ability is heavily taxed for now we fail to see the receiver as being lovable. The receiver is always lovable, because in reality we give but to our SELF. Which form the SELF assumes as the receiver matters not at all. I AM gives to I AM, that is 'All-There-Is' to it. However, as these last few sentences will cause many a reader to swallow hard, an expanded definition seems appropriate:

The officialdom of any nation merely reflects the Spirit of that nation. There are those who would, and do, sell their soul for positions of power and the rest are the lukewarm who have abdicated their ability and right to think for themselves, hence have reduced themselves to receivers of orders. There is no one to blame. The attitude suggested above does not suppose that we enthusiastically agree with every claim officialdom issues forth, thus only helping to finance the prison it builds around its brothers. It does not suggest we condone attitudes of total lovelessness. If bureaucracy had its way, then it would draw every single soul into the cobwebs of its joyless, grizzling world of stifling rules and regulations and make the rest of mankind the cow to be eternally milked. What it does advocate is this: Hardened hearts are still children of God, however steeped in egotistic schemes, therefore they are lovable all the same. Whatever their conduct may be, they are part of humanity as you and I. It is one humanity growing and learning, working its way through from darkness to Light, even though mostly by mistakes. Singling out groups within humanity as undesirable on grounds of misconduct would create an imbalance of polarities once more. That many of these brothers have forgotten their role as servants to the whole and want to play masters and rulers instead does not change the fact of their Being being the same as ours. Remember, this is a free-will universe where 'everything goes'. They have come here to learn, the same as you and I, although they, as most others, forgot this very fact and are lost in their sandbox instead. But they are still learning. Their hunger for control is simply born of the fear of not being in control. They have not discovered love as a principle of State as yet. They, as everyone else reluctant in stepping into the light of love, have a very rude awakening in store. The coming years will see every single recalcitrant heart mightily humbled and many a troubled soul will wish he had listened to the chimes of his conscience. Seeing these fellow humans in this light does away with the them and us attitude. Now we see anew and with this new perspective we recognize bureaucracy as perceiving itself as extremely unloved, hence unwanted. Whatever is unloved will try to substitute this lack with the imposition of power and enslavement or attack. Seeing thus we do not blame but understand. Now when it comes to the act of giving, whatever it is we give, we shall give freely and not in a begrudging spirit. We give without blame. If anything, then these fellow humans are deserving of our compassion and unconditional love, for they experience not the profound enrichment of the soul, the joy which comes from deeply and truly caring for one's brothers and sisters. The only reward their frigid hearts encounter is the transient and shallow satisfaction of Self-gain. Perhaps we should consider that it is only complacency and apathy on our behalf which allows souls in their infancy positions of control. Ultimately their presence serves as an excellent opportunity for forgiveness. Only love will heal – real love and not conformity, which will only cement the belief in those brothers, that happiness is attainable through power and Self-gratification.

Returning to the subject of bargaining, examining the real reasoning behind this concept reveals unpleasant facts. We imagine two people in love. The world adores lovers and romance, for it senses union here and true giving – the giving of Self to SELF. But altered state of Being is quickly off its mark and offers its reversed version of truth again. The giving of Self to SELF becomes the gift of Self to Self.

Before we continue with this examination, the assurance seems in place here that no judgment at all is laid upon the lovers of this world. They too are here to learn as every other soul. The following illustration touches a very delicate chord in all of us. Although our understanding of love is a reversed one, for love is reality – exactly what we deny – we nevertheless regard it as our highest virtue. Observing our lovers now, we see this: They ache for each other, seek each other's company wherever possible – in short, they need each other. The most noble feelings the heart contains are now experienced here. And truly, this is the closest man ever comes to see his SELF in the other's heart. This is the reason for romance's appeal. She worships him – he worships her. 'Ask what you will – I shall surrender it with ease, if only I can be ONE with you,' says each to the other soul.

Beauty is here, trust and open hearts and wonderful it is indeed, there is no doubt at all, if it were not for the value each one puts onto its Self. But what is really taking place here is a bargain, which robs the romance of its true virtue: union. The soul, yearning for completion, knowing in its heart of hearts it is not complete, seeks to complete itself with its Divine SELF. The altered state of mind obscures this goal and leads away from where union could be found. Its identity being the body, it now points to another body and says: 'Unite'. Two Body Selves make not ONE SELF.

In truth, each lover values the other more than his or her own Self. And so the bargain is struck. What these two do not say in words is really this: 'I give my Self, which I value less than you, to you and in return I receive your Self, which I value more. This way I shall be complete'. Obviously, the one I gave my discounted Self to must have picked the shorter straw. Therefore both made a bad 'deal', each one believing to have won the lottery. What bad deals have in common is that they leave a bad aftertaste, which burps up at the time of divorce.

We may, perhaps, observe our own resistance, if not outright indignation, to the acceptance of this version – for this touches the very core of our hearts – and our own Ego feels very threatened. Its instant reaction would most likely be total rejection of such insane claims or at best, be extremely resourceful in finding arguments for its case.

Instead of the lovers, we could have observed the purchase of a second-hand car: 'Give me the best for the least.' We might as well say: 'Give me two Dollars for one' or: 'Give me more for less.' In truth we say: 'I want to give as little love as possible and in return I want as much as I can get!' As both parties are motivated by the same upside-down philosophy, their true gift to each other is rejection instead of love. Cold 'pricklies' instead of warm 'fuzzies'.

The thought of a bargain always implies the notion of getting a value for a lesser value. This implies the subconscious assumption that nature tolerates imbalances. However, the Law of Compensation ensures that this cannot work. The gain a man withholds from his brother, becomes his own deprivation.

For example: a person, on receiving a gift, thinks; 'I got this for nothing.' This thought alone is the evaluation of the gift. The equivalent value of the gift was estimated as zero – as nothing. The Law of Compensation will now create a balance – it zeroes the gift. There are of course a thousand ways for nature to do that. The way the balance is created is not so interesting as the fact that a delay in its execution adds 'interest' to the value, which will have to be balanced. Another most enlightening point concerning the matter is this: the more we are aware of this law, the more immediate is its execution as a result of its transgression. There is no element of punishment in the process of balance, it is simply a balance. The execution of this law in the case of the person with the gift happens most likely in one of three manners: we lose or break the gift, or secondly purchase an item of equal value and lose or break that one. The third most likely manner of balance would see us being disadvantaged in some transaction, exactly to the value of the devalued gift plus 'interest'.

As long as we remain under the influence of the Law of Compensation by virtue of false perception, an item purchased holds the exact value which we ascribe to our payment of it. If we think we overpaid and the item should have been, say, twenty per cent less than its price, then what we purchased will hold the value we ascribed to it, and not what we paid. This should reveal the fallacy of bargaining. The more we haggle the price down, the less we value the item; and this is the value the item holds for us once received. This ought to be news for those among us who believe in getting by simply taking from another's property.

Another illustration: we purchase a second-hand car and feel quite smart in beating down the price. Say, the price is $8,000 and we 'succeed' in achieving a discount of ten percent. What we are really doing is this: we decree the value of the car, and that is $7,200, yet believe we received $8,000 for $7,200, unaware of the fact of having created an imbalance to the value of $800. The correction of the imbalance occurs now most likely after the expiry date of the car's warranty. Now we have to face repairs to the value of the discount plus accrued interest.

Let no man doubt this law by saying the vendor overpriced the vehicle in the first place, expecting the car to be discounted. If the discount is offered as a sales gimmick without encouragement on our behalf, then this is acceptable, if not, then the vehicle shall give us extra joy and pleasure to the extent of the inflated price. This law does not only apply to material things, it covers ad infinitum every experience. The value we give a person, condition or situation, is the value given back to us. To evaluate a situation as bad must inevitably result in the experience of another bad situation. It must be so, for nature has to create a balance. Thus the reason for balancing polarities. To free oneself from the Law of Compensation or 'Karma', that is to live by Grace, we have to unify polarities and acknowledge SELF as the Source of unlimited supply.

Having examined bargaining as such, one begins to contemplate the virtue in a beggar. At least his demand for gain is based on honesty. He foregoes pretence. So much for bargaining, which is one edge of a two-edged sword.

The other we know as competition; the rivalry between parties or individuals to outdo, outsell, outrun, outsmart, in brief: outgain one another altogether. This is plainly based on the fear of one party succeeding in biting off a greater chunk from a limited supply than oneself. The stress is here on limited supply, the underlying false perception of Life's bounty.

Competition necessitates the devaluation of one's fellowman and inflation of oneself. This is very evident in the field of sport. At closer inspection, the friendly competition reveals jealousies, grim ambitions and many a broken dream. Major games, originally designed to bring nations together, display the fierce intent for victory to such extent one feels a hint of shame while looking on. Here are nations assembled to create a hierarchy of heroes, and under smiling faces one detects the pain and melancholy of loss. These must certainly be heydays for the altered state of mind. Victory implies loss, the Ego's preferred battleground.

Commerce, on the other hand, prefers a low key environment for its dubious deeds. But here the Ego's forces are unleashed and often, nation rises against nation in the devouring game of competition, justified as the 'name of the game'. However, commerce stands not so much in need of Self-aggrandizement. Instead, the naked force of greed assumes the place of ancient virtues, such as honesty, fair play and the sincere desire to satisfy its brother's needs with the intent to please. Cooperation replacing competition, would demonstrate the choice of True perception. Be it the owner of a small market stand, tycoons, stock markets or the 'big' world of finance and politics, all are motivated by the fear of lack. Greed for power is fear of lack of supply all the same. If man only knew how different it could be at no price to him at all but the release of fear. The cost of his game is beyond estimate, because the price he lays down at the Ego's altar is his very SELF.

Love must be allowed to rush in and this we can do only by releasing fear. To love we first must learn the love of SELF, the God in us, before it can be extended to those around. If we do not love our SELF, how can we love another? In a different way: if contact has not been made with our own Source, how can we let love flow to others – from which source could it spring forth and flow?

Currency Is Consciousness.

Some of the most beautiful and uplifting words ever spoken on the Law of Supply we find in the Sermon on the Mount, [Matthew 7:24]:

24. No man can serve two masters: for either he will hate the one, or love the other; or else he will hold to the one, and despise the other. Ye cannot serve God and mammon.

25. Therefore I say unto you, Take no thought for your life, what ye shall eat, or what ye shall drink, nor yet for your body, what ye shall put on. Is not the life more than meat, and the body than raiment?

26. Behold the fowls of the air: for they sow not, neither do they reap, nor gather into barns; yet your heavenly father feedeth them. Are ye not much better than they?

27. Which of you by taking thought can add one cubit unto his stature?

28. And why take ye thought for raiment? Consider the lilies of the field, how they grow; they toil not, neither do they spin:

29. And yet I say unto you, That even Solomon in all his glory was not arrayed like one of these.

30. Wherefore, if God so clothe the grass of the field, which today is, and tomorrow is cast into the oven, shall he not much more clothe you, O ye of little faith?

31. Therefore take no thought, saying, What shall we eat? or, What shall we drink? or, Wherewithal shall we be clothed?

32. (For after all those things the Gentiles seek:) for your heavenly Father knoweth that ye have need of all these things.

33. But seek ye first the kingdom of God, and his righteousness; and all these things shall be added onto you.

How much more clearly can the message be expressed? The kingdom of God is within, is our very Being. Two thousand years ago, our awareness did not allow a comprehension of a concept of God as being other than outside of us – a personal God, somewhere beyond the clouds or stars.

Throughout the ages, we insisted on denying Spirit, our God-SELF, and searched in the realm of matter for answers. And in this realm we have, admittedly, come very far – but our creations are not the answer to our quest.

The industrial revolution expanded into the Age of Information, with the electronic media now transmitting data within seconds around the globe. And if the altered state of mind alone had its say, then transmission of negative information would only stabilize false perception further. But fortunately, something else has happened. Spirit uses Man's very creation, the electronic media, on a scale never seen before, to bring the message home. Movies familiarizing us with the picture of a universe teeming with life, songs which trigger an uplifting force in us, music which reaches into the deepest recesses of our hearts, recalling the soul's ancient memories of joy and exuberance, books by the thousands speaking of ONE life, speaking of a joyous, unfolding universe – all reach into the homes and hearts of millions upon millions – we are not alone.

Spirit-Selves are pressing to unite with body-Selves, and in the measure of these truths finding their way into our hearts, we release fear. And gradually fear becomes less until we see it for what it really is – the looming cloud the novice pilot feared. And now it dissipates and reveals what it had covered up so well over eons in time: the radiant, sparkling jewel of love. And with the deepest sigh of relief this universe has ever heard, we say: 'It is done – I shall fear no more!' And it is then when SELF rushes in to unite with the body Self.

Now we are love, and therefore have all that love contains, and love can only increase by giving its SELF. As we give, so we receive. This fact emerges most lucidly in the moral deterioration following an empty purse. Worse is then added to worse.

'For unto everyone that hath, shall be given, and he shall have abundance: but from him that hath not, shall be taken away even that which he hath'. [Matthew 25:29].

The real meaning of this ought to be clear: 'Those who love, their love shall increase. And those who do not love, they shall lose the little they have.' The more love we give, the more we shall have. This is not wishful thinking. Love, the all pervading universal energy, can only be increased by sharing. This thought reverses worldly thinking, especially when we are reminded of money. This world sees giving as giving away. To give, here, is seen as taking from a limited store and now the store is store minus gift.

The above Bible citation is in perfect accordance with the Law of Supply, which states: My Being is my sustenance. God's Being can only be Love.

Currency in the form of money is but one form of the universal energy of love. Love, as the Source of ALL, can assume any form to meet a specific need. The need for a convertible energy on the physical level is met by money, one of the forms of the energy love in the material, the world of matter.

Everything that exists is love in one form or another. Our supply is a direct reflection of our ability to give love and to give with love. It follows then, that Currency is consciousness. The Ego would prefer to see this thought as polarities – rich and poor. But this is not so. The meaning here is not to depict a rich man as having a greater capacity for love than his poorer brother. The meaning is the perfect supply of our needs. The rich man may have more or different needs than the poor. If his need is to be a multimillionaire, then this need shall be met. Caution here – let us not mock this thought, for to this man, being a millionaire is a genuine need. He needs this experience to instruct his soul with the feeling of it. He may have come for that specific reason into this particular lifestream. Notwithstanding its real purpose as a learning aid, it is a need to him all the same. A poor man, in contrast to his richer brother, may take offence to material possessions, thus his needs may not necessarily be furnishable through the medium of monetary currency. Love shall supply here too. So, terms as rich and poor ought to be interpreted on the level of form content, not on the level of form itself. The content simply projects the love capacity of each. The poorer man's capacity could well exceed the rich man's ability to love.

Too easily is quantity, in this world, mistaken for quality. That currency is consciousness is clearly recognized in a nation's economy. At closer inspection, a depressed economy always reveals itself as the material reflection of its national consciousness. If this one is fear-motivated, it shall condense in a depressed state of consciousness. That its economy follows suit is only logical. The same holds true for a business, a family or a single person.

If the entire wealth of this planet would be distributed equally to every man and woman, within two years the rich would be rich and the poor, poor again. Our consciousness is the determining and deciding factor for the degree of our prosperity. It follows then that consciousness is the actual currency. Physical currency is merely another mirror of this consciousness and is therefore instrumental and not causal.

An impoverished state of mind (lack of love) by compulsion projects its image into the world of matter. Love, in the form of currency, has limited power to supply, but love can supply unlimited currency. And currency may appear in countless forms, money being only one of these. This means love is convertible.

A certain wealthy lady may be in a depressed state of mind. Her need is not love in form of money, but love in its formless state. Love will heal her, supply her need. Another person, let us say a poor man, may also be in a depressed state of mind and an observer could easily be forgiven for assuming his poverty to be the cause of his depression. Not so – lack of any kind is always lack of love. His poverty is the result of a depressed state of mind. And it is not – as one could also be easily forgiven for assuming – a case of either lack of Self-love or lack of love of others, but always lack of love of SELF. It has to be, for let us consider: if his Being is his sustenance – for his Being to supply, it has to be contacted first to establish the flow.

Acknowledgment of one's Being as the Source of all supply alone is enough to call it forth. This becomes recognition and love can flow. His Being then brings forth the universal energy of love, which then translates itself into the many forms he requires to satisfy his needs. The emphasis is here on 'bringing forth' – from within, as the Apple Tree does and does without effort.

But back to our poor man: as depression breeds depression, self-help seems unlikely, so we send help in the form of a compassionate lady. Here is a vital point in the understanding of the Law of Supply: our man has put himself in a barren state of mind, his Being is almost completely denied as the source of supply.

He cannot draw on his Source for supply, but the love of a fellowman can. Love can be given in the same way as currency, for love is convertible. Once given, it will convert itself into the forms of supply the poor man requires. So the compassionate lady not only lifts the man from his depression into a sunnier state of mind, but curious little events begin to improve the man's pocketbook affairs. Why? Because love has entered, where it was absent before. Now, if resistance is not offered, this love can supply the man's foremost need: it may open his heart so he may find his own Source of love – his Being.

This little illustration serves the sole purpose of pointing out the convertible power of love. The currency love improved both – mind and purse. Although love in the form of money was not given, all the same, this need was supplied as well. By now the irony of this game we play should be obvious. Currency being but the physical form of the universal energy of love – in pursuit of currency, we really are in pursuit of love.

As love can only be increased by giving, the game of 'getting' achieves the opposite. Again we see: emphasis on one polarity calls the opposite polarity into action.

So when we truly love something within this earthly realm, in a manner which invalidates the unloved, we single it out as a fragment of the puzzle and love only just that. And what we do not love we mostly reject as undesirable – a milder form of hate.

The degree of hate is meaningless. It is still hate, it is a degree of. This should remind us how strongly the learning extracted from the Balance of Polarities is needed here.

To love something in this world as True perception would, we have to love everything alike, meaning we grant every thing an equal right to be. Then we may have our preferences, but still evaluate all as expressions of love. This may very well be a stumbling block for many. For how can we love the unlovable? By learning to see past the form aspect and see the form content.

This learning to see past the form aspect is really not a learning process. We use this word 'learning' throughout this material for convenience of expression. It is rather a remembering of one's knowledge. Rephrasing the above statement we say: by remembering our identity, we look past the form aspect as naturally as breathing. The instant we know who we really are, the unlovable are recognized as the same I AM as ours.

To despise my left hand for being soiled would seem, at best, extremely unreasonable. Insisting on rejecting it, the day might come where I do not recognize it as my own hand. Each time now it wishes to be recognized and accepted, I either slap it or run away from it. An onlooker would, most likely, esteem me a trifle out of touch with reality. Yet this is exactly the case with our response to our brothers and sisters. However much we fear or despise, therefore flee or fight, we cannot get away from them. My brother and my sister are my left and right hand. They are my eyes – they are my heart – they are ME. To 'get rid' of them, the unlovable, I have to 'get rid' of ME, and to do that I have to tear my heart out. And this is precisely what we, as humanity, did. We tore our heart out – meaning we tore love out. Now we have none to give. So to love the unlovable is not to face him and think: 'Wow, how can I love this despicable so and so?' This leads only deeper into the mire of separation. To love these is to love ME! By discovering my BEING I discover theirs as MINE.

Let us stop seeing in these words only words. Let us practice! The very chair we are sitting on is the I AM. Does this come as a shock? Atoms are held together by consciousness. Consciousness is BEING, is the I AM. The chair would disintegrate if consciousness left its atoms. Everything that is, is LOVE in one form or another. The implication of this should send minds spinning, if fully comprehended. The breakdown of our car on the highway is the same as the breakdown of someone's heart in a heart 'attack'. The heart did not attack – IT was attacked (love was denied). The car on the road was not included in the magic of life. It was regarded as just another piece of dead matter.

It was not valued as life, therefore singled out and fixation set in. We heard: fixation is when things do not function any more – be it heart or motor. They are atoms imbued with consciousness.

Everything that enters our field of awareness has not only consciousness, it IS consciousness. The very carpet we walk on is
consciousness. There is no such thing as dead matter. How could
there be, if God is All-There-Is? God does not know how to die!
This is the one truth plaguing the altered Ego most.

So the next time we hear that 'silly' old lady speak to her pot-
plant words of love, we might be in doubt as to who is actually
being silly.

Increase Through Extension.

Our Being is LOVE. There is nothing and no thing love cannot
supply. Be it money, if this be our need, or be it a partner, a
companion, an insight or forgiveness – the form the need requires
to be satisfied is completely irrelevant. Love knows not of degrees
of difficulty in the giving of its SELF. It just simply gives its SELF
in the individually most suitable and required form, if it is allowed
in. Our needs are known to it before our body-Self is even aware
of any need. In the pursuit of money, we constantly affirm its lack.
Why else would we pursue it? Lack is the result of the fear of not
having enough. Our hunt for supply is therefore based on fear. We
even fear each other. We take great care not to be disadvantaged
by our fellowman, yet would have no cause to lose sleep over if
we invested greater care in not cheating him.

Once love has been acknowledged as our Source of ALL
supply – our Being in other words – it must be extended to be able
to flow. This point cannot be repeated enough. This is the real
secret of prosperity. One who sincerely desires to find the secret
of prosperity (not only money, remember?), to learn about the
Law of Supply, cannot and will not do so, unless he comprehends
the fundamental truth of love's increase through extension.

If love is not extended it cannot fulfil its own nature, which IS
extension. Love in the heart of man, when not extended, shrivels
up, recoils within itself. We may be tempted to believe that to
extend love is to walk around this planet and willy-nilly hand out
warm fuzzies, regardless if our brothers like it or not. Being
sincere about this we recognize: love is extending Being – is
acknowledging the same Being as ours in our brother. To share

my Being with my brother, I must look past his body at his real SELF, his Being. Inevitably I see his Being as his Source and before long, I recognize both, my SELF and his, to be of the same Source. That is true sharing. I can do this very well without ever speaking a word to him. This sharing occurs within the quiet of one's heart. It then may very well take on any form this life can possibly provide, but must, of need, be born first in the heart.

Now when a fellowman approaches, claiming a response to his need, whatever it may be – how can we possibly withhold? For all he is really asking for is love. He may be still immersed in his own game of 'getting', but this matters not. We learned – what does not matter will not materialize. His values are based on his reality of loss, that loss of any kind is possible – through the act of giving away. These, his values, shall never materialize for us.

The currency, the form of love he claims, is totally irrelevant. If it be money – so be it – so we give, to us it is all the SAME. And if his claim exceeds all bounds of decency, we may communicate our argument, not born of scorn, and fear of loss – but rather in the manner a parent corrects a misbehaving child. But we still give, not necessarily all in the form he claimed, but certainly we healed through the response of love. For we communicated, listened to his needs, and this is really what his need was all about.

And should his claim be in form of an attack, let not indignation and outrage direct our response. For if this is what we truly feel, then we must not deceive ourselves. If suppression of such feelings is outright denial of these, then we do more harm, to ourselves and our man, than good. In such a case, we shall air our frustration, it is a safety valve. A righteous anger can cause some wind, but wind can also clean the air. For all it means is we have not understood as yet. And this is perfectly in order. To feign feelings we do not have would certainly not be in order. But if there is a chance to calmly remember what we have learned, we can then look at the idea behind the form of his attack. Deeming himself as a separate Self, he has to be deprived of love. So his attack is just a twisted call for love. And desperate he must be in his thirst for love, so let us not reject his cry for help. Outwardly he may rage and rant just for a little while. If his claim be justified, we give, we pay. If not, with love's approach we will, most likely, find a mutually agreeable solution.

If all this fails, if his heart seems hardened, not approachable by love, then we pay him anyway, whatever the currency he claims, for we know it to be love. To him it is the only form of love acceptable at present.

Love, we know, once accepted in whatever currency, converts itself into the help he really needs – finds its way into his heart – be he aware of this or not. And it begins to open what was hardened until then, and slowly he discovers his own Being as the Source. Love was extended and thus increased. We prosper and our brother too. My Being can only give to his Being, and both in truth are ONE BEING, it follows then, that Love gives unto itself. This is why giving is receiving.

Its very nature being extension, it extends in return and so forever increases. In giving a material thing, it certainly seems as if it has been given away. Seeing its value in its form we are certain this value is now gone. This, of course, is false perception. Now let us see aright: the object given, the material form, is representing of the love we gave it with. Love now extends itself, and always returns in the form we can use best – its value always being greater than the value we ascribed to the gift we gave.

This helps us better understand why not to be concerned if debts are not repaid. The Ego wants to fight and take matters to court, because it sees these matters on the material level, where everything that matters enough to arouse resistance – fight – must materialize its opposite polarity. Neither party in the end is any better off, though on the surface they may seem to be. Yet probing past the form of the legal confrontation into its content, we see both parties embattled in the war of polarities, for both believe in gain and loss. And as we know, the only fruit battlefields produce is further fear.

True perception, however, would rest in complete security on the Law of Supply, which simply states that love given in any form must return increased. Through which particular individual or channel this return flows unto me is of no significance, for Being gives to Being, which is Itself.

Here one subtle point: if love were given in order for love to be returned, then what was given in the first place was certainly not love. Whatever it was – it was given for gain. The very essence of love is to love for love's sake, not for its return. Otherwise we would be back to bargaining. And now it becomes a different matter, for it is easy to love the lovable. But who can love the unlovable? We can put into practice what we learned in the Balance of Polarities regarding this question.

We happen to stroll through a market and discover a stand with sweets. The fellow behind the counter looks at us with shifty lizard eyes and is about as warm and human as a shark. He charges inflated prices and he looks as if he is the type to kick his dog. To make matters worse – he shouts rudely at our oh-so-sweet and innocent five year old, who was just in the process of consuming the entire contents of one of his cookie jars. Vibrations now are not exactly harmonious. How can we give him our money – love – with love, when all we feel like is slamming it – cold pricklies – on the counter? Here again: if we feel like slamming, we shall slam.

Remember? Suppression of feelings is denial – transmutation of these is not. The biggest mistake would be Self-denial. As great a mistake it is to deny the God-SELF in us, as great is the mistake to deny, that is suppress, the personality Self. Denial is not required – integration and transmutation is. We ought to be at all times true to ourself and not feign feelings we do not have. So we slam and shout back at him, if it makes us feel better – it is alright.

So back to our question: who can hand money to this man with the genuine feeling that he be deserving of kindness and love? The answer is simple enough: love can. Once our Being, our Source, is acknowledged as the giver of all gifts, and not the personality Self, then giving to this man with love is a pleasure and comes very, very naturally. There is no strain involved in this way of giving. Love gives to his Being, gives to its SELF, which is his Being and mine. We may even be jesting and squeeze a smile out of the sour grape.

A brief recapitulation: MY BEING IS MY SUSTENANCE. This is the Law of Supply. Everything that exists is the energy aspect of love in a limitless diversity of form. Money is only one of these forms. For love to flow it has to spring from its source and must be allowed to flow. As each human being is an individual expression of God, his Being is therefore love's source. Denial of the God in us blocks the flow, therefore blocks supply. Acknowledgment of one's Source releases the flow in proportion to one's identification with one's Source, one's Being, the I AM.

191

We imagine once more our Apple tree. One of its branches has a mad little dream and imagines it is a tree on its own. It has all the power of the tree and as such, makes the dream its reality. It forsakes the tree, dreams it falls to the ground and for a while, things go well. It is still full of juice and even sprouts a few new shoots. But after a while its juices do not flow as they used to, and it begins to struggle. The fruit it so desired to bring forth are, at best, little, shrivelled up, pathetic-looking apples. Besides, all kind of creatures trample on it without any consideration. It feels alone, frail and uncared for, its dark green leaves are dry and but a shadow of their former selves and so the branch begins to accuse the tree for leaving it in such misery. The tree responds with the call to awaken. It sends small birds to it, messengers, which begin to sing to the little branch, that its experience is only a dream and urge it to awaken and to stop pretence.

The tree yearns for its branch to awaken and to participate again in full awareness of its bounteous dance of life. Yet the branch insists on its dream, but feels its juices running dry – it withers and dies. Its death does not release it from its dream, of course, its death is the central theme of the dream. It feels somehow relieved, the place it finds itself in seems untroubled and so peaceful, but soon it remembers again its desire to be a tree on its own. Now it slips from this dream back to its original dream of being a separate branch. Again the birds come, this time larger ones and chirp and sing to it the song of life and plead with it to hurry up and join them in their play.

And so it continues its round of dreams within dreams, until a million dreams go past. Then one day, the song of an especially persistent bird pierces its dream. And somehow, for the first time, an ancient memory begins to stir, it feels the promise of something so much greater than its misery. It takes courage and has a good look at its 'reality', and concludes it to be actually quite boring and laborious.

So it dares to open an eye and lo – it feels its juices flowing and finds itself as part of the tree. It now opens the other eye and before long it knows it IS the tree, for where does the tree begin and where does it end? And now the joy is great. All the birds celebrate together the awakening of the little branch. And their song of jubilance echoes throughout the universe and every star in every galaxy joins the festivity – their light seems so much brighter now. The little branch has finally come home. The Apple tree is complete once more.

A children's bedtime story? Hardly!

The second most vital point in the full comprehension of the Law of Supply is the nature of love: Increase through extension. Love, to be itself, must extend its SELF. This is the reason why giving, in the spirit of love, increases and not diminishes. As ALL IS LOVE, it is irrelevant the form we give. Its content is always love.

My Being is my sustenance – this is the grand Law of Supply. If fully understood and implemented in our lives, lack of any kind is inconceivable. Its implementation serves a seeming double function. At first, it is seen as supplying our every need. This then is a grand self-demonstration to us in pointing to our power Source. Increasingly we now acknowledge it and recognize eventually in IT our very SELF.

Once this occurs, our only need we ever really had is thus supplied, the union with our very SELF.

Chapter 6

Self-Reliance

Or the Practice of True perception

True perception, we know, relies on SELF. Although we begin to walk shakily in its new boots, we take a few more steps – even try an arabesque and we are convinced. We are ready to take the world by storm, open the door and step out into the mainstream of human attitudes, and POW!, are swept right out of our new shoes. And why? The shoes were too big for us, or we were too small for them. Whichever way we look at it, they did not fit.

The Ego is quick to blame the shoes, yet we see through its tricks. So we resign to some more home work and try again. We walk and now get blisters. Why? Because we are too large for our boots. How is this possible, we ponder, but the Ego could tell us why, for it inflated us in its game of spiritual pride. So we take off our boots, soothe our wounds and eat humble pie for a while. But we learn. Now we try again. This time we know the fiercest hurricane could not lift us out of our boots. Now our step has bounce. We walk through thistles and through fire. What powerful boots we have. With these we could kick any attack into oblivion. Chances not wanting, we do just that and break our toes in the process of it. We take off our boots again and hurl them into some forgotten corner. While our bones mend we return to humble diet once more and bemoan our lot. We feel cheated and betrayed. But, as time goes by, we begin to sense that power cannot be possessed and thus cannot be used.

Power IS. As we heard before, the rising sun does not fight the night; by its very presence the night transmutes into a glorious new day, and we begin to comprehend the magnanimity behind the understanding of True perception:

Ultimate Power is ultimate vulnerability. So we learn to walk barefoot.

If God IS then fear is NOT, hence I lay down my sword and shield and bare myself to the partaking of my SELF.

To meet the world and its Global Thoughtform in the budding stage of True perception can be disheartening indeed. It can be likened to a tender plant weathering its first storm. Therefore I say: have mercy on yourself, and do not judge yourself for being sucked back into the world of make-believe at times. It is alright. The young plant having just lived through a storm can barely take the full brunt of the sunshine either. For a while its leaves wilt sadly, yet, in time, the tender shoot becomes a promising sapling and before long we see a mighty oak tree in its making.

The secret in the stabilization of True perception is the unshakeable reliance and trust in one's SELF, the God I AM. This, of course is the reversal of an altered state of mind, which leans on popular attitudes, superstition of all kind and utilizes the crutch of conformity most heavily. To be truthful to one's SELF is the anchor of True perception, for this cannot be shifted even by king tides. The world will resent us for it, mock at times, and ridicule. Yet it is intrigued, because it senses its lost treasure here.

Whenever we encounter nonconformity, we conform. The picture of the prattling adult leaning over the prattling babe tells the whole story in itself. For who causes who to prattle? The babe, vulnerable and helpless, totally true to its SELF, has the adults serve at its tiny feet.

The first to break away from the rigid and stifling rules of society will cause the weaker ones to imitate, often forming a cult, be it saint, hippie, punk or oppressor – it matters not. Power will be given to the one who reclaims his own.

A man does not receive the contempt of the crowd for being saint or punk, but for having dared what they dared not – for breaking away from the herd. Society detests nonconformity, because it always stands in disapproval of the rules of its game, which it knows itself as boring and exhausting, but finds itself unable to leave for the habitual vice of denying the Spirit within, and hence, for want of strength. Nothing great has ever entered through the door of conformity. It is by abandoning the beaten tracks that we shake off their dust. It is by daring and enthusiasm that we step into unknown territory and behold new beauty. It is when the winds blow away the fogs that the rising sun is seen. New horizons are not discovered by staying at home and dusting the books which speak of them. No soul has ever risen to any heights by accepting the boundaries of the stuffy rules and laws of the timid. It was when the 'flat Earth' disciples were mothballed that the Earth became a sphere. It is no challenge to the soul to grizzle with the discontent over the politics and commerce of the day, but to draw grander circles and rise into Light where all things are made new.

In defiance of the Law of God, man made his own, the folly of insulting his own intelligence, for it is debasing and a blatant display of lovelessness. Here the collective lack of character, the void of compassion and absence of sincere care for one's brother is filled with the wizardry of hollow words and meaningless terms, sanctified by a humanity steeped in complacency. It is called moral decay, regardless of the verbal face-lifts we try to hide it under. We allow the noble values of life to be vitiated to the extent that the scheming of Self-gratification receives the stamp of legal consent – the perfect environment to retard the growth of the soul. We, the children of One God, of One Spirit, should BE ONE Spirit, but we have ignored our potential, have lost our way in the sandbox of space and time, the darkness of SELF-denial.

A man with trust in his SELF sets himself free, in the truest sense of the word, by surrendering to Divine Law, hence he sets his own standards, whether the world adopts these or not. He returns to the essence of man and that is I AM and abides by the Law of God. Therefore he is Law unto Himself. Let such a man be fool enough and proclaim this truth aloud and the mob is ready to stone him. How dare the Son of God be Law unto his SELF (which is God)! This is the one thing which outrages the Ego most – to dare to break the corral and leave its herd of mindless sheep and put power back where it belongs. Nothing reflects its insanity as clearly back to it as this, for it can only conceive of an image of a Self and not of the God-SELF, of which an awakened soul speaks.

This leads us to the biggest hurdle in the path of any awakening soul: the practice of SELF-reliance. Truth may have been under-stood but now it must be lived. So we shall define the hurdle and then see how we can remove it best.

The spiritual awakening of any individual is in the rarest of cases a swift process. Like a growing plant the soul unfolds and stretches in its own time. The ideal environment conducive for this unfoldment would see such a person surrounded by like-minded company. And this is exactly where the hurdle begins, for such a favourable climate hardly lends itself naturally. On the contrary, for now we are confronted with a world which does not speak our language, for now we recognize it as a mere regurgitation of the Ego's affirmations of negativity – where every hint at truth is watered down or avoided like the black plague. In short, we are surrounded by shallow living. Whereas only a short while ago we felt quite comfortable and at home in the grizzling world of Dollar arithmetics and survival – in this dark cloud we defined as our reality – we now begin to feel quite homeless.

This 'stretch' on our path between leaving our 'home' in society's reality and finding our true home in the God I AM within us is the march through the desert. Every awakening soul has to walk this distance eventually. It is the time when society's false God's have lost their grip on us, but by the same token we are not quite certain as yet of our true destiny. It is a time of vulnerability. It is here where one needs all the help one can get for it is this period in our development which exposes us to the distractions of society most, to its constant discouragement, and if not on guard, there is the danger of falling back into complacency, the stupor of SELF-denial. It is easy to be truthful to oneself in the shelter of one's home. But it needs a triumphant soul to step out into the midst of society and uphold its principles in the face of all adversity. It takes courage to proclaim: 'Henceforth I am my SELF, humbly and truly'. Differently expressed: it is easy to behold God in a blossom – it demands a deep rooted knowing to see nothing but that same God when faced with cruelty and chaos.

We said before, it is a lean march – like walking through a desert. Some attention is required here, so we better pack a backpack with supplies to see us safely through. The supplies in the main are faith and a one-pointed mind. The first no man can be taught – he either has it or he has it not. If he does not, he might as well turn back to where he came from. The second, the ability to focus, can be and must be acquired before we can hold our attention for any length of time. An altered state of mind is 'monkey-mind', is scattered (and cluttered) – jumps from one subject to another and can be likened to the flickering light of a candle – subject to the slightest draft. Spiritual mind is like a laser beam, and that is highly focused light, therefore very, very powerful. The issue then is to become one-pointed. The Global Thoughtform cannot enter into a one-pointed mind.

This process of focusing is not a doing, it is a process of becoming aware. In general it is a grossly misunderstood concept for what is it that we need to focus on? On the surface it appears as a paradox because the focus required is on un-focusing! A scientist, for example, studying an object under a microscope, of necessity restricts his awareness to the object he focuses his attention on. His whole attention is absorbed by the object he studies. In the measure of his focus he loses awareness of everything contained within the realms of his non-focus. It is exactly the same with souls journeying through the physical plane. In order to experience the physical realm we have to fine-focus. We pay a price for this and the price is called overview. To recapture the grander picture – the overview – we have to step back, meaning we un-focus. So this focus on un-focusing has nothing to do with furrowed brows and stressful concentration but it has all to do with allowance. We allow ourself to step back to take in the panorama. To focus then in this context is to hold the mind steadfast on a universal perspective in preference to limiting one's reality to the trivia of daily survival thinking.

The ability to focus, to become one-pointed, can be self-taught and this, of course, depends entirely on the intensity of one's desire to do so. There exist, of course, countless books suggesting equally countless methods and 'techniques' of how to gain 'mind-control', many of them claiming superiority over all others. In the end one is left as high and dry as before one was introduced to such methods. The reason for this is very simple: the majority of these suggestions work within the confines of the altered Ego's realm (because fear was not surrendered as yet), which will either leave us in a state of boredom or these methods become, most likely, distractions in themselves. With the exception of light visualizations, most techniques are rather useless. In fact they can create enormous pressure, because the energies generated with some of these methods cannot go anywhere, so to speak – they are held down by the lid, or plug, of survival-consciousness. The focus we speak of here bears no semblance to mind-control. On the contrary, we allow the mind to retreat, to step back, and in that measure the heart takes over. Control is the language of masculine energy. Allowance is the mark of feminine energy. Control restricts. Allowance sets free. The entire process of transmuting fear to love is the balance of masculine with feminine energy.

No, the answer is not a technique, it is something different. It is a replacement of habit. The greater part of an altered state of mind consists of habitual thinking (stabilized perception). The easiest way to release a habit is by replacing it with another one. This is done best not by ritual or technique but by schedule, which is the setting aside of certain time periods during each day dedicated to the Spirit within us. If followed through on a daily regular basis, it will develop into a most constructive habit. These periods of dedication to higher thought should be seen as the most sacred activity of our day. If undertaken in earnest, born of the deep desire to bring about real change, the benefit of these periods will soon spill over into the rest of our day. Not to mention that this move toward self-help is soon reinforced by that part of our SELF which perceives truly already, that which is still wholly Spirit in us, however much denied, regardless if we can accept this fact at our present stage of awakening or not.

The objective of this material is not to tell the reader what to do – that would be rather silly. The objective is to develop the tool of True perception, which is an understanding, a new way of seeing life. This is the tool the reader can take away from this material, a tool which he can apply in every walk of life. An understanding is something real, a technique is not, although the Ego would see it the other way around. A technique is at best but a crutch.

The above suggestion is not a recipe telling one what to do. Each person sincerely desiring an expansion of consciousness will gravitate naturally toward the kind of schedule best for him or her. No two souls are alike in their make-up, therefore each has different needs. The heart will tell if listened to. However, there are general guidelines and any suggestion made here should be understood in this context. The suggestion then in essence is this: To seek time to be alone in the sanctum within, away from the hustle and bustle of 'monkey-mind'. This we can do wherever we feel that our environment is most conducive to aloneness. Aloneness is not loneliness, it is all-oneness. It is a return to our natural state of Being. It is the essence of nature, the energy of the wild, the pure and simple. Though only to be found within, many would be well advised to spend time alone (all-one) in nature as often as they can, especially those of us who dwell in cities. Nature's energy is pure – is God-vibration – and has great healing potential to help us realign. It also affords a respite from the incessant shower of destructive electromagnetic frequencies many among us expose themselves to in an electronic environment. To prevent a misinterpretation of the word destructive we should bear in mind that the meaning here pertains to a mind which is still fear-oriented. Once fear is transmuted nothing can affect us adversely.

These times we spend all alone with our SELF are true prayer. Here we become honest again and eventually find the lost great prize: God I AM. Prayer need not be words, love need not be action – both may express themselves as such but are really one and the same: Sacred Being, the God-SELF within us. True prayer is praise, is living a life for the joy of it. This is veneration of life and thus its glorification. So let my prayer be my very own and never that of any creed or any other man.

The heart asks not for favours, it does not beg, nor does it command. It simply states its truth and that truth IS. To illustrate this understanding I desire to relate a true story, for stories often crystallize a truth far clearer than any dissertation could.

I know a man who was taught the secret of prayer by the grandest of all teachers, nature herself, and that in one single afternoon. Many years ago, after eleven days of torrential rain, he accompanied a farmer and his young son in search of the farmer's lost horse. The terrain was rough and their feet sunk deep into the slushy ground. They came upon the ruins of a hut built of solid logs and there was the chestnut stallion. It had sought shelter in the hut but this one had slowly caved in as the logs lacked firm ground to uphold the structure, thereby trapping the fine steed in a hollow four foot high formed by the logs. The animal lay on its side unscathed, patiently and quietly, with a dignity only nature can call her own.

There was no way to free the creature, for how could the heavy machinery needed be brought across the soggy land to this isolated spot? The man noticed a pool of water in the animal's nostril and, kneeling, comforted it by gently stroking its soft nose. 'Be not concerned' – the farmer said – 'three days, or so, and he'll be dead'. The man, however, insisted on a method somewhat more humane and so, sad as it may seem, it was agreed to release the creature from its misery by the shot of a gun.

The young boy was sent back home to fetch a rifle and almost two hours went by before the young lad returned with a rifle without a bolt. Reluctantly the boy made his way back to the farm once more, eventually returning with the bolt – but now where was the ammunition? Close to four hours had passed by now and farmer and son cancelled the mission in disgust, leaving the man behind, for he had not the heart to desert the suffering creature.

Alone now with horse and wind the man stepped around the huge pile of fallen logs and stood for a long moment before the helpless stallion, whose neck and head protruded from the pile. He gazed into its knowing, velvet eye and knew that it knew. Its gentle eye looking at him pained, it pleaded silently.

The man felt a tenderness fill his being and an ache so great it made him shiver. The ache grew and pierced his heart and rent it asunder with an explosive burst; with an all-consuming flame of compassion he bent his knee and clasped his hands, his heart expanded by a might that could have made the earth tremble and mountains tumble, he whispered: 'Oh Father, set its Spirit free!'

With one sudden sweeping movement of its neck the steed raised its head – only to sink back with wide open jaws, exhaling its last breath – its beautiful and polished eye now veiled.

Instantly, by the high nature of the moment, the man was given a vision in crystal clarity: He beheld a plane of open bushland and staggering on shaky legs the steed recapturing his freedom. When firm in pose, with head thrown high, it neighed, and never had the man heard so much joy expressed in one single cry.

Unashamedly the man fell to the grass and sobbed. His river of tears were pearls of joy for the treasure he had found. Indeed, the treasure was twofold for not only had he touched the creature heart-to-heart, creating an eternal bond, but he had found a power so awesome, it pales man's bayonets and cannons to mere tinker toys – the power of love. He had found the secret of prayer – he knew it to be the language of the heart – desire embraced and propelled by emotion.

That man was I and – ennobled by the experience – henceforth I knew the heart only need as much as whisper and nature holds its breath. When praying thusly, what could even Yeshua add? So let Thine prayer be Thine own and pray Thee not in numbers but in the hallowed chambers of Thine heart.

Yeshua suggested to pray in the quiet of our closet. The closet is the heart. We can be alone in our room, walking in a park or sitting quietly by a brook, listening to the whisper of the wind. This may not have, initially, the same appeal as dramatic exercises, but rest assured: techniques attempting the activation of chakras do not lead to God, but seeking the God within with the deepest longing of one's heart activates the chakras, with absolute certainty. There is a good reason for this. Desire for God raises one's vibrations to the highest possible frequencies. As always, simplicity is the answer.

Flushing one's mental, emotional and physical being of the daily impurities, we may augment this inner cleansing process by visualizing a flood of vibrant, white light entering our body through the crown chakra, washing our being clean. We allow this light to exit our physical body at the solar plexus, spreading and enveloping us entirely. We may alternate this cleansing procedure with different colours of light. Pink (unconditional love), blue (protection), green (healing and reconnecting with the energy of Earth). Yellow (Feeling, compassion for animals and fellow human beings), violet and purple (the colours of freedom and sacredness, reuniting us with Spirit). We may even hug a tree at times. (Do not underestimate this suggestion, there is more to it than meets the eye). Some will have noticed that red was not part of the process. Pure red is the colour of the Rebel Ray, the altered Ego. Much damage was caused in the past by exercises which aimed at raising the base chakra energy (red), the Kundalini, again, because the altered Ego led astray and reversed directions. Light cannot be raised where there is none. Light comes from above, as sunlight does, as rain does, as seeds fall off a tree and gently settle on the ground. Filling the base chakra with orange light purifies the resident energy, if this light treatment is accompanied by the greater process of releasing survival thoughts. So, as long as we seek these periods of stillness on a regular basis, we establish a rhythm, which leads us away from thoughts of chaos and violence, dispersion and restlessness – negativity in short. That is the secret, only in the calm of aloneness can we contemplate truth, the things of the Spirit. This is true meditation, not rigorous techniques but the return to the sanctum within our heart. It is here where we become simple, honest and childlike again. Here we make contact with our Source and begin to walk with God once more, with the almighty Spirit that causes us to be. We speak to it, tell it what troubles our heart, tell it that we feel lost and want to come home to our true identity, even weep for a while., it is alright. There is not a single tear, when given to the God I AM within, that He does not turn into a river of joy. But we can give Him our laughter too, our giggles and delights, we can give Him everything, but above all we listen. We do not bring the gravity of Self-importance into these periods – that is not what is meant with sincerity. But we come unto the Spirit with the light-heartedness of the young who are in awe and wonder of the first morning in Spring, where all things are new and germinate. There is a sense of adventure, as with the young eagle when spreading his wings for his virgin flight. He knows he has to abandon his nest to soar the skies – he also knows he has to be bold. It is something he must do on his own, there is no help. There is expectancy of newness, of wide and bright horizons, and the promise that all is well. It is by dropping the shackles of the known that we glimpse our possibilities and in the moment of forgetfulness of nest-security the thrilling flight of the soul is born. It is in these moments of solitude that we experience the elation of being, that we become knowing.

In these revered times of quietude we begin to hear the acuter notes of a song in our heart, which was there all along, but was drowned out by the clamour of survival living. We begin to hear what ears do not hear and see what eyes do not see. We touch the intangible. We transcend the kingdom of the senses and draw a strength of Spirit which is unknown to worldly thinking. It fills our Being with substance, hope and purpose, and cleanses our mind, bringing it back to sanity and purity. Once this habit is established, we soon learn to give these sacred periods predomi-nance above all else and we will not allow anything or anyone, neither husband nor wife, child nor pet, to dilute our dedication to the God within.

With this strength we step out into society, into our daily field of activities and the day is changed. This consecration to regular periods of inner quietude and communion with the Creator on a habitual basis, if not allowed to be degraded to a mere ritual, makes us one-pointed and brings us eventually to a point where we are constantly working from the centre of the inner sanctum. This is the practice of focusing, of holding our attention on the Divine intent. Once this develops into a natural state of mind, it matters little if we are alone or in a crowd. The mental pollution of society has then lost its influence on us, although our preference will always be solitude. Now the principles of True perception shift from the realm of theory and become our natural understanding. Ours is then a spiritual and not a materialistic sight. We begin to see with the eyes of God-man instead of Clay-man. We invest in God and not in the superficial values of society. As a result our life begins to change. Irritations drop away, most 'friends' too and fewer, but lasting, friendships are formed. The drag of 'nine to five' transforms into the thrill of now. Thus we may stand in the midst of the scattered thought and noise of this world, yet we really stand in the centre of our sanctum, the God I AM, the quiet pool of peace, joy and knowing. We become poised. We then stand in the light and warmth of the spiritual Sun, the God I AM, and illness, upset and lack of any kind drop from us like dried crusts of mud.

Moments of confusion will certainly come, they are a natural part of our growth. Yet, confusion is co-fusion, an act of unfocusing from old values and refocusing on a greater reality. It is a process of reorientation. With some this process projects itself right down into the material level. It materializes to the extent that one's physical eyesight becomes blurred at times – the eyes have difficulty in focusing. Be not concerned then – it is part of the process. If it causes discomfort, simply seek stillness in the sanctum within and say: 'From the Almighty I AM Presence I call forth clarity', and clarity will come.

Mentioning discomfort as part of an expansion process in consciousness brings to mind a few other sensations, which may accompany the activation of chakras. Pressure may be felt at times to the extent of acute pain in the solar plexus area during the revitalization of that energy centre. Actual physical pain in the heart area, rather short lived, is known to occasionally go parallel with the opening of one's heart aspect. An experience of strong pressure from inside the lower throat area in the vicinity of the thyroid gland, going hand in hand with frequent heatwaves more or less restricted to the neck's collar-line, should be no reason for concern. The sensation of a dull pressure, a 'squiggly' sensation or a very local icy feeling in one's central forehead indicate activity in the 'third eye'. Frequent, short dizzy spells, not necessarily unpleasant, mostly point to an expanding pituitary gland, which corresponds with the crown chakra. Overall, headaches and a stronger flow of body fluids (e.g. runny noses) seem to be common side-effects of greater energy releases in the upper four chakras. A most certain indication of increased activity in the heart chakra is the ease with which tears begin to flow. We tend to become mellow for no obvious reason, and that at the 'weirdest' times. A sunset, a starry sky or the sight of a retarded little one may release waves of love, causing our eyes to be quite disobedient, as they 'keep on leaking'. But it is rather all very wonderful; it shows we are opening up and love is flowing, to an extent that our being cannot quite cope with as yet. Perhaps some reader can relate to one or another of the above mentioned symptoms of an expansion of Being.

This then, in sum and substance, is how we learn to hold our attention, the art of focusing: by establishing the habit of regular periods of quietude. Initially it is a decision, the decision to let nothing interfere with our new direction. It is quite easy, if we remind ourself that the old direction did not exactly deliver us to the realms of bliss in the first place. In these moments of stillness we do not let our mind wander from the conscious communion with the I AM. As the mind wanders anyway, we make these periods very short at first, perhaps two or three minutes, but still adhere to their regularity. After some time we feel, to our pleasant surprise, the growing desire to extend these intervals. As soon as we notice our mind drifting off to mundane subjects, we should earnestly consider this advice: not to force the mind back to attention but to gently coax it back 'in line'. It is quite astonishing how favourably the mind responds to a determined but gentle approach. The bottom line of this procedure is that it becomes alluring, thus self-generative. The more we tend to it the more we want it. To say it differently: The more we focus the less we need to focus, because our entire Being becomes the focus of the Divine SELF.

The mind can be likened to a body of water, perhaps a lake. The surface of the lake is roughed up, rippled by the winds of day-to-day living in the state of social consciousness, preventing a recognition of its crystal depth. Yet underneath the lake is tranquil and clear. Our periods of quietude smoothe the ripples and allow us to penetrate beneath the surface, where the waters are still. Thus we prepare for the grandest step and eventually dare to pierce behind the veil where all movement is suspended; and however much we have prepared, what we behold halts our breath, bends our knee. The soul knows then, that what it sought for so desperately on the highways and byways of lives beyond count, was all the while within, was its very own SELF. Trembling in awe of its own Being, in the face of the unspeakable, it stammers the most sacred words a soul can ever voice: I AM that I AM. I AM the very Spirit that causes Me to be. I AM All-there-is, I AM humanity, I AM life, I AM the God I AM. The soul has come home – it is at peace – it is free, for it is born anew.

This is the grand prize, the end of all darkness and the beginning of walking in the Light of Spirit. An individual experiencing this distinctly distinguishes between the Self the world identifies with and the SELF it discovers as the I AM. When doubts come as to the authenticity of the above statement, then we know we are listening to our altered Ego. The difficulty lies in the acceptance of this assertion, which springs from the Ego's tendency to contradict: to inflate or deflate the personality Self, always according to what denies the true SELF best. The Ego will be ready and on its mark to judge: 'How can 'I' be God? How blasphemous!', because as we said, its identity, the I it refers to, rests in an image only, the body-Self. Our success, on the other hand, relies on utter simplicity, the totally unassuming acceptance of our Being as the God I AM. It is the recognition of the incontestable truth, that there are no two beings in all the universes combined. It is one Being only, expressing as many. Yeshua expressed the same truth as this: 'I and the Father are One.' We can rephrase this statement: The I AM of us and what we term God is One and the same. The I (and the eye) of God is the I AM of you and me. God speaks to God. Knowing this reveals the utter insanity of any form of attack, for who could we harm, judge or attack but ourself. The recognition of this is SELF-realization, which is only possible when judgment has been released. For whosoever finds the God I AM must see the same God in the I AM of every one of his brothers. Therefore he is compelled to see him as innocent, which is an impossibility while still under the 'guidance' of the altered Ego. Seeing him as innocent does not suggest naivety to his mistaken ways, on the contrary, we become more discerning than ever, but with an attitude of forbearance, forgiveness and good will.

The Ego is always judgmental, and judgment serves as an impenetrable wall, hiding the truth which is its purpose. Its revenue is amnesia, the loss of identity. Now we understand why the balance of polarities was afforded so much emphasis, because it leads to the release of judgment. Enlightenment or SELF-realization are one and the same. It does not require strenuous exercises, ascetic living, untold meditation techniques or sitting under pyramidal shapes, facing east or north. If these methods help an individual to stay focused, then so be it, but in principle such endeavours are aimed at achieving something. There is nothing to DO. Doing is merely an apology for BEING. 'Doing' in the understanding of achieving never creates joy and exuberance, only being does. There is nothing to be achieved. Such exercises are only food for the Ego, because they represent distractions in themselves, becoming trips, deviate the mind from the real objective: the simple recognition of one's true nature. All that is ever required is the deepest sincerity of the heart.

So many seem compelled to improve themselves, to master themselves, to do something to enlarge their spiritual stature somehow, to become something – so they think – that they are not as yet. Yeshua's statement: Which of you by taking thought can add one cubit unto his stature? addresses this same issue. Spiritual evolution is certainly a becoming – not becoming what we are not as yet, but becoming aware of what we already are!

There is this misconstrued idea of becoming 'spiritual', which is in itself confirming separation, for I ask you: what is there that is not spiritual? If God is All-There-Is then ALL is spiritual. This desire to aspire to the image of some role model is falling prey once more to the thoughtform. The 'spiritual' walk not on water or through a wall, it suffices they walk tall. They are the housewife next door, the cobbler, the farmer, the businessman, living in our midst. They are the sunny Spirits who lay bare their great heart in charity and compassion and find it not beyond their ability to accommodate the confused, the lonely, the half-crazed, the im-poverished – all those who hurt – and these will leave accepted and uplifted, enriched with promising glimmers of hope upon their dark horizons.

Blessed are the simple and kind hearted; they truly are the salt of the Earth. Old George is one of them. Meet him on Easter Sunday or at a funeral, it matters not what day, and there is an air of Christmas about him. Sally reports her migraine simply dissi-pates by merely exchanging a few courtesies with him across the rusty garden gate. In his presence felicity is tangible and suddenly the world becomes a safe and cheerful place, so peaceful and so kind; yet speak to him of things spiritual and he has the whim to change the subject to Azaleas. He resides somewhere in Stanford Lane, but I suppose he really dwells elsewhere, as his own sovereign God on his own Olympus.

Then there is young Maggie, who must have missed out somehow on the general concept of a God reduced to a personage, and she would be hard pressed to see the difference between a rose and a dimwit.

Above all, there are our very little ones who still have the capacity for wonderment and awe, for they give God a chance. There is no lack of Self-worth as yet, but total Self-acceptance.

Striving to be more confesses to being less, testifies to a nonacceptance of SELF, whilst the crowning glory of spiritual awakening is the exact opposite, is unconditional acceptance of Self as it IS – this is unconditional love of SELF. So the achievers will achieve the opposite, for they constantly affirm their lack of Self-approval, which, in essence, is Self-judgment.

The doers, the strivers, I invite to contemplate this thought: God loves you unconditionally. His love is not conditional on who, how or what you are. He accepts you already, however you are; how could he not, if you are the very expression of that God? So, if you are acceptable in God's sight, then why are you not in your own? The pebble by the roadside will ascend with you when the time is ripe. It will not be left behind, yet it strives not, nor does it observe ritual. It simply IS. Then what is the pebble's secret? Exactly that. It does not resist, neither does it judge – it simply IS.

The elation of Being that comes from the union with the God I AM is unknown to the man of society, for one centred in the I AM, the sanctum within, lives in reality. He has left the 'reality' of Self-images, the world of make-believe, where a soul is valued for its power, its race, its nationality and creed, moneys and external appearance.

Life always mirrors our state of Being back to us and tells us exactly where we are at. What if we were kneeling in our garden planting a tree, wearing bedraggled clothes, splattered with mud and the night watchman from down the road dropped in for a chat – would we wash up and change our shirt? Most likely not. On the contrary, we might even say: 'Listen, Jack, while we are talking, could you just hold the tree in position, while I fill the hole?' And when the job is done we make a cup of coffee and sit down with him and converse. What if we exchanged this visitor for the leader of a nation or some celebrity? Would we act in like manner? Would we remain composed? Or would we not drop everything and get into a frizzle trying to please this one? The insufficiency of character is thus revealed by the very cover made to hide. We can learn much from our little ones in this respect. They know not of

Self-images. They treat everyone alike. True perception does the same. Such an understanding identifies itself with the I AM in a person and does not identify the person with the role he or she plays. If the celebrity is worthy of a feast, then so is Jack. Why is it that the celebrity is rendered so much respect and worship? Because he has what we would like to have, the things we really value – wealth and fame – our values which he stands for. Hence it is this we identify with, an image and not the God I AM he represents.

If approached by Truth, the sneer of the altered Ego is only too familiar, because it perceives Truth as the threat, and not itself. Such a Self tends to give way to lowly doubt, by asking True perception: 'How do you know? Where do you know it from?' It would be the same as walking in the rain and being wet, the question being asked: 'How come you know you're wet?' We know we are wet because we are wet, it is as simple as that. The Soul issuing forth Truth knows because it is Truth.

If we only cared to slow down, lift our eyes but for a moment from our daily busy-ness or find stillness in the silent thunder of a sunrise and dared to look within, we would find something so precious against which all things pale into nothingness. If we braved ourselves to look where we constantly look from, we would discover that we are really much wiser than we think.

If two or three gather to communicate and thoughts should ascend from the personal to the impersonal, that is from the material to the things of the Spirit, then greatness is born. Then the I AM gushes forth its truth and we are surprised at the wealth of knowing we carry in the depths of our heart. Then the intellect is bypassed, and communication occurs along the golden thread which runs through all men – simpleton and genius alike – and that is the heart. It is here and not in intellect where virtue resides. It is here where Spirit dwells, and Spirit is wild and free, it cannot be tamed by creeds, dogmas and concepts, it cannot feed on dollars or the things dollars can buy, but on greater thought which lifts the Soul above the petty bickerings of the marketplace.

If men communicate thus, they become conscious of their unity, then it matters not who utters words of Truth, for they know it is the property of all, it is the nectar of the Soul. It is eternal, and Man's treasured progress becomes as fugitive dust in the light of the Soul. This is true sustenance, and lifts a man beyond his private Self, transmutes him into the knowing of his essence, his God-SELF, thus each of such men shall part a greater man than when he came. According to his truth shall a man avail. Such a one need not conform – he owns his truth – he finds true security in his Being, and that is God.

The conformist, in lack of his own truth, quotes Kahlil Gibran, Shakespeare or Epiktet – the man who has the wisdom of his soul will speak his own and it shall become the rule of the day. He puts his roots not in outer property but in the eternal wealth of his SELF. He has risen above the personality Self, therefore draws his substance from the eternality of universal Being, and knows himself but as an individualized expression of that Being, which is Spirit, and that is God. Thus he recognizes his brother as the same I AM, regardless if his brother be asleep or not. There is a magnetism that touches the millman and the clerk alike, as he brushes by and leaves a spark to pierce their souls, and they begin to wonder. For like remembers like and Self has stirred a little in its sleep.

True perception walks with the Almighty at its side. It comes as no surprise that the world, having denied its Source, yet simultaneously yearning for it, will display a love-hate attitude toward things of God.

Society is separation's expression on a collective level. True perception knows society as the great whore, who sells herself to the highest bidder, because the price she asks is a man's most precious possession – his SELF. She is a fickle lady, to be sure. As she cannot please herself, she desires to be pleased forever. No one shall ever please another, until he pleases his SELF. A man relying on the God within, his I AM, shall not be apologetic of his being, neither shall he cumber himself for society's approval. He shall not conform to its hollow demands and shallow ethics – he will not suffer it to lose his way. His intent is not to provoke, yet he is provocation. Yeshua, Gautama, Confucius, Lao Tse or Luther, they are the true rebels of history. They earned the resentment of society, because they challenged their brothers, they inspired new thought.

A man relying on himself lives already, while society makes plans for a future which it decrees to be uncertain, and thus knows not what the future holds. True perception determines every now-moment, therefore holds the future. SELF-reliance gives away the values of society and is thus secure.

Society can buy a house but not a home – can bar the front door with lock and bolt and call this security, but it is not peace. It can consume caviar and champagne – but it is not sustenance. It can rest the body on the finest linens – but these do not make for sweet slumber. It can buy tickets for amusement – but it cannot purchase joy. It can illumine a hall of festivity with a thousand lights – but it cannot illumine the soul. It pursues its aims with passion – yet it knows not of compassion. It 'makes' love – but it cannot love.

Social consciousness divides mankind into classes, but it cannot create class. True perception is as comfortable on the silky cushions of aristocracy as it is on the straw of a poor man's hut. In all probability the latter would be its preference. That is class. It esteems SELF – that is true humility, for all it sees is I AM. Therefore his brother is the same as he, be it a lady moving in a cloud of perfume, or the farmer kneeling in his field surrounded by the stench of manure. To him it is I AM, is God in all his appearances.

True perception relics on SELF and does not succumb to the suggestions of society's Global Thoughtform, which are always based on fear, and fear always labours to obstruct truth. To false perception all truth must seem paradox. It is the irony of a separated mind which sees a man in union with his SELF as standing apart from itself. In proportion to the emergence of an awakening Christ in man, this unifying force seems as the sword of division to the fearful. For those who do not choose SELF as their guiding star put themselves in the camp of fear, as chaff is sorted from the wheat.

This contrast is more and more noticeable. In the measure of the awakening God in man the fearful amplify their fear. For example, we see increasingly public warnings, therefore affirmations, of diseases of all kind. TV advertisements proclaim the proof of statistics, claiming so many out of so many are doomed to die of heart disease, cancer, diabetes, AIDS and what not. True perception shakes its head at such 'scientific' nonsense, for it sees the blatant contradiction in its claim: statisticians believe the dice falls by pure chance, yet derive a regularity from that chance. As if sickness or any condition is ever by chance. The smoker smoking his smoke-stick through the filter of love shall never suffer cancer. Yet, the nonsmoker shall suffer what he fears (for the smoker). The fortunate man owes nothing to fortune but all to his truth.

Once we see with the eyes of True perception, we realize clearly that everyone makes his own choices, hence is responsible for his own life. This then leads to two main tendencies: to either withdraw in the sense that we cannot be bothered with the woes of society or the irresistible urge to impart that greater knowing to our brothers, to tell there is another way. Both reactions can turn into tripping stones. To prevent that from happening, revealing the inherent traps is advisable at this point.

In the case of withdrawal there is definitely the need for a period of respite, however, the aspirant to truth cannot remain there. If he does, the process of spiritual unfoldment becomes retrogressive, for now he lives for the personality Self again, whereas true awakening transcends this Self and identifies with the impersonal, universal SELF, which will always forgo personal choices in favour of the greater whole. It has realized that what this world needs is real love and that can only be increased through extension, meaning it has to be shared. Which brings us to the trap hidden in the sharing of knowledge: real knowledge is truth and truth has to be lived first before it can be extended. Only when we live our truth will it come across as true. A fellowman may be ignorant of truth, but he will soon sense if our words vibrate at the rate of intellectual theory or carry the wisdom of our heart. The latter is only possible when we live our truth in thought and deed, when every word is backed up by the very life we live. If not, then what we project remains mere hypothesis, tickles his intellect on the surface but does not reach his soul. To keep our distance from him while he sneezes and coughs, in case we 'catch' his cold, does very little to support the claim that a virus is not the cause of his cold. However, the claim becomes convincing after we have spent two or three days in his presence, perhaps in a closed working environment, breathing in his entire menagerie of viruses and bacteria and all the rest of the friendly companions of a nasty flu.

To tell him that his Being is his sustenance and nothing else is a most helpful act, if he cannot detect the slightest worry or apprehension in our own life. Should he, however, witness us fretting over a bill or some other concern, then our statement becomes a laugh. Our personal life must testify to our words. Let there be no misunderstanding: the issue is not to display a halo – they do not balance very well and tend to slip. No, the issue is definitely not to project a saint-like image, for this would only be another Self-image, but to be honest, to be true to oneself with all one's shortcomings. This our brother can relate to. If we speak our truth thus, then he knows he can trust.

If none of our words contradict one another or the life we live then we have become honest. Then we live by a power that is within us, though not of us. This our brother cannot fail but notice and he begins to ponder, and looks at the laws which really govern life and eventually drops the ones he assumed were real and his life changes for the better.

The last major trap in the budding stages of our new way of seeing is the conversion syndrome. It is not a serious hurdle, but serious enough to warrant a closer look. Although the desire to share is a natural one, there is a world of difference between imparting and converting. To convert is to enslave, to share is to enrich. The act of sharing offers knowledge for the purpose of consideration – no more. The converter, on the other hand, has not really made his words his own, meaning he does not really believe himself in what he says, therefore he doubts and needs confirmation by way of a witness, hence he stands in ludicrous contrast to his words. This is called seeking safety in numbers. One who truly knows himself has genuine self-respect and as such respects his brother equally, whatever his brother's views may be, thus he will never impose anything. To impose is to enslave.

There is more to imparting our truth: One who knows also knows his responsibility, and this in the most literal sense, that is when to respond or not. More often than not it is more important to know when not to speak than when to speak. Although some needy soul may have asked for help, we nevertheless may risk feeding him more than he might be able to digest. For this reason alone it becomes imperative to 'stay tuned' to the God I AM whenever we are asked to help. And this is why: Facing our brother in the consciousness of I AM, which means seeing him as the exact same I AM as we are, we become him. In this consciousness we instantly understand him. Understanding him we know his needs, therefore we know exactly when and what to speak or when to be silent. More damage than good is done by the 'do-gooders' of this world, however sincere they may be in their desire to help, for to extend true help, we have to step aside and let the God I AM lead the way. To do that we must have found that God first ourself. We cannot share what we do not have. It is the God in us which then becomes a benediction to our fellowman and not the personality Self, as this one at best will only make a nuisance of itself. Once in tune, we will be prompted from within as to when and what to speak, regardless if we would much rather be elsewhere and carry on with our own personal tasks. Then again, it is not always words our brother is in need of; often we just listen, but above all we see him aright. His need is not a lecture, but acceptance, an open ear and love. The secret of our help lies in seeing him aright. If he is recognized as the exact same I AM that we are, then a process is initiated which obeys no worldly law. It is called a miracle, and only so because its workings escape our understanding entirely. This is what really sets him free and not so much our words or silence, although their genuine support cannot be denied.

Where lack of any kind is experienced, the I AM is not acknowledged. Self identity rests then in a Self image but not in the I AM. True perception sees his fellowman bedecked with jewels, even if it be a starving child, for it sees God. If that particular expression of God appears not to be prosperous, it knows it as prosperity all the same. For such a one garners the pearls of wisdom from his experience, and these are the only wealth there is. Once such a soul is laden with the pearls of wisdom, or in different words: if all it beholds is the I AM, the universe resonates to this wealth with prosperity on every level. Thus the man relying on his SELF, the I AM in him, relishes I AM's reflections. Should the world panic in the thought of depression, he shall be the calm within the storm. If there be a need he asks of SELF and so he shall receive.

If the world around him moans and groans he knows it but to be their choice. So he attends to the joy of the moment and that is attending to the business of the Father, the SELF, and thus his garden of life blossoms and blooms and is heavy with the perfume of the flowers of divine provision. He lives in the now and that is eternity, therefore he is assured of eternal support. He does not search for things outside himself, this way they never come, for where would they come from if he has cut himself off from their Source? He knows his SELF to be the Source of ALL-GOOD and knowing this he determines not how it comes. He just allows divine providence to flow. He has learned how not to block the waters of life.

True perception sees but its SELF in all around, therefore to it beauty is truly in the eyes of the beholder, because it beholds God in all it perceives. It knows that all is possible to those who know. Happiness is a choice. The profound wisdom of this we learned in the Balance of Polarities. There is but one choice: Reality or Illusion. Reality is happiness and joy.

And this is achieved through the transcendence of judgment and that is true forgiveness. It is security and Peace. It is total SELF-reliance. It is trust in God. If now we read the words on our legal tender: 'In God we trust', we may understand it differently. The Law of Supply showed us the secret of prosperity: My Being is my sustenance – if understood, then freedom is understood, the utter non-dependence on outer circumstances or conditions. For if My Being is my sustenance then my I AM brings forth this sustenance and nothing else. This understanding makes us the master of our life and does away with reversed thinking, which is victim-consciousness. Thus we go forth unafraid and share our only wealth we have and that is All-There-Is and that is God. Nature is always lavish and abundant and produces in excess.

This is the flow we now allow in and life delights in heaping it onto those who can accept. This is the art of receiving. The greatest gift is not given if it is not received! This should spark some thought in us, because of its profound implication. It means we remain paupers because we do not accept and not because the gift is not there.

Acknowledgment and love of the God I AM is the stone of wisdom. When SELF is shared the wealth of God has its way to work itself into the affairs of those who accept.

****

I thank you from my heart, the mighty I AM Presence within me, for allowing me to share my wealth with you, my SELF – it shall double and quadruple in your life in the measure of your acceptance. Go forth then, and share with your brothers and sisters what you have made your own and it shall return increased, for this is the nature of love. It is the greatest gift you can possibly give to anyone. For you give SELF.

Tell the downtrodden that there is true hope – show the cynics another way. Teach the sad ones how to laugh again and say to the victims: happiness is a choice.

Rebuke not the unkind and the heartless but testify to a compassionate heart for all living things. Pardon not your antagonizers but embrace them with forgiveness. Soften hardened hearts with love and restore the destitute to their dignity of Spirit.

Spare our little ones the regurgitation of ancient platitudes – the reaffirmations of fear – and lead them to a greater destiny instead.

Above all speak to your brothers and sisters of the Oneness of all life. Be the God I AM that they may remember their own – and you shall be remembered in the heavens.

If there be a drought in your life, or hurricane – judge it not, for judgment is divisive and a barren ground for seeds. Rather see it for what it truly is: an expansion into awareness. And when you feel the need to pray, pray not to a God outside yourself, but to the I AM of you – for that is God. This way your prayer shall be answered – always.

Decree your every now and you need no designs on the future; and I beseech you: always be gentle with yourself, for this is true strength. Celebrate life with laughter and dance, for this is the will of God. Jubilate – sing from the mountain top and know that you are forever. Revel and frolic in this knowing. Praise your SELF, thus you praise God.

The destination of the journey, which we made together, is the I AM of you. The journey never ends, for life is unlimited adventure for all eternity. Thus our ways do not part. I AM always with I AM.

So, I say to you Namaste, that ancient Sanskrit salute, which means the God in me honours the God in you. Blessed you must be – for you have opened your heart to God – the only wealth there is. Thus you shall come to know that your I AM is my I AM, and that is Innocence, is Joy, is Abundance, is Love, is You – is GOD.

NAMASTE.

Epilogue

Or A Cosmic View

Gazing at the night sky, I behold myriads of shimmering diamonds in a sea of dark. Silent companions throughout our odyssey of millions of lifetimes lived on Earth. How many poets have been inspired by their magnificence to contemplate the deeper mystery of Creation? How many hearts found solace and hope at the sight of their splendour? How many searching souls have been reminded of eternal poise by their sublime lustre – of a greater destiny – of God in the most High – of the Spirit that causes all things to be?

I give thanks for their dazzling beauty – I take their grandeur into my innermost. Though my vista shall be transformed to one immensely more encompassing, I nonetheless treasure the stars as precious beyond expression, for there soon comes a time when I shall not see them the same ever again.

* * *

It is not a prerequisite for an expanding consciousness to have a structural understanding of the overall process which is taking place – but it does give it support in the sense a young climbing plant uses a lattice to reach its own heights. So, we shall look at what is actually occurring globally and universally in this our time.

That we are part of a universal current of energy flow – the Divine Intent – still does not change the fact of us being the masters of our destiny.

Let us be once more reminded: the future holds no thing. On its own it is a blank. It 'holds' what we hold in our thought. We decree what is to be – we determine our next now moment. Global consciousness determines the global next now moment. Individual consciousness decrees its individual next now moment.

Any prediction for the future of Mankind merely illustrates the most probable reality created by humanity's moment-by-moment choices. We have entered a cyclic change and are approaching a massive transformation – a rebirth in consciousness – involving the alignment of entire galaxies. As mentioned before, it is a culmination of cycles within cycles within cycles, of eons of time.

We would do well in stretching our mind a little to understand the universal, magnanimous process which is occurring at this time, of which we are not only an integral part, but which occurs because of us.

Our solar system is part of the galaxy we call the Milky Way. Our Milky Way contains billions of solar systems. This Milky Way is part of a loose group of 20 other galaxies, and science knows today that our Milky Way is but one of billions of such galaxies. Astronomer Allan Sandage once said: 'Galaxies are to astronomers as atoms are to physics.'

A physical universe is the densest and smallest condensation of a greater, non-physical universe and this is part of a greater universe again. In a three-dimensional understanding, creation as such is incomprehensible. There are universes contained within a super universe – super universes are again contained within a 'super-super' universe and so forth. The process is literally unlimited, each universe orbiting around a central sun, and this not only laterally in the physical plane but vertically in non-physical dimensions. And all this expands at a rate of 90 percent of the speed of light. The ultimate Central Sun of it all is what we vaguely call God, the Spirit that causes all things to be. The fact that creation as such is virtually teeming with life can only be obscured to the blindest among us.

Approximately every 25,000 to 26,000 years our Solar System completes one orbit around the central sun of the Pleiades (Alcione – see diagram last page). Ancient Eastern wisdom knows this cycle as the various Yugas. This orbit has a point closest to Alcione and one farthest away from it. The furthest point from the central sun – symbolizing Light – correlates with ignorance, here Man's consciousness is 'in the dark'. The nearest point correlates with what we term an awakening or Enlightenment. Alcione is known to the East as Brahma, the seat of creative power or universal magnetism (concerning our particular universe).

In 1961 science discovered, by means of satellites, a photon belt encircling the Pleiades. This photon belt circles the Pleiadean system at an absolute right angle to its orbital planes. As our Sun (and we with it) orbits the Pleiades once every 25860 years, it reaches the midpoint of this photon belt approximately every 12500 years. It requires some 2,000 years to traverse it. Meaning that after departing this realm, another 10,500 years pass before it enters it again.

In 1962 we entered the sphere of influence of this photon belt. Calculations approximate the year of the actual entry into its mainstream to be 2011. This correlates with the time when the universe reaches its point of maximum expansion. The East familiarizes us with the contraction and expansion rhythm of the universe as the Inbreath and Outbreath of God – each breath covering a time span (in this density) in the vicinity of 11,000 years. It is no coincidence that this time frame corresponds with the Grand Cycles, the orbit of our Sun around the central sun Alcione. The transition into super-consciousness, the second Coming of Christ, is to occur at the precise moment of suspension of movement between expansion and contraction, going parallel with the entry into the radiation of the photon belt. This energy is also referred to as the Manasic Vibration or Radiation. Astrophysical calculations, based on the Sun's speed travelling through space (29 km/s) – and Earth's own movement – indicate that we will enter the photon belt at a speed of 208,800 km/h. The actual entry of Earth into the Manasic Vibration will occur in the twinkling of an eye. The energy of the photon belt is of etheric and spiritual nature, not physical, but interacts with, and affects the physical. The 10,500 years of darkness between the 2000 year periods of light afford incarnating man repeatedly his spiritual evolution. As the majority of humans become forgetful of their Divine Source and purpose during these earthly sojourns, the periods of light serve a dual purpose. They represent a sorting-out process, gathering matured souls into the Light of the Spirit and affording the weaker, just maturing souls a stabilization period of respite and an opportunity for further spiritual growth. The individuals who could not or would not acknowledge Divine Love as the essence of their being during the 10,500 year period of incarnations are removed and given another chance elsewhere. In this sense – and in this sense only – it is The Day of Judgment, for it is man who judges himself.

One of our brothers from the unseen, St. Germain, refers to the photon-belt as the Golden Nebula; we quote: (Date: Thursday August 20, 1987)

'Now, your astronomers, and your quantum physicists have understood [discovered] that which is grand golden nebula at the ridge of your universe, allowing itself to embrace and absorb all the electrums in the universe. Bit by bit it is absorbing your universe. And they are scratching their heads a bit in non-understanding of what be this grand golden essence that is there upon the horizon of the universe. It has not been seen before. It is the understanding of the golden essence that you call the Christus. It is the physical manifestation of the second coming of the Christus. It is indeed a parallel universe. The parallel universe and the golden nebula is the New Age perceived. When you traverse this threshold, when you become One with the golden nebula, you are in super-consciousness'. End of quote.

The entry of Earth into the Manasic Radiation constitutes the fulfillment of the deepest hopes of the human soul. Much scare has been generated since the time of David, prophesying the coming transition into Light. This may have been justified in order to shake the apathy from man, inciting him to look within. Today's generations however are less in need of pressure induced through fear of coming events than an enlightening approach addressing their intelligence. It is not that the prophecies are false – they are right in two points: We are nearing the End Time and moving into the Age of God. In regard to the projections of calamities, however, the following clarification seems mandatory. Trepidations are a direct reflection of Man's resistance to a change of heart. And it is here where we can see glad tidings on the horizon. True intelligence is surfacing in man, slowly replacing the reasoning of an altered state of mind.

The predictions of dire circumstances and trepidation need not come to pass if man aligns with the energy of love and releases fear.

It is not the Earth causing quakes and shakes, it is a humanity paralysed by fear, where one brother mistrusts the other and fears him to the extent that he bolts and bars his hovel to keep him out – God in fear of God.

As it is not at all the purpose and intention of this material to delve into and uncover the petty conspiracies among the worldly hierarchy, it would be of benefit to many a reader to acquaint himself with material which sheds light on official manipulations on a global scale, which are purposely designed to keep humanity in fear. It is a fast method to shake off complacency. For you see, as long as humanity fears, it can be manipulated and enslaved.

Those who have difficulty accepting this as fact should consider that the transition from Darkness to Light is a universal one, not just concerning Earth, however, it is acted out on Earth. Therefore both forces, light and dark, are attracted to Earth from all corners of this universe trying to make their stand. Consciousness is food. Fear is consciousness all the same, therefore feeding the manipulated and manipulators alike. What we are witnessing is a culmination of events merging into one final sorting-out process. Although the outcome of this process is certain, be assured that you are, in the meantime, constantly exposed to manipulations of all sorts to keep you under fear's spell. This keeps you in survival mode, hence makes you a food source for the greater forces of Darkness.

That these forces, known also as the 'Greys', work in conjunction with key governments and those who pull the strings of the world's purse, should be almost common knowledge by now. But be at ease – they are experiencing already their own medicine. They fear the collapse of their plans, they fear the emerging Light Force, for they are lackeys all the same – lackeys of the Rebel Ray – the universal altered Ego. What these 'Greys' and their servants fear most is the Family of Light. To those not familiar with this term, a brief explanation: The Family of Light are souls not actually native to the evolution on Earth, but native enough through numerous incarnations on Earth, which accustomed these souls to the heavy and dense vibrations of this plane. They have come here in great numbers prior to the great transition, for the specific purpose of helping humanity to awaken by unmasking fear and reminding their brothers of the Spirit that causes all to be. They represent one half of a huge force – the other half is the Family of Love. The latter are here already, but for the greater part still as children. The Light Force educates, the Love Force will influence and change events directly by means of highly unusual methods. The Grey's very own ranks are already being infiltrated by the Light Force. Their greatest fear is the gigantic wave of education being set into motion by the forces of Light, teaching man the truth: that a withdrawal of credence to fear will lead humanity into the light of the Spirit and render fear's disciples impotent. We withdraw their power by withdrawing our fear. It is solely our survival consciousness which empowers them. Without this power they become helpless individuals, having to seek new ways. As the only other way is love, it is this they will find. This they cannot do if we constantly reinforce their ways of enslavement and suppression by feeding them with fear. Have pity for them, have compassion, for they delay the purpose of their soul, but have no fear. Evil cringes and consumes itself in the face of Spirit, in the Light of love. They are God's children all the same, regardless of rank or form. The voice of conscience of those collaborating with the ancient forces of Jehovah or Yahweh, whichever name one prefers, is deafened by the greed for power – leaving no room for higher degrees of moral sentiment. They will seem to succeed, yet it will be very short-lived. It is fast coming to an end. If some reader may find all this rather far-fetched, then to him I say, with all due respect: 'You had better wake up, or you will be shaken up'. The system is rotten almost to the core. It is crumbling and it is crumbling fast. However, the core is not rotten. The core is the human soul. It is innocent, it is beautiful, however, it is also very, very complacent and the coming years will see little accommodation for complacency.

Our gift to these forces should not be judgment and condemnation, but a deeper understanding of their motives, therefore forgiveness and unconditional love. Think not: 'What difference will that make'; for if you do, then this material taught you little. It is forgiveness of their state of separation which sets these mistaken souls free. Remember, it is True perception which paves the way for the miracle. If the forces of Darkness are seen as the same I AM as you and I, but as having lost their way in the denial of this very God I AM, then they are thought of in love and cannot have the slightest power over you. Any evil, if faced with love, yet resisting a change of heart, will consume itself. It is a universal

Law. If an approach suggests a fearful response, simply say: 'You play in your sandbox – I play in mine'. For that is all it is: souls in their infancy, playing their game of illusion, powerless in the Light of God.

During a conversation with Archangel Michael about the coming changes, he emphasized that, due to the fact that at present negativity is by far outweighing positivity, Man's only hope for a smooth transition is to at least balance negativity with positivity. Upheavals would then be rendered superfluous. If not, he stressed, then a great cleansing process would have to be imposed. Michael advised not to rely on a date in regard to the transition. 'It could come today or in millennia'. Meaning, despite the photon belt, it might not come at all for most, if fear is not released and transmuted into love.

However, the winds are changing. There is every indication that the transition will be relatively smooth. Already many individuals in key positions around the world are plagued by their conscience. In addition, members of the Family of Light, who are millions in number, are establishing their presence in their midst. Gloom and doom merchants will soon run out of customers. Projections of gloom serve the altered Ego, but not the God I AM. That there are changes in store for us is obvious, and great turmoil in places, is obvious too, but all are constructive changes, regardless of their seeming negativity. These so-called negative events have begun since quite some time already. No one need to fear, though it is certain that those not being able to let go of their old thought-patterns of vengeance and attack, hatred, fear, suppression, greed and unforgiveness, will have no place in the Age of Light and will therefore remove themselves. This process is in progress already, as can be seen with every earthquake, flood and the like, which lift thousands of those souls from this plane who are too steeped in materialism to show any promise for change.

Any individual aligning with the Divine Intent, which is love, will be at the right place at the right time. He can literally be careless of his whereabouts.

The End Time is the end of time as such, but not the end of life, instead it is a new beginning. We will experience life as it really is, as an eternal now. The Mayan Calendar's time ends at the approximate equivalent of the year 2012[1]. We enter the last katun of this calendar in 1992 (1 katun = 20 years). The Bible speaks of the Day of Rapture as the 'End Time', the time of the Second Coming of Christ. Prophecies beyond count confirm these projections. It is the ancient promise of a New Heaven and a New Earth coming true.

We heard that whenever life initiates a transition into another state of Being, it comes as a sudden shift – without graduation. To speak then of the forthcoming transition and the period following is very much like telling the egg what it is like to be a chicken, or to explain to the caterpillar the state of being a butterfly. So we simply have to make the best of the information, which seeped through to us from higher realms, from our brothers in the unseen, from fellow souls who received clear visions, from what we call the White Brotherhood and from our space brothers. Considering our present limited awareness the clarity of the picture emerging is staggering.

The poles will not shift, the Earth's axis will not tilt but the magnetic poles will reverse their electromagnetic charge.

The Manasic Radiation operates on a subatomic level, causing each and every atom to radiate its own auric field visibly. The entire Earth's biosphere will be aglow and human bodies will glow in the radiance of their own aura. There will not be a dark place on and in the entire Earth, not even a shadow, as all is bathed in the radiance of the Light of the Spirit. Every living thing – man, animal, plant and mineral will be luminous in its own auric field. It is the end of the duality of day and night – the end of polarity altogether. The Earth shall keep on rotating, the Sun shall keep on shining, but a starry sky will be a sight of the past, as the brilliance of the radiance will outshine everything else. Those who feel a sadness creeping in with this thought should take consolation in the fact that they will not even miss the stars in a higher consciousness. What is to come is the marriage of Light with darkness, of Heaven with Earth. Our real SELF enters the physical realm in its fullness, thus in a very real sense we will be here for the first time. We will be born. Time as such then ceases to be, which implies that ageing cannot be possible. Disease will be a dream of the past. ('...and there shall be no more death, neither sorrow nor crying, neither shall there be any more pain; for the former things are passed away'), [Rev. 21:4].

('And Ye shall be changed to immortality without the separation of Death in the twinkling of an eye.')

The word Manasic has its root in the word Manaseh (Hebrew: menasseh), its literal meaning being: causing to forget. As a departed soul does not remember its earthly life for any length of time, so will the remaining humanity forget its history, for it experiences a shift from third density into the fourth – we shall actually expand into the next dimension, suggesting a complete new beginning.

Beside the Earth, other planets and celestial bodies will merge with this radiation as well. This appears optically as if such a body is burning up, though this light is of a cold nature and does not burn. On the contrary – every living thing shall be blessed with it. It encourages the growth of plants and causes wild animals to surrender aggression. ('..and the lion shall lie with the lamb'). The interaction of the photon belt with our atmosphere shall cause our sky, initially, to look as if being full of falling stars. The following biblical prophecy then seems not so far fetched: 'All the stars will fall from the sky and the sky will be no more...'

These are but a few of the physical effects of the Manasic Radiation. Now to the real changes: Our communication with one another will be rather direct and in a most honest manner, as the slightest conceit or rejection will cause our aura to contract to a dim glow. Man, the word, is expressing as light: The word becomes Light. As Paul Otto Hesse put it: 'No need for lawyers then, when agreeing to a contract.'

Although it was several times stated that we shall move from third to fourth density, from the physical to the etheric, a more refined definition expresses this: The statement is fundamentally true, but we do not lose awareness of the physical. On the contrary, we remain in the physical but expand our awareness to the etheric. Our consciousness becomes enlarged to the extent of encompassing the next dimension. The process depicts a joining of the two dimensions. A thought so thrilling that it should leave anyone speechless with joy who can comprehend its implication. The entire shift is one from fear to love.

Our bodies will be lighter, that is less dense, and many will nourish their bodies with physical food, purer and more vital, to be sure – many will not, they simply sustain their bodies directly from the ether. Manipulation and creation of matter is then the novel aspect. Sciences will flourish, as they are balanced with Spirit now. Technological advances will grace humanity, which will make 'Space Encounters of the Third Kind' look like lullabies for infants, mainly due to the assistance offered to us by our space brothers. Transport systems shall evolve to levels which, when compared, reduce our present jet-planes to clumsy ox-carts, this predominantly through the discovery of magnetic force-field and crystal technology. However, some – according to their stage of soul development – will simply discover how to teleport.

The grandest change of all is the shift from our terribly limited awareness to a superior consciousness, therefore Super-consciousness – to God consciousness, to the bliss of Oneness with our Creator. It is the long awaited Golden Age – the Age of God. Beyond this there are no words.

The human souls who have merged already into Christ-consciousness during their 10,500-year cycle of incarnations are to become the helpers giving guidance to the rest. It is mentioned that their number is approximately 144,000 – we call them avatars – though my understanding of this figure is a symbolic one, therefore I understand it not as a specific number of beings but as a consciousness expressing itself through helpers in general.

Anyone desiring a more detailed picture of the grand transition is advised to read Paul Otto Hesse's book (in German): 'Der Juengste Tag[1]' (The Last Judgment). Hesse had been blessed with a profound revelation of the Manasic Vibration and felt urged to publish his insights in order to help humanity prepare itself for this final event of this grand cyclic change.

Although the forthcoming transition is not a secret and its gift is upliftment and joy, it is to be expected that the event will send the unprepared into shock, mainly because of the suddenness of entry into the photon belt. All the more it is of benefit to be prepared with the knowing that it is a universal rebirth into love and Light and nothing to be feared. Visitations of extraterrestrials will already occur before the transition. Those who desire this as

---

1 Der Jüngste Tag, by Paul Otto Hesse. Published by Turm Verlag, Postfach 229, D-7120, Bietigheim, Württemberg, Germany.

a personal experience may put themselves to the test for eligibility. They may 'scan' their hearts for any man or creature who or which they still invalidate. If there is one single living thing they still exclude from the Divinity of life, then how can they make their peace and acknowledge in equality beings of non-humanoid appearance? If I cannot break bread with the Pigmy, the Muslim or the Black man, how can I sup with an Alpha-Centaurian?

It seems appropriate here to mention an 'outside' reference made regarding the phenomenon of the Manasic Radiation.

For many years, starting in June 1942, a certain Eduard B. Meier in Switzerland was regularly contacted and taught by our ancestors, the Pleiadeans. Their aim is to assist humanity in the preparation for the coming changes. Meier's role was to publicize his findings, photographs, and conversations with the Pleiadeans, in order to help man expand his limited views beyond his narrow scope of religious dogma – belief systems which limit mankind to the unbelievable arrogance that we are alone in the universe. Meier was given the unique chance to travel with these Pleiadeans, human beings as we are, to distant star systems to convince himself. Unfortunately, since the publication of his contact notes, Meier, a most courageous and humble man – was exposed to incredible hardship, humiliation, and seventeen assassination attempts. All these attempts to deter Meier from his mission came from his 'uniformed fellow-beings on this planet', notwithstanding the fact that the message of the Pleiadeans was one of love, peace, and cooperation.

The main individual (Pleiadean) working with Meier was a woman by the name of Semjase, daughter of a certain P'taah, the commander of the Pleiadean mother-ship stationed in our cosmic vicinity. From the book 'Message From The Pleiades – the Contact Notes of Eduard 'Billy' Meier', (ninth contact, Friday March 21, 1975 – 16:18 hr.) we quote the following in regard to the photon belt (Semjase speaking to Meier in person):

'The origin of this epochal change is the radiation effect of the huge central sun around which your system circles once in 25,860 years, and passes through 12 epochs within the meaning of your astrologists' Zodiac. The Earth has already touched the outer borders of the 'Golden Radiation' of the central sun, which are the strongest and most revolutionary radiations.'

We may view the Manasic or Golden Radiation as the trigger force for an expansion in consciousness of such magnitude that we may compare this process to a cosmic birth. It is our birth into a new day of creation – our spiritual rebirth. Terms such as the Second Coming of Christ, New Age, Super-consciousness, are but different labels for one and the same transition.

Depending on what enters the photon belt first, Earth or Sun, the initial entry shall result in a series of days of darkness followed by a series of days of light, or vice versa. Recent forecasts by channelled entities predict a period of twelve days of light followed by twelve days of darkness, designed as an intimidation to stimulate the last 'dawdlers' into a change of heart, to choose love instead of fear. Those souls not releasing fear, who choose not to partake in the unfoldment into light, shall sleep the long sleep. They shall have another opportunity to make that choice. Unfortunately, or perhaps fortunately after all, each new beginning for such a civilization cannot even lean on traces of the previous one, in fact has to start all over from the very rudimentary basics. Perhaps we have an explanation now for the puzzling fact that civilizations such as Atlantis have left no trace, because normally at the end and beginning of each of the 10,500 year cycles of darkness a global cleanup assures the removal of all impurities. However, the message conveyed makes clear that such geophysical changes are not necessary prior to this present transition, as humanity had never before reached such a high level of intelligent comprehension as now. It now remains a matter of awakening the dawdlers, yet not against their will. Although the awakening has begun already, the decade before the turn of the century will witness the forces of Light emerging to an extent as humanity has never seen.

Over and above all, the picture emerging then from the understanding of these recurring cycles is one of Earth being a schoolhouse, where one 'passes' one's exam or repeats the class.

What will happen to humanity after the 2,000 year period of Light? If Earth enters darkness once more, must humanity that made the 'jump', follow suit? No, certainly not. Governed by our tendency to think in linear terms we think of Earth as being the only one – but there are many. Picturing a spiral, rather than a circle, we can imagine a 'different' Earth on any given point along the spiral. This is the multi-dimensionality of which we speak. The coming transition shifts us into the next Earth-reality along the spiral, still occupying the same space but a different time continuum. It is not really a different Earth, rather of different density. As no reality along the 'spiral' is exempt from the changes, third-density Earth will certainly go through its own changes, but those not desiring the 'jump' into fourth dimension shall remain in third density. As the evolutionary direction on every level is one of 'up', none can escape their growth.

So for fourth-density humanity there is again a nobler destiny in store: According to reliable sources we shall take to the stars. However tempting to elaborate further, I believe this would lead into the realms of speculation and is beyond the purpose of this material.

So let us shift our focus now from a galactic view, back to Terra itself. In 1987, our brothers in the unseen, the White Brotherhood, have laid a special energy band around this planet. The purpose of this energy is to amplify, therefore accelerate, emotions. Thus we see the oppressors becoming more oppressive, the fearful becoming more fearful, the loving becoming more loving. In other words, the split in consciousness, (the sword of division), becomes increasingly accentuated. This is designed to stimulate choice, for only what is aligned to the frequency of Light shall move into Light – what remains with fear, cannot partake of Light. Hence the purpose of this material, to aid us in aligning ourselves with the help of True perception.

Now to Earth itself. In every process of growth and expansion, as in our physical bodies, energy is assimilated, and those energies we term unresolved, which cannot be assimilated, much like waste products, have to be released. The same applies to our universe. These energies, which we may call negative, have to be stored somewhere, else they could affect the rest of the universal system, in the same manner as toxins would affect our bodies. Within the evolutionary process of expansion and growth in our universe, Earth was given the task of storing these waste energies in her dense matter, where they could not cause any harm. Here they could be slowly and gradually released to be transmuted and returned back into the greater cycle of creation. The souls incarnating on this planet were the transmuters and those who wanted to learn the process of transmutation. So Earth served as a university, teaching us to deal with negative energies. Thus Earth and all it contains became a grand redeemer.

This process is so excellently recorded in David Spangler's 'Links with Space', under 'Communication from an Angelic Source' (21st June 1970).

We may begin to understand now how our altered state of mind fits into the universal puzzle. Only here are we afforded the opportunity of awakening to a true knowledge of SELF, for only here can we be separated from our SELF. Earth in its side track of evolution, while in its transmutational process, certainly became a place where 'angels fear to tread'. For here was the risk of losing one's identity – and this is precisely what we did. For this reason alone each single soul ever having incarnated on this planet deserves a 'medal'. It takes great courage to come knowingly to a place where one shall suffer amnesia.

These universal energies of unintegrated nature are not channelled any more toward Terra, for she is entering her mainstream of evolution. Another planet, not in our solar system, has been given this sacrificial task.

For Terra, the time of pain and suffering is past. What we still see as such is the sum total of negative energies running out on its own momentum. Earth and every soul in alignment with her energies is preparing for an event of such magnitude as this universe has never seen. The reunification with the Spirit. The marriage of Star light with Matter. An embrace of love. An act of making love. A universal, spiritual orgasm. Earth, the emerald sapphire, is the bride – Spirit the bridegroom. That beings from the seen and unseen, our space brothers, are attracted to our planet to witness and partake of this event should not come as a surprise.

In her process of stretching and realigning, Earth encounters the recalcitrant energies of those reluctant to align with love. Those who love will come to know a depth of joy undreamt-of before, in contrast to those who adhere to fear, for these shall find themselves in an increasing measure exposed to situations of discordant nature, designed to trigger a change of heart. Eventually all will have to make a choice. We might remind ourselves that those reluctant in making a choice for love can do without contempt and judgment. This would again result in fixation and achieve the opposite of a release from fear.

To focus now on the forthcoming transition would only propel us back to false perception. To project forward in time is to eject from the now. Future is the now-potential. We determine the future now, for what else is the future but another now. Thus it is of no avail to the aspiring soul to overly concern itself with the timing, stagelights and settings of however grand an event to be. Let it suffice to know that a mass awakening in consciousness is to occur, yet let it be also known that any soul may come into super-consciousness, the union with the God I AM, well before the great, but silent, 'bang'. This way an individual can become a grand helper to his struggling brother, much in the way a midwife helps in the birth of a newborn. So let us view any 'will be' in this spirit.

The beauty of this birth of humanity into Christ-consciousness is totally beyond words. It truly represents the end of time as we know it to be. Human history shall be less than a feeble memory, as little as the butterfly remembers its caterpillar stage. If all of humanity would release judgment now (Balance of Polarities), we would be in Christ-consciousness within three days. And this without one single calamity taking place.

The union of starlight with matter, of Spirit with separated Selves, can only occur via the bridge of True perception, which in essence is the surrender of judgment, therefore the release of fear.

Apart from her inception, it is the greatest event ever to grace the Earth. We, as her children, have stood the severe test of Separation. Thus we have become her cleansers and purifiers. We have entered the great mystery of creation and as such shall always carry the essence of Earth in our hearts. She, and we, are beautiful beyond measure. Since eons Earth supported humanity in its struggle from darkness to Light and absorbed negative energies – she did this without judgment. It was for her children to learn to do the same. Now she shall emerge as the Goddess she is – a radiant being of love. Her children, who align with her, she embraces and takes with her into a new adventure. The rest must sleep until a new day in creation offers them another opportunity to choose the way of love.

The universe with all its beings, in seen and unseen dimensions, joins with us in this greatest of all celebrations, the jubilance of rebirth into Light – the dance of the Gods – for where Earth and we as her children go, is the fulfillment of the soul's ancient cry:

We are coming home.

Diagram of the Sun's orbit
around the central sun Alcyone

As the diagram illustrates, the transition occurs at the entry of the Sun system into the light sphere, and accordingly the exit marks the fall from light.

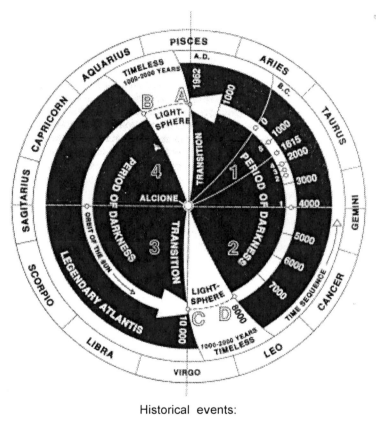

Historical events:

1. The beginning of Biblical Chronology 4128 B.C.
2. Noah's flood 2473 B.C.
3. Erection of the Cheops Pyramid
4. Sodom 2050 B.C.
5. David 1039 B.C.

Diagram by courtesy of Turm Verlag, Bietigheim/Württ., Germany

Other compatible books by Triad include:

GARDEN OF GODS

By Peter O. Erbe

From the author of the highly acclaimed spiritual classic 'GOD I AM', comes 'GARDEN OF GODS', a deeply inspired collection of wisdoms, presented in the form of an 'open at any page' book, which may serve as a daily companion, offering profound insights.

GARDEN OF GODS

ISBN: 0 9586707 0 6
Size 11.5 x 17.5 cm, 164 pages, PB

Excerpt:

At your evening tide in the twilight of dusk
when the land is still, then go to the grove.
Let meadow and forest enfold you in their peace,
and when a calm balms your soul,
speak to ME in your heart and you shall find ME there.
And when we meet, the night bird shall hush -
your lips shall quiver in speechless wonder
and your heart tremble - in awe your knee shall bend,
for nothing so lovely have your eyes ever beheld
and no such love has your heart ever felt,
for you will find YOU - that which I AM.
And together as ONE, in silent wonderment,
shall we merge in the sweet ecstasy
of our communion.

St. Germain

TWIN SOULS
&
SOULMATES

Channelled by Azena
and Claire Heartsong

ISBN: 0 646 21150 1
A5, 160 pages, PB

This is a fascinating account of St. Germain's merging and ascension with his own soulmate Portia, and also an eye opener to the deeper spiritual mystery of this most misunderstood subject.

'Experiencing Christ-consciousness within yourself, loving unconditionally that which you are as you exist and abide in your reality at this point in time, creates the resonance within your being that attracts the identical essence within the opposite body of soul energy - your soulmate will manifest in physicality as a natural progression and merges with your energy and you with it. And as you merge together closer and closer and drink more and more of one another's cups, you become One, and you become one another's strength and one another's love. As this occurs, you experience what is called enlightenment. The physical expression of your soulmate automatically appears.

Your twin flame is the identical vibration of the vibration you emit in your personality Self in this your now moment. And if you will recognize that you already embody the principle of love, then you will merge with your soulmate and the merging of soulmates creates miracles.'

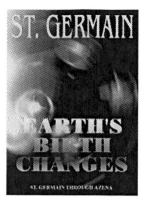

St. Germain
EARTH'S
BIRTH
CHANGES

St. Germain
through Azena

ISBN: 0 646 21388 1
A5, 280 pages, PB.

Apart from revealing unknown, revolutionary facts about Earth's and humanity's history, St. Germain affords the reader elating and in depth insights into matters spiritual.

The upheavals, the unrest and torment within humanity at this time are the contractions and labour pains heralding a birth of an incomprehensible, cosmic magnitude. The decade before and after the turn of the century represent the culmination - the Harmonic Convergence - of a 200 million year evolutionary cycle: Earth and her children, in unison with the Solar system and thousands of galaxies, are birthing into a new dimension.

From the shores of eternal being, from the Council of Light, comes one called St. Germain to assist in this birthing process. As he bares his heart in love and compassion, rekindling an ancient memory, he transforms the prophecies of Old, of looming calamities and trepidation, into shining, new horizons without circumference. His words are carried by an air of urgency for the changes are imminent; quote: 'the acceleration is becoming exponential'. His gift to us is not approximate statement but the promise of fact: freedom for humanity.

What is more, he unfolds a vision for humanity of such grandeur, that it renders the uninitiated speechless. If the historian and the scientist only as much as consider the information presented here, they will have to revise their certainties, for their facts are at risk. Unravelling a tapestry of dazzling beauty for humanity, the thrilling joy of St. Germain's message is contagious, is of effervescence and jubilance: the transition from separation to the union of Oneness with all Life - the age of Love -

THE GOLDEN AGE OF GOD

He treats 3000 people per day, 15 million people treated in 30 years.
He makes the blind see and the quadriplegics walk again.
More operations per day than a large hospital in a month.
Why is there no bleeding?
How is it possible without anesthetic?
He cured 139 cases of AIDS.
How does he remove tumors without touching the patient?
Why does he refuse payment?

ISBN: 0 646 33767 X
13 x 20 cm, PB

ROBERT PELLEGRINO-ESTRICH

THE MIRACLE MAN

The Life Story Of Joao De Deus

A man dies in hospital from cardiac arrest. After thirty minutes of clinical death, a phone call to Joao de Deus, 1200 km away in central Brazil, raises the man from death, completely healed; verified by his doctors.

Is Joao a modern Christ? Read this rivetting account of the greatest healing phenomenon of our time. When people, totally paralysed, rise from their wheelchairs and the profoundly blind have their eyesight restored, when modern medicine has given up on them, one feels deeply stirred to ask some fundamental questions.

Joao de Deus puts our reality at risk, defying the certainties of medical science, forcing us to replace it with one of hope and joy. The story of Joao de Deus shakes the bedrock of common beliefs, kindling an ancient memory that rings only too true: that with love all things are possible.

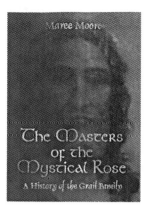

Maree Moore

The Masters
of the
Mystical Rose
A History of the Grail Family

ISBN: 0958670757 750 pages, PB

Inspirational – Educational – Historical

'The Masters of the Mystical Rose' presents a fascinating and in-depth account of the Grail family from Noah to Saint Germain – from the Knights Templar to the Royal House of Scotland. Meticulously researched, this book gathers the scattered pieces of the puzzle of history to form a meaningful picture, revealing stunning information and insights as to the Teachings of the Mystical Rose and the Masters who shaped the destiny of Mankind.

Did Atlantis and Lemuria really exist? Who was the mysterious Joseph of Arimathea? Did Merlin and Arthur exist? Where was Avalon? What was the Grail? Who were the Fisher Kings? Who was the Teacher of Righteousness of whom the Essenes wrote in the Dead Sea Scrolls? Learn the answers to these and hundreds of more questions.

This inspirational work ranks among the classics of human history.

Printed in the United States
74328LV00002B/11

9 780646 052557